CONTRACT

The University of Law

CONTRACT
SECOND EDITION

Alison Smith

The University of Law
2 Bunhill Row
London EC1Y 8HQ

© The University of Law 2024

All rights reserved. No part of this publication may be reproduced, stored in a retrieval system, or transmitted, in any form or by any means, without the prior written permission of the copyright holder, application for which should be addressed to the publisher.

Contains public sector information licensed under the Open Government Licence v3.0

British Library Cataloguing in Publication Data

A catalogue record for this book is available from the British Library

ISBN 978 1 80502 099 8

Preface

This book is part of the 'Foundations of Law' series of textbooks, designed to support postgraduates in their study of the core subjects of English law.

It is anticipated that the reader can then move on to studies for their professional examinations (eg the SQE and BSB assessments) comfortable that they have an understanding of foundational legal principles.

Each textbook aims to provide the reader with a solid knowledge and understanding of fundamental legal principles and rules. The series aims to give the reader the opportunity to identify and explore areas of critical interest whilst also identifying practice-based context.

For those readers who are students at The University of Law, the textbooks are used alongside other learning resources to best prepare students to meet outcomes of the Postgraduate Diploma in Law and related programmes.

We wish you every success as you learn about English Law and in your future career.

The legal principles and rules contained within this textbook are stated as at 1 May 2024.

Contents

Preface			v
Table of Cases			xiii
Table of Legislation			xix
Chapter 1	**Agreement and Contractual Intention**		**1**
	Learning outcomes		1
	1.1	Agreement (offer and acceptance)	1
	1.2	Offer or invitation to treat?	2
		1.2.1 Distinction between an offer and an invitation to treat	2
		1.2.2 Self-service and shop window displays	3
		1.2.3 Advertisements	3
		1.2.4 Auctions	5
		1.2.5 Tenders	6
	1.3	Termination of offer	6
		1.3.1 Revocation	7
		1.3.2 Rejection by the offeree	9
		1.3.3 Lapse of time	10
	1.4	Acceptance	10
		1.4.1 Certainty and completeness	13
		1.4.2 Communication of acceptance	14
		1.4.3 Acceptance by post	15
		1.4.4 Acceptance by electronic communication	17
	1.5	Intention to create legal relations	20
		1.5.1 Domestic and social agreements	21
		1.5.2 Commercial agreements	21
	Summary		25
Chapter 2	**Consideration, Privity, Agency and Capacity**		**27**
	Learning outcomes		27
	2.1	What is consideration?	27
		2.1.1 Definitions of consideration	27
	2.2	Adequacy and sufficiency	28
	2.3	Past consideration	30
		2.3.1 Past consideration will not be sufficient	30
		2.3.2 Exception to the rule that past consideration will not be sufficient	30

2.4		Performance of existing duties	31
	2.4.1	Existing duty imposed by law	31
	2.4.2	Existing contractual duty owed to a third party	32
	2.4.3	Existing contractual duty owed to the other party	33
2.5		Part payment of undisputed debts	36
	2.5.1	Promissory estoppel	37
	2.5.2	Conditions for promissory estoppel to apply	38
	2.5.3	The effect of the doctrine of promissory estoppel	38
	2.5.4	Review of promissory estoppel	40
2.6		Performance of existing contractual duty owed to other party and part payment of debt: can the legal principles be reconciled?	43
2.7		Doctrine of privity of contract	44
2.8		Agency	45
	2.8.1	What is agency?	45
	2.8.2	How is agency created?	45
	2.8.3	Effects of agency	47
2.9		Capacity	48
	2.9.1	Minors	48
	2.9.2	Mental incapacity	48
	2.9.3	Corporations	49
Summary			52

Chapter 3 Contents of a Contract — 53

Learning outcomes			53
3.1		Identifying the express terms of the contract	54
3.2		Implied terms	54
	3.2.1	Terms implied by the courts	55
	3.2.2	Terms implied by statute	57
3.3		Classification of terms	65
	3.3.1	Conditions and warranties: the traditional approach	65
	3.3.2	Innominate terms: a more recent approach	66
	3.3.3	Which approach should the court adopt?	67
3.4		Exemption clauses	68
	3.4.1	What are exemption clauses?	68
	3.4.2	Establishing liability	68
	3.4.3	Common law rules on exemption clauses	69
	3.4.4	Unfair Contract Terms Act 1977	74
	3.4.5	Consumer Rights Act 2015	83
	3.4.6	Exemption clauses and third parties	84
Summary			87

Chapter 4	**Remedies for Breach of Contract**		**89**
	Learning outcomes		89
4.1	Damages		89
	4.1.1	Introduction	89
	4.1.2	Assessment and measure of damages	90
	4.1.3	Types of loss	94
	4.1.4	The remoteness rule	96
	4.1.5	Mitigation	101
	4.1.6	Contributory negligence	102
	4.1.7	Time for assessment of damages	102
	4.1.8	Specified damages and penalty clauses	103
4.2	Action for an agreed sum		106
	4.2.1	Introduction	106
	4.2.2	The duty to pay must have arisen	106
4.3	Termination of the contract		106
	4.3.1	When can a party terminate the contract?	106
	4.3.2	Right of election of the innocent party	108
	4.3.3	Effect of termination	108
	4.3.4	Effect of affirmation	108
	4.3.5	Special rules for sale of goods contracts	108
	4.3.6	Anticipatory breach	108
4.4	Specific performance		109
	4.4.1	Introduction	109
	4.4.2	Restrictions on the availability of specific performance	109
4.5	Injunctions		110
4.6	Restitution		111
	4.6.1	Introduction	111
	4.6.2	Recovery of money which has been paid where there has been a total failure of consideration	112
	4.6.3	Compensation for work done or goods supplied	112
	4.6.4	Restitutionary damages	114
4.7	Guarantees and indemnities		115
	4.7.1	Guarantees	115
	4.7.2	Indemnities	116
	Summary		118
Chapter 5	**Performance and Discharge of a Contract**		**119**
	Learning outcomes		119
5.1	Order of performance		119
5.2	The doctrine of complete performance		119
	5.2.1	Exceptions to the doctrine of complete performance	120

	5.3	Discharge by agreement	127
	5.4	Discharge by frustration	127
		5.4.1 What constitutes frustration	127
		5.4.2 The original common law rule	129
		5.4.3 Modification of the original common law rule	129
		5.4.4 Review	130
		5.4.5 Events which will frustrate a contract	130
		5.4.6 Restrictions on the doctrine of frustration	136
		5.4.7 Frustration and leases of land	138
		5.4.8 Effect of frustration at common law	139
		5.4.9 The effect of frustration under the Law Reform (Frustrated Contracts) Act 1943	140
	Summary		145
Chapter 6	**False Preliminary Statements**		**147**
	Learning outcomes		147
	6.1	False preliminary statements made by a contracting party	147
	6.2	Distinguishing between terms and representations	148
		6.2.1 The relative skill and knowledge of the parties	148
		6.2.2 Whether a statement made verbally was repeated in a written contract before it was agreed	149
		6.2.3 Whether the recipient of the statement made clear it was of vital importance	149
		6.2.4 Whether the statement maker invited the other party to verify it	150
		6.2.5 Whether there was a lapse of time between the statement being made and the contract being formed	150
		6.2.6 Summary – classification of actionable pre-contractual statements	150
	6.3	Misrepresentation	150
		6.3.1 What is a misrepresentation?	150
		6.3.2 Remedies for misrepresentation	153
	6.4	Negligent misstatements	160
	6.5	Conclusion	161
	Summary		164
Chapter 7	**Duress and Undue Influence**		**165**
	Learning outcomes		165
	7.1	Duress	165
		7.1.1 What constitutes duress in contract law?	165
		7.1.2 Effect of duress and remedy	167

7.2	Undue influence		168
	7.2.1	Actual undue influence	169
	7.2.2	Presumed undue influence	169
	7.2.3	Undue influence and the position of third parties	171
Summary			179

Chapter 8 Mistake and Illegality — 181

Learning outcomes			181
8.1	Mistake		181
	8.1.1	What is mistake?	181
	8.1.2	Types of mistake	181
8.2	Illegal contracts		184
	8.2.1	Illegality	184
	8.2.2	Contracts illegal under statute	185
	8.2.3	Contracts illegal at common law	185
Summary			186

Appendix Resource Materials — 187

Reading 1 Standard Conditions of Sale	187
Reading 2 Consumer Rights Act 2015	190
Reading 3 Sale of Goods Act 1979	194
Reading 4 Supply of Goods and Services Act 1982	195
Reading 5 Unfair Contract Terms Act 1977	196
Index	199

Table of Cases

A

Adam Opel GmbH and Renault SA v Mitras Automobile (UK) Ltd [2007] EWHC 3205 (QB)	167
Adams v Lindsell (1818) 1 B & Ald 681	15, 18, 20, 24
Addis v Gramophone Co Ltd [1909] AC 488, HL	95
Adler v Dickson [1955] 1 QB 158	84
Allied Marine Transport v Vale do Rio Doce Navegacao SA (The Leonidas) [1985] 1 WLR 925	2
Anglia Television v Reed [1972] 1 QB 60, CA	93
Ashmore, Benson, Pease & Co Ltd v AV Dawson Ltd [1973] 1 WLR 828	184
Atlas Express v Kafco [1989] 1 All ER 641	166, 167, 168, 177
Attorney-General v Blake [2001] 1 AC 268	114
Attwood v Small (1938) 6 Cl&F 232	152, 163
Azimut-Benetti SpA (Benetti Division) v Healey [2010] EWHC 2234 (Comm)	105

B

Balfour Beatty Construction (Scotland) Ltd v Scottish Power plc 1994 SLT 807, HL	97
Balfour v Balfour [1919] 2 KB 571, CA	21, 22
Bannerman v White (1861) 10 CB NS 844	149
Barclays Bank v O'Brien [1994] 1 AC 340	172
Barry v Davies (t/a Heathcote Ball & Co) [2000] 1 WLR 1962, CA	5
Barton v Armstrong [1975] AC 104	165
Beale v Taylor [1967] 3 All ER 253	59
Bell v Lever Bros [1932] AC 161	182
Birch v Paramount Estates (1956)	149
Bisset v Wilkinson [1927] AC 177	151, 163
Blackpool & Fylde Aero Club Ltd v Blackpool Borough Council [1990] 1 WLR 1195, CA	6, 94
Blu-Sky Solutions Ltd v Be Caring Ltd [2021] EWHC 2619 (Comm)	70
Bolton v Mahadeva [1972] 1 WLR 1009, CA	123, 126
BP Exploration Co (Libya) Ltd v Hunt [1979] 1 WLR 783	141, 142, 145
Brimnes, The [1975] QB 929	8, 10
Brinkibon Ltd v Stahag Stahl und Stahlwarenhandelsgesellschaft GmbH [1983] 2 AC 34	17
British Steel Corp v Cleveland Bridge and Engineering Co Ltd [1984] 1 All ER 504	113, 114
British Westinghouse Electric & Manufacturing Co Ltd v Underground Electric Railway Company of London Ltd [1912] AC 673	99–100
Brogden v Metropolitan Railway Co (1877) LR2 App Cas 666, HL	12
Brown v KMR Services Ltd [1995] 4 All ER 598, CA	100
Butler Machine Tool v Ex-Cell-O Corp [1979] 1 WLR 401	11
Byrne & Co v Van Tienhoven & Co (1880) 5 CPD 344	7, 19, 24

C

Canada Steamship Lines v The King [1952] AC 192	73, 74
Car and Universal Finance Co Ltd v Caldwell [1964] 1 All ER 290	153, 154
Carillion Construction Ltd v Felix (UK) Ltd [2001] BLR 1	167, 168, 177
Carlill v Carbolic Smoke Ball Company [1893] 1 QB 256 (CA)	4, 7, 14, 18

Table of Cases

Casey's Patents, Re, Stewart v Casey [1892] 1 Ch 104	30, 31, 51
Cavendish Square Holding BV v Makdessi; ParkingEye Ltd v Beavis [2015] 3 WLR 1373	105
Central London Property Trust v High Trees House [1947] KB 130	37
Chandler v Webster [1904] 1 KB 493	139, 140, 144
Chapelton v Barry Urban District Council [1940] 1 KB 532	70
Chaplin v Hicks [1911] 2 KB 786	94
Chappell & Co Ltd v Nestlé Co Ltd [1960] AC 87, HL	28, 29, 37, 50, 176
CIBC Mortgages plc v Pitt [1993] 4 All ER 433	172, 173
Collen v Wright (1857) 8 E & B 647	47
Collins v Godefroy (1831) 1 B & Ad 950	31, 32, 36
Combe v Combe [1951] 1 All ER 62	38, 41, 51
Condor v Barron Knights [1966] 1 WLR 87	131, 135
Credit Lyonnais Bank Nederland NV v Burch [1997] 1 All ER 144	173, 174
Crystal Palace FC (2000) Ltd v Iain Dowie [2007] EWHC 1392 (QB)	156
Cundy v Lindsay (1878) 3 App Cas 459	183
Currie v Misa (1875) LR 10 Ex 153	27, 50
Curtis v Chemical Cleaning & Dyeing Co [1951] 1 KB 805, CA	69, 151, 152
Cutter v Powell (1795) 6 TR 320	120, 124

D

D&C Builders v Rees [1966] 2 QB 617	38, 39, 40, 41, 51
Daniel v Drew [2005] EWCA Civ 507	169
Davis Contractors Ltd v Fareham Urban District Council [1956] AC 696, HL	130, 134, 136, 137
Derry v Peek (1889) 14 App Cas 337	158
Dick Bentley Productions Ltd v Harold Smith (Motors) Ltd [1965] 1 WLR 623	149, 162
Dickinson v Dodds (1876) 2 Ch D 463, CA	8, 10, 14, 19
Dunlop Pneumatic Tyre Co Ltd v New Garage & Motor Co Ltd [1915] AC 79	104, 106

E

East v Maurer [1991] 2 All ER 733	158
Ecay v Godfrey (1947) 80 Ll L Rep 286	150, 162
Edgington v Fitzmaurice (1885) 24 Ch D 459	152, 163
Edwards v Skyways [1964] 1 WLR 349	21, 22, 23
Emanual Ajayi v RT Briscoe (Nigeria) Ltd [1964] 3 All ER 556	38, 39
Entores Ltd v Miles Far East Corp [1955] 2 QB 327, CA	14, 15, 16, 17, 18, 20, 24
Erlanger v New Sombrero Phosphate Co (1878) 3 App Cas 1218	155, 156
Errington v Errington and Woods [1952] 1 KB 290, CA	9, 10
Eugenia, The [1964] 2 QB 226	137

F

Farley v Skinner [2001] 3 WLR 899, HL	96
Felthouse v Bindley (1862) 11 CB NS 869	14, 15, 18
Fibrosa Spolka Akcyjna v Fairbairn Lawson Combe Barbour Ltd [1943] AC 32, HL	135, 136, 140, 144
Fisher v Bell and Pharmaceutical Society of Great Britain v Boots Cash Chemists [1961] 1 QB 394	3, 4
Foakes v Beer (1884) 9 App Cas 605	36, 37, 40, 41, 43, 44, 51, 127

G

Gamerco SA v ICM/Fair Warning (Agency) Ltd [1995] 1 WLR 1226	141, 142, 145
Glasbrook Bros Ltd v Glamorgan County Council [1925] AC 270	32, 36
Golden Strait Corporation v Nippon Yusen Kubishiki Kaisha (The Golden Victory) [2007] 1 CLC 352 HL	103
Goodlife Foods Ltd v Hall Fire Protection Ltd [2018] EWCA Civ 1371	78, 79, 80

Table of Cases

H

H Dakin & Co Ltd v Lee [1916] 1 KB 578	123
Hadley v Baxendale (1854) 9 Exch 341	96, 97, 98, 101
Hamer v Sidway (1891) 27 NE 256	29, 30
Hamilton and Others v Allied Domecq plc [2007] UKHL 33	151
Harlingdon & Leinster Enterprises Ltd v Christopher Hull Fine Art Ltd [1991] 1 QB 564	59
Harris v Watson (1791) Peak 102	33
Hartley v Ponsonby (1857) 7 E1 & B1 872	33, 36, 176
Harvela Investments Ltd v Royal Trust Company of Canada Ltd [1986] AC 207, HL	6
Hedley Byrne & Co v Heller [1964] AC 465	160, 161
Herne Bay Steamboat Co v Hutton [1903] 2 KB 683, CA	132, 133, 135
Hillas v Arcos (1932) 147 LT 503	13
Hoenig v Isaacs [1952] 2 All ER 176, CA	123, 124, 126
Hollier v Rambler Motors [1972] 2 QB 71, CA	72
Holwell Securities Ltd v Hughes [1974] 1 WLR 155, CA	16, 18, 20, 24
Hong Kong Fir Shipping Co Ltd v Kawasaki Kisen Kaisha Ltd [1962] 2 QB 26, CA	67
Houghton v Trafalgar Insurance [1954] 1 QB 247	73, 74
Household Fire and Carriage Accident Insurance Co (Ltd) v Grant (1879) 4 Ex D 216, CA	15, 16, 20, 24
Howard Marine & Dredging v Ogden [1978] 2 All ER 1134, CA	160, 163
Hutton v Warren (1836) 1 M & W 466	55
Hyde v Wrench (1840) 3 Beav 334	9, 10, 11, 19, 20, 23

I

Interfoto Picture Library Ltd v Stiletto Visual Programmes Ltd [1989] QB 433, CA	71

J

Jarvis v Swans Tours [1973] 1 QB 233, CA	95
John Grimes Partnership Ltd v Gubbins [2013] EWCA Civ 37	101
Joseph Constantine Steamship Line Ltd v Imperial Smelting Corporation Ltd [1942] AC 154	138

K

Kendall (Henry) & Sons v Lillico & Sons Ltd [1969] AC 31, HL	72
Koufos v C Czarnikow Ltd, The Heron II [1969] 1 AC 350, HL	98
Krell v Henry [1903] 2 KB 740, CA	132, 133, 135, 139, 140, 144

L

L'Estrange v Graucob Ltd [1934] 2 KB 394	69
Lampleigh v Brathwait (1615) Hob 105	30, 31, 51
Leaf v International Galleries [1950] 2 KB 86	155, 163
Lewis v Averay [1972] 1 QB 198	183
Liverpool City Council v Irwin and Another [1977] AC 239, HL	56

M

Maritime Fish Ltd v Ocean Trawlers Ltd [1935] AC 524	137
McCutcheon v David MacBrayne Ltd [1964] 1 WLR 125, HL	72
Merritt v Merritt [1970] 1 WLR 1211, CA	21
Metropolitan Water Board v Dick Kerr [1918] AC 119	133, 134, 135, 137
Monarch Airlines Ltd v London Luton Airport Ltd [1997] CLC 698	74
Moorcock, The (1889) 14 PD 64, CA	56
Morgan v Manser [1948] 1 KB 184	131, 135
Morris-Garner & Another v One Step (Support) Ltd [2018] UKSC 20	115
Mountford v Scott [1975] 1 All ER 198	7, 10

Table of Cases

N	National Carriers Ltd v Panalpina (Northern) Ltd [1981] AC 675	138
	North Ocean Shipping v Hyundai Construction Co (The Atlantic Baron) [1979] QB 705	168
O	O'Sullivan v Management Agency Ltd [1985] QB 428	169
	Obagi v Stanborough (Developments) Ltd [1993] TLR 646	90
	Olley v Marlborough Court Ltd [1949] 1 KB 532	72
	Omak Maritime Ltd v Mamola Challenger Shipping Co (The Mamola Challenger) [2010] EWHC 2026	94
	Oscar Chess Ltd v Williams [1957] 1 WLR 370, CA	149, 162
P	Page One Records v Britton [1968] WLR 157	111
	Pakistan International Airline Corporation v Times Travel (UK) Ltd [2021] UKSC 40	167
	Pao On v Lau Yiu Long [1980] AC 614	166
	Paradine v Jane (1647) Aleyn 26	129, 143, 144
	Parker v South Eastern Railway (1877) 2 CPD 416, CA	70
	Parsons (Livestock) Ltd v Uttley Ingham Ltd [1978] 1 QB 791	99, 100
	Partridge v Crittenden [1968] 1 WLR 1204	3, 4, 19
	Peekay Intermark Ltd v Australia and New Zealand Banking Group Ltd [2006] 2 Lloyd's Rep 511	152
	Pharmaceutical Society of Great Britain v Boots Cash Chemists [1953] 1 QB 401, CA	3, 19
	Philips Hong Kong Ltd v Attorney-General of Hong Kong (1993) 61 BLR 41	104
	Photo Productions Ltd v Securicor Transport Ltd [1980] AC 827, HL	74
	Pinnel's Case (1602) 5 Co Rep 117a	36, 37, 51, 127
	Planché v Colburn (1831) 8 Bing 14	121
	Powell v Lee (1908) 99 LT 284	14
	Proform Sports Management Ltd v Proactive Sports Management [2006] EWHC 2903 (Ch)	48
R	R v Clarke (1927) 40 CLR 227	11, 19, 20
	Raffles v Wickelhaus (1864) 2 Hurl & C 906	182
	Redgrave v Hurd (1881) 20 Ch 1	152
	Robinson v Harman (1848) 1 Ex 850	90, 121, 158
	Rock Advertising Ltd v MWB Business Exchange Centres Ltd [2018] UKSC 24	43
	Roscorla v Thomas [1842] QB 234	30, 31, 50
	Rose and Frank Co v Crompton Bros [1925] AC 445, HL	22
	Routledge v Grant (1828) 4 Bing 653	7, 10, 19, 24
	Routledge v McKay [1954] 1 WLR 615	150, 162
	Royal Bank of Scotland v Etridge (No 2) [2001] 4 All ER 449	169, 170, 172, 175, 178
	Royscot Trust Ltd v Rogerson [1991] 3 All ER 294; [1991] 2 QB 297	158, 159, 161
	Ruxley Electronics v Forsyth [1996] AC 344	92, 109, 118
S	Scammell v Ouston [1941] AC 251 (HL)	13
	Schawel v Reade [1913] 2 IR 81, HL	150
	Schuler v Wickman Machine Tool Sales Ltd [1974] AC 235, HL	66
	Scotson v Pegg (1861) 6 H & N 3295	33, 36
	Selectmove, Re [1995] 1 WLR 474 CA	15, 43, 47
	Shirlaw v Southern Foundries Ltd [1939] 2 KB 206, CA	56

Table of Cases

	Shuey v United States (1875) 92 US 73	8
	Smith New Court Ltd v Scrimgeour Vickers Ltd [1996] 4 All ER 769	159
	Smith v Eric Bush [1990] 1 AC 831, HL	80, 81
	Smith v Hughes (1871) LR 6 QB 597	1, 19
	Smith v Land and House Property Corporation (1884) 28 Ch D 7	151, 152, 163
	Spice Girls v Aprilia World Service BV [2000] EMLR 748	151
	Spurling J Ltd v Bradshaw [1956] 1 WLR 461, CA	55, 71, 72
	St Albans City and District Council v International Computers Ltd [1995] FSR 686	81
	St John Shipping Corp v Joseph Rank Ltd [1957] 1 QB 267	184
	Stevenson Jacques and Co v McLean (1880) 5 QBD 346	10, 11, 18, 19, 23, 24
	Stewart Gill Ltd v Horatio Myer & Co Ltd [1992] 1 QB 600	79
	Stilk v Myrick (1809) 2 Camp 317	33, 34, 35, 36, 43, 44, 166, 176
	Sumpter v Hedges [1898] 1 QB 673	122
	Super Servant Two, The [1990] 1 Lloyd's Rep 1	137, 138
T	Tate v Williamson (1866) 2 Ch App 55	169
	Taylor v Caldwell (1863) 3 B & S 826	129, 132, 138
	Thornton v Shoe Lane Parking Ltd [1971] 2 QB 163	72
	Tool Metal Manufacturing Co v Tungsten Electric Co Ltd [1955] 1 WLR 761	39
	Transfield Shipping Inc v Mercator Shipping Inc (The Achilleas) [2008] UKHL 48	100, 101
	TRW Ltd v Panasonic Industry Europe GmbH and another company [2021] EWHC (TCC)	12
	Tsakiroglou & Co Ltd v Noblee Thorl [1962] AC 93	134
	Tweddle v Atkinson (1861) 1 B & S 393	44
V	Victoria Laundry (Windsor) Ltd v Newman Industries Ltd [1949] 2 KB 528, CA	97, 98, 100
W	Ward v Byham [1956] 1 WLR 496, CA	31, 32
	Warner Brothers Pictures Incorporated v Nelson [1937] 1 KB 209	110, 111
	Watford Electronics v Sanderson CFL Ltd [2001] EWCA Civ 317, CA	78, 79
	White v Bluett (1853) 23 LJ Ex 36	29, 30
	Whittington v Seale-Hayne (1900) 82 LT 49	156, 157
	Williams v Carwardine (1833) 5 C & P 566	3, 4, 11, 19, 20
	Williams v Roffey Bros & Nicholls (Contractors) Ltd [1991] 1 QB 1	34, 35, 36, 43, 44, 51, 166, 167, 176
	Williams v Williams [1957] 1 All ER 305	32
	With v O'Flanagan [1936] Ch 575	151
	WJ Alan & Co v El Nasr [1972] 2 All ER 127	38
	Wrotham Park Estate Co Ltd v Parkside Homes Ltd [1974] 1 WLR 798	115

Table of Legislation

C

Companies Act 2006
- s 31 — 49
- s 39 — 49
- s 40(1) — 49

Competition Act 1998 — 185

Consumer Rights Act 2015 — 53, 57, 61, 65, 75, 84, 86, 190–193
- s 2 — 63
- s 5 — 62, 190
- s 5(1) — 190
- s 5(1)(a) — 190
- s 5(1)(b) — 190
- s 8 — 190
- s 8(a) — 190
- s 8(b) — 190
- s 9 — 63, 64, 83, 108, 191
- s 9(1)–(4) — 191
- s 10 — 63, 64, 83, 108, 191
- s 10(1) — 191
- s 10(3) — 191
- s 11 — 63, 64, 83, 108, 150, 162, 191
- s 11(1) — 191
- s 17 — 183
- s 19 — 63, 191
- s 19(3) — 191
- s 19(4) — 191
- s 20 — 63, 191, 192
- s 22 — 63, 191
- s 23 — 63, 192
- s 24 — 63, 192
- s 25(1) — 122
- s 31 — 192, 197
- s 31(1) — 83, 192
- s 31(2) — 83, 192
- s 31(3) — 83, 192
- s 48 — 192
- s 48(1) — 192
- s 49 — 63, 64, 83, 89, 192
- s 49(1)–(2) — 192
- ss 49–52 — 193
- s 50 — 193
- s 50(2) — 193
- s 51 — 63, 64, 83, 193
- s 51(1)–(3) — 193
- s 52 — 63, 64, 83, 193

Table of Legislation

s 52(1)–(3)	193
s 54	64, 192
s 57	83, 193
s 57(1)	83
s 57(3)	83
s 57(4)	83
s 57(5)	83, 194
s 62	197
s 65	197
Part 1	62
Part 1, chp 2	194, 195
Part 2	83, 193
Sch 2	84
Contracts (Rights of Third Parties) Act 1999	44, 85, 87
s 1	44
s 1(1)(a)	84
s 1(1)(b)	84
s 1(2)	84
s 1(6)	84

L

Law Reform (Frustrated Contracts) Act 1943	136, 140, 145
s 1(2)	140, 141, 142, 144, 145
s 1(3)	141, 142, 144, 145
s 1(3)(b)	141
s 1(5)	141
s 2	141
Law Reform (Contributory Negligence) Act 1945	102
Limited Liability Partnerships Act 2000	50

M

Misrepresentation Act 1967	148, 160
s 2(1)	158, 159, 160, 161, 163, 164
s 2(2)	157, 160, 161, 163
s 3	148

P

Protection of Birds Act 1954	
s 6(1)	3

R

Restriction of Offensive Weapons Act 1959	
s 1(1)	3

S

Sale of Goods Act 1979	48, 53, 57, 65, 75, 84, 119, 194–195
s 8	194
s 11(4)	60
s 12	183
s 13	58, 59, 60, 63, 75, 77, 82, 108, 150, 194, 197
s 13(1)	58
s 14	58, 59, 60, 63, 77, 82, 94, 108, 194–195, 197
s 14(1)	194
s 14(2)	58, 59, 60, 75, 194
s 14(2A)	194

	s 14(2B)	194
	s 14(2C)	195
	s 14(3)	58, 59, 60, 75, 195
	s 14(6)	195
	s 14(9)	195
	s 15	197
	s 30(1)	122
	s 35	108
	s 57(2)	5
	s 57(3)	5
	Supply of Goods and Services Act 1982	53, 57, 60, 61, 65, 75, 84
	s 2(1)	61
	s 3	61, 63, 75, 77, 82, 150, 195
	s 3(1)–(2)	195
	s 4	63, 77, 82, 195
	s 4(1)	195
	s 4(2)	61, 75, 196
	s 4(4)	196
	s 4(5)	61, 75, 196
	s 4(6)	196
	s 13	61, 63, 67, 76, 82, 85, 102, 122, 126, 196
	s 14	61, 63, 67, 196
	s 14(1)–(2)	196
	s 15	61, 63, 195
	s 15(1)–(2)	196
U	Unfair Contract Terms Act 1977	73, 74, 75, 80, 84, 86
	s 1(3)	75
	s 2	75, 76, 82, 196
	s 2(1)	75, 76, 85, 196
	s 2(2)	75, 76, 80, 82, 85, 197
	s 2(5)	197
	s 3	75, 76, 81, 82, 137, 148, 197
	s 3(1)–(3)	197
	s 4	75
	s 6	75, 76, 77, 78, 82, 197
	s 6(1A)	197
	s 6(5)	197
	s 7	75, 76, 77, 78, 82
	s 11	75, 77, 78, 79, 86, 148
	s 11(1)	77
	s 11(4)	79, 81
	s 11(5)	77
	s 13	75
	Sch 1	75
	Sch 2	75, 78, 80, 81

1 Agreement and Contractual Intention

LEARNING OUTCOMES

When you have completed this chapter, you should be able to:

- explain and discuss the rules governing offer and acceptance and contractual certainty;
- explain and apply the presumptions governing contractual intention;
- use a structured approach to identify legal, factual and practical issues involved in contract formation problems and to advise a client on the options.

For a binding contract there must be agreement, consideration (ie something given in exchange for the other party's promise) and an intention that the agreement should have legal consequences. For the moment we are going to be focusing on agreement (which manifests itself in terms of offer and acceptance) and contractual intention. We shall be looking at consideration in **Chapter 2**.

1.1 Agreement (offer and acceptance)

In order for parties to reach an agreement, one party must make an offer (ie a definite promise to be bound by specified terms) which is accepted by the other. So the first thing you really need to know is what is meant by an 'offer' in the eyes of the law.

Professor Treitel has defined an offer as 'an expression of willingness to contract on certain terms, made with the intention that it shall become binding as soon as it is accepted by the person to whom it is addressed' (Treitel, *The Law of Contract*, 13th edn, p 8).

- The person who makes the offer is called the offeror and the person to whom the offer is made is called the offeree.
- The 'expression' referred to in the definition may take many different forms, eg a letter, newspaper advertisement, email and even conduct, as long as it communicates the basis on which the offeror is prepared to contract.
- The 'intention' referred to in the definition does not necessarily mean the offeror's actual intention. The courts adopt what is primarily an 'objective' approach to deciding whether there was agreement between the parties (*Smith v Hughes* (1871) LR 6 QB 597). Clearly, they cannot discover as a matter of fact what was going on in the minds of the parties at the time of the alleged agreement. Nor are they prepared simply to accept what the parties themselves say was their intention at that time (which would be a 'subjective' approach). Instead, the courts look at what was said and done between the parties, from

the point of view of a 'reasonable person', and try to decide what a reasonable person would have thought was going on.

> ⭐ **Example**
>
> *Faheem had been advised by a motorcycle dealer to ask at least £6,000 for his motorcycle. Faheem texted John offering to sell it to him for £5,000. On reading the text message, John immediately telephoned Faheem and agreed to pay £5,000 for the motorcycle. Faheem told him that he would not accept less than £6,000 for the motorcycle. He said he was sorry if the price stated in the text message was not £6,000, but that it must have been an error, which he had not noticed.*
>
> *Although Faheem in fact intended to sell the motorcycle for £6,000, the price mentioned in his text message was £5,000. Assuming that this communication was the only one between the parties regarding the price, a reasonable person would assume that £5,000 was the intended asking price. Also, as far as we can determine, John believed that Faheem was making an offer to sell the motorcycle for £5,000. Faheem would be bound to sell the motorcycle to John for £5,000.*

In *Allied Marine Transport v Vale do Rio Doce Navegacao SA (The Leonidas)* [1985] 1 WLR 925, Goff LJ approved the following statement of the law relating to the making of an offer:

> If the offeror so acts that his conduct, objectively considered, constitutes an offer, and the offeree, believing that the conduct of the offeror represents his actual intention, accepts the offer, then a contract will come into existence.

Note from the quotation that, although the test is predominantly an objective one, the offeree must believe that the offeror actually intended to make an offer. This introduces a subjective element to what is otherwise an objective test of intention.

Finally, Treitel's definition of an offer refers to 'the person to whom it is addressed'. This may be one person, a class of persons or even the whole world. The point is that you can only accept an offer that was addressed to you.

1.2 Offer or invitation to treat?

1.2.1 Distinction between an offer and an invitation to treat

An offer must be distinguished from an invitation to treat.

Imagine I said to you: 'I am thinking of selling my car. I have been told that £7,000 would be a realistic asking price. Would you be interested in buying it?' Do you think that would amount to an offer to sell you my car? Is it a definite promise to be bound by specified terms?

This would not amount to an offer as I have only said that I am 'thinking' of selling my car, and the price is only a potential asking price. I have not committed myself to selling you the car at a specific price. The legal terminology for such preliminary statements is 'invitation to treat'. The statements are simply inviting negotiation and so the buyer could not by agreeing to pay £7,000 for the car create a binding contract. Compare this invitation to treat with an offer, eg 'I will sell you my car for £7,000'.

The distinction between an offer and an invitation to treat is important, but not always easy to draw.

1.2.2 Self-service and shop window displays

One area of difficulty arises in relation to goods on display in a shop, either in the window or on the shelves of a supermarket or other self-service shop. Such goods are commonly referred to as being 'on offer' and may well be labelled 'special offer', but in terms of contract law are they 'offers' or simply invitations to treat?

Goods on display in supermarkets and self-service shops are generally regarded as invitations to treat and not offers. The authority for this general principle is the case of *Pharmaceutical Society of Great Britain v Boots Cash Chemists* [1953] 1 QB 401, CA.

If goods on display were held to be an offer then a customer might be regarded as accepting that offer as soon as the customer selected the goods and put them in the trolley or basket. If that was the case the contract would be made at that point, and the customer would be unable to change their mind and put the goods back. The customer would be bound to buy or be in breach of contract.

The customer offers to buy the goods when the customer presents them at the payment point, and acceptance takes place when the shop takes payment for the goods (*Pharmaceutical Society of Great Britain v Boots Cash Chemists*).

In *Fisher v Bell* [1961] 1 QB 394, the defendant was charged with offering for sale a flick knife contrary to s 1(1) of the Restriction of Offensive Weapons Act 1959. The defendant had displayed the knife in a shop window, labelled 'Ejector knife -4s' (4s (ie 4 shillings) was the price of the knife).

In *Fisher v Bell* the court held that the display of the knife was simply an invitation to treat and acquitted the defendant of the charge.

So we have seen that goods on display (either in a shop window or on the shelves of a supermarket) are normally just an invitation to treat. The offer to buy is made by the customer and acceptance takes place at the payment point. It is only then that a binding contract is concluded.

A display of goods may amount to an offer in very limited circumstances where there is a clear intention to be bound (eg a display of goods in a special sale).

1.2.3 Advertisements

In this section we are going to consider the effect of advertisements, menus, promotional material and the like. Are they offers or invitations to treat?

Generally, they are regarded as invitations to treat. An authority for this is the case of *Partridge v Crittenden* [1968] 1 WLR 1204. Here the defendant was charged with 'offering for sale' a live wild bird contrary to s 6(1) of the Protection of Birds Act 1954. The defendant had placed the following advertisement in a periodical: 'Bramblefinch cocks, bramblefinch hens 25s each' (25s (ie 25 shillings) was the price of the birds).

The court held that the defendant was not guilty of the offence, as the advertisement was simply an invitation to treat (ie inviting the public to offer to buy a bird at 25s).

If such advertisements were offers, it would mean that anyone asking for the advertised goods would be accepting, in which case it would be a problem if the advertiser had run out of stock.

However, an advertisement of a reward has traditionally been treated as an offer as there is an intention to be bound as soon as the information is given (*Williams v Carwardine* (1833) 5 C & P 566). We shall look at this case later in this chapter. There is a policy reason behind this approach to rewards. Treating the advertisement of a reward as an offer means that the money has to be paid once the offer is accepted by the supply of the information. No negotiation is involved. This should encourage people who have information to come forward.

Advertisements of reward, then, are offers, but other types of advertisement will usually be invitations to treat. However, if there are special circumstances which show an intention to be bound, an advert may amount to an offer – an offer of a unilateral contract.

Most contracts are bilateral (ie a promise in return for a promise), but with unilateral contracts only one party is making a promise (eg a promise to pay a reward); hence they are said to be unilateral. No one is bound to do the specified act. This is why unilateral contracts are sometimes referred to as 'If' contracts: 'If you do X, I promise to do Y.'

The distinction between unilateral and bilateral contracts is particularly important in relation to 'acceptance' and 'consideration' (which we will cover at **1.4** below and in **Chapter 2** respectively).

The formation of a unilateral contract can be demonstrated in the famous case of *Carlill v Carbolic Smoke Ball Company* [1893] 1 QB 256 (CA).

In order to guarantee the effectiveness of the smoke ball remedy, the company offered a reward of £100 to anyone who used the remedy and contracted flu. The company also confirmed that it had deposited £1,000 in a bank account ready to make any payments under its promise, showing great confidence in the smoke ball and further tempting customers to buy one (see **Figure 1.1**).

Figure 1.1   Carbolic Smoke Ball offer

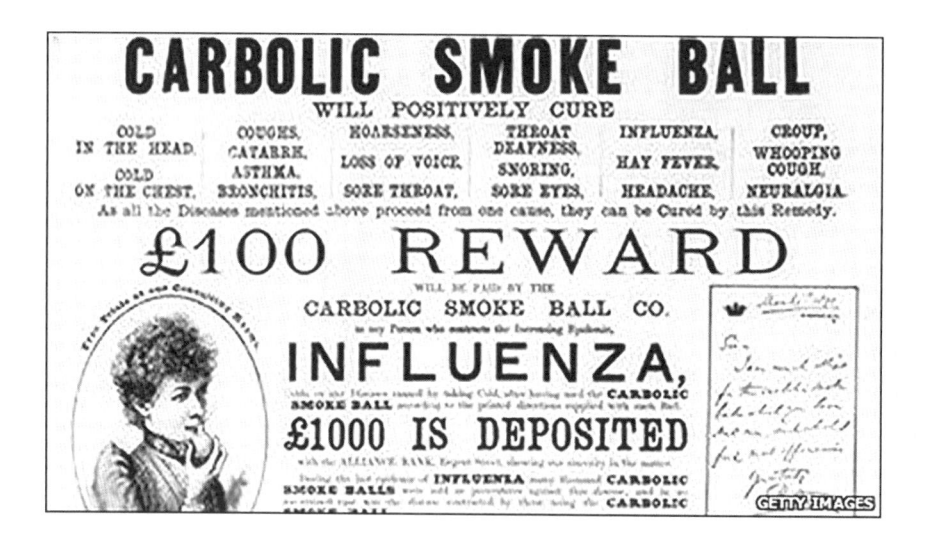

Once aware of the offer, Mrs Carlill accepted it when she purchased the smoke ball, completed the prescribed course and then contracted flu. She sued for the £100 and the court held that the company's promise to pay £100 was an offer of a unilateral contract, ie a promise in return for the specified act that Mrs Carlill had performed.

Carlill therefore is authority for the proposition that an advertisement can constitute an offer to 'the world' (that is anyone who learns of it).

Offer or invitation to treat – summary

- An offer is a definite promise to be bound by specified terms and must be distinguished from an invitation to treat where there is no such intention to be bound.

- Goods displayed in shop windows and inside shops will normally be invitations to treat (*Fisher v Bell* and *Pharmaceutical Society of Great Britain v Boots Cash Chemists*). However, a display may amount to an offer in very limited circumstances where there is a clear intention to be bound, eg a display of goods in a special sale.

- An advertisement will normally be an invitation to treat (*Partridge v Crittenden*) but in exceptional cases may be an offer of a unilateral contract if there is a clear intention to be bound – see, for example, *Carlill v Carbolic Smoke Ball*.

- Advertisements of reward will normally be offers of unilateral contracts (*Williams v Carwardine*).

1.2.4 Auctions

If you attend an auction, at what point do you think a sale is concluded? When is an 'offer' accepted? A contract for the sale of goods concluded at an auction is regarded by the law as a particular situation to which special rules apply.

According to s 57(2) of the Sale of Goods Act 1979, a sale by auction is complete on the fall of the auctioneer's hammer, in which case that is the acceptance. The bids are offers which can be withdrawn at any time before acceptance. When the auctioneer calls for bids, the auctioneer is therefore inviting offers, and as such the call for bids is an invitation to treat.

If the auctioneer accepts a bid by the fall of the hammer, a contract of sale is formed between the bidder and the owner of the goods. The auctioneer acts as the agent of the owner in order to form the contract.

Section 57(3) of the 1979 Act refers to a 'reserve price'. This is a price agreed between the auctioneer and the seller as being the lowest price which the auctioneer may accept for the lot; in other words, if the bidding does not reach the reserve price, the lot will be withdrawn from the sale. Most substantial lots will have a reserve price.

Occasionally, however, auction lots will not have a reserve price and the auction sale may be advertised as being 'without reserve'.

In *Barry v Davies (t/a Heathcote Ball & Co)* [2000] 1 WLR 1962, CA, two machines being sold at an auction were advertised by the auctioneer as being 'sold without reserve'; in other words they would be sold to whoever made the highest bid (however much that might be). Mr Barry made the highest bid for the machines, but the auctioneer did not accept it as he knew he could get a much higher price for them elsewhere. Mr Barry successfully sued the auctioneer for breach of contract; more specifically for breach of a unilateral contract. Why unilateral? Only one party had made a promise, namely the auctioneer. He had promised to sell the machines to whoever might make the highest bid. Why would it have been pointless for Mr Barry to sue the owner of the machines? The auctioneer had not accepted his bid and so there was no contract of sale with the owner. At an auction, a contract of sale arises only when a bid is accepted on the fall of the auctioneer's hammer (Sale of Goods Act 1979, s 57(2)) and here that had not happened.

The measure of Mr Barry's damages was the difference between the amount of his bid (£400) and the total value of the machines (£28,000) ie £27,600. That sum represented his loss of expectation: he had expected to buy the machines for £400 but it would cost Mr Barry another £27,600 to buy similar machines elsewhere. The amount the auctioneer sold the machines for elsewhere was irrelevant. We will consider damages in detail in **Chapter 4**.

Auctions – summary

- An auctioneer's request for bids is an invitation to treat.
- The bid is an offer which the auctioneer may accept or reject (Sale of Goods Act 1979, s 57(2)).
- If the auctioneer accepts a bid then, as the auctioneer is acting as agent for the owner, a bilateral contract is formed between the owner and the bidder.
- If the auctioneer refuses to accept a bid then there cannot be a contract between owner and bidder. However, if the auction is without reserve, the highest bidder may be able to bring an action against the auctioneer.
- If an auction is advertised 'without reserve', there is an offer of a unilateral contract by the auctioneer (ie a promise to accept the highest bid) which is accepted by the highest bidder. If the auctioneer refuses to accept the bid, the highest bidder will have a claim in damages against the auctioneer (*Barry v Davies*) but will not have a claim against the owner.

1.2.5 Tenders

Many businesses outsource functions (such as cleaning) on the basis that it is more commercially viable to pay outside contractors to do the work rather than employees. When businesses decide to outsource a function, they will invite a number of contractors to submit written tenders for the job. Generally, such requests for tenders will be invitations to treat and the tenders will be the offers, which may, or may not, be accepted by the business which has invited them.

There may be situations, however, where an invitation to tender does constitute an offer.

In *Harvela Investments Ltd v Royal Trust Company of Canada Ltd* [1986] AC 207, HL, two parties (the claimant and the second defendant) were invited to tender (ie put in an offer) for the first defendant's shares in a company. They were each sent identical telexes stating, 'We confirm that if any offer made by you is the highest offer received by us we bind ourselves to accept such offer ...'. The House of Lords held that the telexes were offers of a unilateral contract to sell to the highest bidder, which would be followed by a bilateral contract for the sale of the shares.

So, depending on the circumstances, an invitation for tenders may give rise to a unilateral contract.

This was the issue faced by the Court of Appeal in *Blackpool & Fylde Aero Club Ltd v Blackpool Borough Council* [1990] 1 WLR 1195, CA. The Aero Club had been granted a number of concessions to operate pleasure flights from Blackpool airport. When the last concession was nearing expiry, the council sent invitations to tender to the claimant and six other interested parties. The invitation said that the tenders had to be received not later than noon on 17 March 1983. The Aero Club posted its tender in the Town Hall letter box at 11am on 17 March. The letter box was supposed to be emptied at noon each day, but due to an oversight was not emptied at noon on 17 March. Consequently, the claimant's tender was recorded as late and not considered. The Aero Club sued for breach of an implied promise that a tender, returned on time, would at least be considered.

On the grounds that tenders had been invited from a small number of selected parties connected with the airport and that the invitation had laid down 'a clear, orderly and familiar procedure', tenderers obviously would assume that if they submitted a conforming tender they had a right to have it considered. On that basis, the court held that there was an implied promise to that effect which the Club had accepted by submitting a conforming tender. As the council had not considered the Club's tender, it was liable to the Club in damages for loss of opportunity. We will be looking at damages in **Chapter 4**.

Note that in *Blackpool & Fylde Aero Club*, the council had entered into a bilateral contract with the person whose tender had been accepted, but also had a separate implied unilateral contract with Blackpool & Fylde Aero Club.

However, the decision is a controversial one, and it is not clear exactly when the court will imply that there has been an offer to consider all tenders. In the *Blackpool & Fylde Aero Club* case, the court emphasised that tenders had been invited from a small number of parties connected with the airport, a 'clear, orderly and familiar procedure' had been laid down, and the tenderers would obviously assume that if they submitted a tender which complied with this procedure, the tender would be considered. It is not clear how the case would have been decided if one of these factors had been absent, or whether there were other factors which influenced the decision, eg the Club was the existing holder of the concession and so had even more reason for feeling their tender should be considered.

1.3 Termination of offer

What if an offeror changes their mind and wishes to withdraw their offer? For how long does an offer remain open for acceptance? What if the offeree does not fully agree to the terms of the offer? These are just some of the issues that you will be looking at in this section, dealing with how, and when, an offer may be brought to an end.

An offer may be terminated in the following ways:

- revocation (ie withdrawal) of the offer by the offeror;
- rejection by the offeree;
- lapse of time.

1.3.1 Revocation

As a general rule, an offer can be withdrawn any time before acceptance. Once an offer has been accepted, however, it is irrevocable.

What if an offeror promises to keep an offer open for a certain period of time? Can the offeror then change their mind and withdraw the offer?

Sometimes people make offers and promise to keep them open for a certain period of time. For example, they may offer to sell something and say that the offer will remain open for a week.

Routledge v Grant (1828) 4 Bing 653 is authority for the principle that such promises are not binding if they are gratuitous promises (in the sense that the offeree has not given or promised anything in return for the promise to keep the offer open).

So, generally, a promise to keep an offer open is not binding. The offeror can revoke the offer within the specified time as long as it has not been accepted. However, there is an exception to this rule. In *Mountford v Scott* [1975] 1 All ER 198, the claimant paid £1 for the option to buy V's house for £10,000. The option was exercisable within six months. V purported to revoke the offer. The claimant subsequently sought to exercise the option. The court held that the offer was irrevocable as the claimant had paid for the option (albeit a nominal amount). In paying £1, the claimant had given consideration for the offeror's promise to leave the offer open for six months. We shall look at consideration in **Chapter 2**.

1.3.1.1 Revocation must be communicated to the offeree

Notice of withdrawal of the offer must be given and must be communicated to the offeree to be effective. This was implicit in the decision in *Byrne & Co v Van Tienhoven & Co* (1880) 5 CPD 344, in which withdrawal of an offer by telegram was held to take effect only on receipt.

According to Professor Treitel, however, there are some exceptions to this general rule that revocation must be communicated. For example, notice of withdrawal sent to the offeree's last known address would be effective if they had moved without notifying the offeror. Similarly, a withdrawal which reaches the offeree may be effective if the offeree simply chooses not to read it (Treitel, *The Law of Contract*, 13th edn, p 43).

At **1.2.3** above you considered the case of *Carlill v Carbolic Smoke Ball*. If you cannot remember the facts of the case, please re-read them. If the Smoke Ball Company had decided to retract the offer it had made in the newspaper advertisements, how would you suggest that it should have gone about it, bearing in mind the general principle that revocation must be communicated? In other words, how could the company ensure that any person who had read its advertisements was notified that the offer had been withdrawn?

Clearly it would be impossible to notify everyone who had read the advertisements. In the first place, how would the Smoke Ball Company know exactly who had seen the offer apart from regular subscribers to the newspapers? Surely the best the company could do to revoke the offer in these circumstances would be to publish a sufficiently prominent notice of withdrawal in the relevant newspapers, eg by a notice that was at least as prominent as the original advertisement and in the same section of the newspapers.

This conclusion is confirmed by the decision in *Shuey v United States* (1875) 92 US 73. As *Shuey* is a US authority, it is not binding on an English court, but it seems reasonable that similar principles would be applied.

Notice of revocation sent to a business

You have seen that the general rule is that revocation must be communicated, and you have looked at some exceptions to this rule. There is one further issue to consider in relation to communication of revocation.

Suppose a notice of revocation (eg by email) is sent to a business during normal office hours. When do you think it would be effective: when it arrives, or when it is actually read by a member of staff, or at some point in between?

It would appear from the case of *The Brimnes* [1975] QB 929 that in this situation the notice will be effective on receipt where it is reasonable to expect a member of staff to be available to read a notice of revocation. The offeree cannot complain that they did not know of the notice if failure to read it was due to their oversight or oversight on the part of their staff. This case was not concerned with revocation of an offer but may be applied by the court by analogy.

In *The Brimnes*, a telex arrived between 5.30pm and 6pm but was not read until the next day. The Court of Appeal decided that it was communicated on arrival. Megaw LJ said:

> ... if a notice arrives at the address of the person to be notified, at such a time and by such a means of communication that it would in the normal course of business come to the attention of that person on its arrival, that person cannot rely on some failure of himself or his servants to act in a normal business-like manner in respect of taking cognisance of the communication so as to postpone the effective time of the notice until some later time when it in fact came to his attention.

Therefore, if a notice of revocation is sent to a business and arrives during normal office hours, it is likely to be effective at that point, even if not read until the next day. However, it all depends on what is reasonable, bearing in mind the particular context and the situation as a whole.

So, apart from a few exceptions, the general rule is that revocation must be communicated. The next question for you to consider is whether it necessarily has to be communicated by the offeror. Is it enough if somebody else tells the offeree that the offer has been revoked?

1.3.1.2 Revocation may be communicated by a reliable third party

Dickinson v Dodds (1876) 2 Ch D 463, CA is authority for the principle that revocation can be communicated by a reliable third party. Note that the third party need not have been authorised by the offeror to communicate notice of revocation, but must be objectively perceived as being reliable.

In his judgment in *Dickinson v Dodds*, James LJ said: 'In this case, beyond all question, the plaintiff knew that Dodds was no longer minded to sell the property to him as plainly and clearly as if Dodds had told him in so many words.' The informant was known to Dickinson. Dickinson knew he could rely on what he had been told.

1.3.1.3 Revocation of offers of unilateral contracts

Particular difficulty arises in relation to revocation of offers of unilateral contracts. As you saw at **1.2.3** above, a unilateral contract is formed when a promise is made in return for an act. As you have also seen, an offer can be withdrawn at any time before acceptance. The problem that arises in connection with unilateral contracts is concerned with when acceptance takes place. Is it when the promisee starts to perform, or is it on completion of the act?

Professor Treitel gives the example of someone offering to pay you £100 if you walk from London to York (*Law of Contract*, 13th edn, p 38). Do you accept this offer when you first embark on the walk, or when you actually arrive at York? The general view is that with unilateral contracts no obligations arise until the specified act is completed; in other words, acceptance only occurs when performance is complete. That being so, it would mean that the offer of £100 could be withdrawn at any time before you complete your walk to York. You could be just five miles away from York when you are told that the offer no longer stands and you would have no redress. It would be grossly unfair, and accordingly there are a number of judicial authorities which suggest that partial performance of a unilateral contract is sufficient to prevent revocation by the offeror.

It has been suggested by McGovney (27 *Harvard Law Review* 644) that there are two offers in this situation. In addition to the express offer, there is an implied promise not to revoke if the specified act is started within a reasonable time. The acceptance and consideration for the implied promise is the commencement of the act.

We shall look at consideration in detail in **Chapter 2**, but consideration is what a party does, or promises to do, in return for the other party's promise.

A case which involved the revocation of a unilateral offer is *Errington v Errington and Woods* [1952] 1 KB 290, CA. A father had bought a house in his own name and allowed his son and daughter-in-law to live in it. He promised them that if they paid the mortgage instalments, he would transfer the house to them. It was an offer of a unilateral contract as the couple did not promise to repay the mortgage; they simply did so (ie they performed the required act in reliance on the father's promise). When the father died, his widow sought possession of the house. It was held that the father's promise was irrevocable so long as the couple continued to pay the instalments.

The reasons behind this conclusion are not absolutely clear, but at one point Denning LJ does refer to an implied promise not to dispossess the couple as long as they paid the mortgage instalments. Denning LJ said: '... the father expressly promised the couple that the property should belong to them as soon as the mortgage was paid, and impliedly promised that so long as they paid the instalments to the building society they should be allowed to remain in possession.'

The second way in which an offer may come to an end is if it is rejected by the offeree. We will consider this next.

1.3.2 Rejection by the offeree

An offeree may reject an offer either expressly or impliedly.

As you will see later in this chapter, an acceptance must match exactly the terms of an offer; otherwise there can be no contract. Consequently, where the response to an offer suggests something different, it will not be an acceptance but a 'counter offer' and as such an implied rejection of the original offer.

In *Hyde v Wrench* (1840) 3 Beav 334, the defendant offered to sell a farm for £1,000. The claimant at first made a counter offer of £950, but two days later agreed to pay £1,000 and tried to accept the original offer. The defendant refused to complete the sale and the claimant sued. It was held that there was no contract since the offer to buy for £950 was an implied rejection of the original offer and as such had destroyed it. Consequently, it was no longer available to be accepted.

What if the claimant in *Hyde v Wrench* had not put forward a different price but simply asked about possible methods of payment? Would that have been a counter offer? No, because by simply querying the method of payment, a prospective buyer is not impliedly saying 'I do not want to buy at the stated price', but simply making an inquiry, the reply to which may determine whether or not to accept. It is for this reason that a simple request for information does not affect the offer. It still stands and can be accepted. Authority for this principle is *Stevenson Jacques and Co v McLean* (1880) 5 QBD 346.

1.3.3 Lapse of time

An offer may become incapable of acceptance through lapse of time. If the offer contains an express condition that it will lapse after a specified time, any acceptance received outside that time limit cannot create a contract. For example, if you look at the Specimen Standard Conditions of Sale in **Reading 1** of the **Appendix**, you will see that clause 3 specifically states, 'Any quotation given by the Seller is valid for 21 days only' (ie it will lapse after that time).

In all other cases, an offer will lapse after a reasonable time. What is a reasonable time depends on all the circumstances (eg how the offer was made and the subject matter of the offer). Thus, an offer to sell perishable goods would terminate after a short time.

Termination of offer – summary

An offer may terminate in the following ways:

(a) *Revocation*

- An offer can generally be revoked at any time before acceptance, even if the offeror has said they will leave it open for a specified period of time (*Routledge v Grant*).
- An exception to this is if the offeree has given (or promised) something to the offeror in return for keeping the offer open (*Mountford v Scott*).
- Revocation must be communicated to the offeree (*Byrne v Van Tienhoven*), although there are some exceptions.
- An offer made to the public at large may be revoked through the same channel as it was made, provided the revocation is given the same prominence (*Shuey v United States*).
- If a notice of revocation is received (eg an email) but not read until the following day, the court will have to decide when communication takes place, and this will depend on the reasonable expectation of the sender (*The Brimnes*).
- Revocation may be communicated by a reliable third party (*Dickinson v Dodds*).
- In the case of offers of a unilateral contract, it is likely that the offeror cannot revoke once the offeree has started to perform the act of acceptance (*Errington v Errington and Woods*).

(b) *Rejection by offeree*

- If the offeree rejects the offer either expressly or by implication (eg by making a counter offer), the offer will terminate (*Hyde v Wrench*). A request for information will not have the effect of terminating an offer (*Stevenson v McLean*).

(c) *Lapse of time*

- The offeror may specify that the offer will stay open only for a particular time. If not, the offer will terminate after a reasonable time.

1.4 Acceptance

So far you have considered 'offer', which is the first constituent of agreement. An offer must be in a form whereby a simple assent to it is enough to lead to agreement. In many cases, therefore, it is enough if the person to whom the offer is made simply says, 'Yes, I agree.' In some situations, however, it may be more difficult to decide precisely if, and when, a matching offer and acceptance have been made.

An acceptance must be a complete and unqualified acceptance of all of the terms of the offer. Also, the offeree must know of the offer in order to accept. An authority for this is the

Australian case of *R v Clarke* (1927) 40 CLR 227. The Australian Government had advertised an offer of reward for information leading to the arrest of certain murderers. Clarke saw the offer but subsequently gave the information only when he himself was suspected of the murders. By that time he had forgotten about the offer of a reward. In his judgment, Higgins J said: 'There cannot be assent without knowledge of the offer; and ignorance of the offer is the same thing whether it is due to never hearing of it or forgetting it after hearing.'

Williams v Carwardine is another case which involved an offer of reward for information leading to the conviction of a murderer. The claimant knew of the reward, but in fact only provided the information because the claimant was dying and wanted to ease their conscience. The court held that this did not preclude a valid acceptance of the offer; the motive itself was irrelevant.

Professor Treitel's definition of acceptance is 'a final and unqualified expression of assent to the terms of an offer' (Treitel, *The Law of Contract*, 13th edn, p 17). So first and foremost, acceptance must be 'unqualified' in so far as it must correspond exactly with the terms of the offer. If the offeree suggests even slightly different terms in response to an offer, it cannot be an acceptance. It will be a counter offer and an implied rejection of the offer. A counter offer destroys the original offer, which cannot then be accepted (*Hyde v Wrench*).

If the offeree responds to the offer by making an inquiry, this will not be an acceptance, but neither will it be a counter offer. It will be a request for further information, which does not destroy the original offer (*Stevenson Jacques v McLean*).

Sometimes there may be clear acceptance followed by a request for information, in which case the acceptance will be valid.

One situation where it may become vital to decide whether a particular communication is an acceptance or a counter offer is where there is a so-called 'battle of the forms' between two businesses.

Businesses generally want to contract on their own standard terms and conditions (Ts & Cs) rather than those of the other party. In an attempt to achieve this, they will attach their Ts & Cs to any document they submit to the other side (whether that be a quotation or, say, an order form). A so-called battle of the forms may result, with both sides passing their own Ts & Cs to the other side for agreement. These can be seen as counter-offer after counter-offer. The parties battle it out and the prize is having your own terms prevail. In other words, the last shot wins.

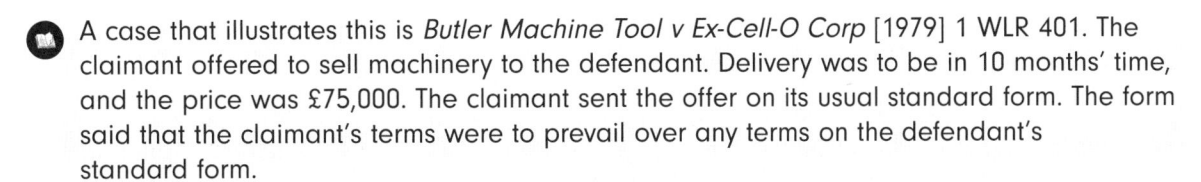

A case that illustrates this is *Butler Machine Tool v Ex-Cell-O Corp* [1979] 1 WLR 401. The claimant offered to sell machinery to the defendant. Delivery was to be in 10 months' time, and the price was £75,000. The claimant sent the offer on its usual standard form. The form said that the claimant's terms were to prevail over any terms on the defendant's standard form.

The claimant's terms included a price variation clause which allowed the claimant to increase the price of the machinery to keep pace with inflation.

The defendant sent back a form purporting to accept the claimant's offer. The defendant's form of acceptance, however, said that the price must be fixed at £75,000.

The defendant's form of acceptance asked the claimant to sign and return a tear-off slip. This slip provided that the terms of the defendant should prevail.

The claimant signed and returned the tear-off slip. When the claimant delivered the machinery, it tried to invoke the price variation clause in its original offer and claimed an extra £2,800. The defendant refused to pay and the claimant sued.

The Court found a contract on the defendant's terms. The claimant made the initial offer. However, it was held that the defendant's form of acceptance amounted to a counter offer. This had been accepted by the claimant returning the tear-off acknowledgement slip which provided that the terms of the defendant were to prevail. Consequently, the defendant was not subject to the price variation clause and did not have to pay the extra £2,800.

If you look at the Specimen Standard Conditions of Sale in **Reading 1** of the **Appendix**, you will see that they include a prevail clause (clause 2.1). From what you have just read, you will appreciate that such a clause will not necessarily help to win the battle of the forms. In *Butler Machine Tool* it was of no use at all to the claimant. It was simply one of the claimant's many terms that were impliedly rejected by submission of the defendant's terms.

The decision in *Butler Machine Tool* did little to resolve a true 'battle of the forms', such as might have arisen if there had been no acknowledgement slip, but simply an exchange of incompatible terms, followed by the delivery of the machine. In such a situation, delivery of the machine might be regarded as acceptance by conduct of the last set of standard terms to be proffered (*Brogden v Metropolitan Railway Co* (1877) LR2 App Cas 666, HL). It is for this reason that 'the last shot' will often win 'the battle' and explains why businesses persist in putting forward their own standard terms. By continuing to put them forward, there is more chance of them being the 'last shot', but, as shown by the recent case of *TRW Ltd v Panasonic Industry Europe GmbH and another company* [2021] EWHC (TCC), there is no guarantee the 'last shot' will necessarily win the battle.

TRW v Panasonic concerned a purchase by an English-based company, TRW, of electronic resistors from Panasonic (in Germany). Each party had supplied its own standard terms and conditions (Ts & Cs) as part of the negotiation of the sale/purchase of resistors. Each set of Ts & Cs contained a term on jurisdiction. The TRW Ts & Cs provided that the English courts would have jurisdiction and the Panasonic Ts & Cs stated that the German courts would have jurisdiction. Panasonic supplied its Ts & Cs upon the proposed sale. TRW responded with a purchase order, along with its own Ts & Cs, which was effectively the 'last shot'.

But this does not tell the whole story. TRW and Panasonic had negotiated sales and purchases for quite a considerable amount of time (since around 1998, in fact). In 2011, TRW had signed Panasonic's 'customer file' which confirmed that it had 'received and acknowledged' Panasonic's Ts & Cs.

Crucially, those Ts & Cs stated that German law would apply to the contract which would be subject to the jurisdiction of the courts in Hamburg. They also contained a provision to clearly disapply any terms that may be received in response to Panasonic's general conditions, unless Panasonic agreed to such terms in writing.

In 2020, TRW issued a claim (in the English courts) against Panasonic on the grounds that resistors that had been supplied as a result of the 2015/2016 purchase were allegedly defective.

Panasonic alleged that service of the claim was invalid as the German courts had exclusive jurisdiction over any claim; but TRW argued that as its Ts & Cs had been the 'last shot', they should prevail.

The court sided with Panasonic. The court relied upon the provision in Panasonic's Ts & Cs that prohibited any contrary terms applying, unless specifically confirmed in writing, and the fact of TRW having signed the 'customer file' in 2011 meant that Panasonic's Ts & Cs would apply to subsequent orders placed by TRW, notwithstanding what terms TRW may elect to send with such orders.

The court considered that if signing the Panasonic 'customer file' did not mean that Panasonic's Ts & Cs were incorporated, then obtaining the buyer's signature would have been a pointless exercise. It was therefore appropriate to put weight on this positive act, and the court found that the 'first shot' won the battle and that the 'last shot' missed its target.

You will be considering incorporation of Ts & Cs by signature in detail in **Chapter 3**.

1.4.1 Certainty and completeness

Even though the parties may appear to have made an agreement by exchange of a corresponding offer and acceptance, the courts may refuse to enforce it if there appears to be uncertainty about what has been agreed, or if some important matter is still left to be determined.

Whether, or not, parties have reached complete agreement in relation to all the material terms of a deal is generally judged objectively, but the facts have to be judged in context, eg:

(a) whether the parties are in the same trade;

(b) trade usage;

(c) whether the agreement has been acted on for any length of time; and

(d) whether there is an objective mechanism for resolving any uncertainty such as an arbitration clause.

> ⭐ *Examples*
>
> *(a) You go to a car dealership and say you are interested in buying a particular car priced at £10,500. You agree to buy it on 'hire purchase terms'. In the absence of any other details of the hire purchase agreement (eg duration, number and amount of repayments), it would be too vague to be a contract (Scammell v Ouston [1941] AC 251 (HL)).*
>
> *(b) An agreement to buy 'timber of fair specification'. This may seem vague, but in Hillas v Arcos (1932) 147 LT 503 the court held that there was a binding contract on the particular facts. The parties had dealt with each other in the past; they were well acquainted with the timber trade; and the contract had been partly performed. In other words, as far as the parties themselves were concerned, there was no uncertainty.*
>
> *(c) An agreement between a petrol company and filling station to supply petrol at the market price prevailing at the date of delivery. Although the exact price has not been agreed, if the agreement provides a mechanism by which the uncertainty can be resolved there would be a binding contract.*
>
> *(d) A 'provisional agreement' is drawn up and is to operate until a fully legalised agreement drawn up by a solicitor and embodying the conditions of the provisional agreement is signed. The fact that a formalised agreement has yet to be drawn up is irrelevant. Generally, contracts do not have to be in any particular form, and clearly the parties are in agreement and so there would be a contract.*

1.4.2 Communication of acceptance

The general rule is that acceptance must be communicated (*Entores Ltd v Miles Far East Corp* [1955] 2 QB 327) and communicated either by the offeree or its duly authorised agent (*Powell v Lee* (1908) 99 LT 284). (This is in stark contrast to notice of withdrawal of an offer, which if you recall, can be through a reliable third party (*Dickinson v Dodds*).)

It is possible for the offeror to waive the need for communication of acceptance in certain situations. For example, if there is an offer of a unilateral contract, the offeror is generally taken to have impliedly waived the need for communication. As we saw earlier, a unilateral contract is formed where the offeror makes a promise in return for an act. In this case, the performance of the act will amount to acceptance.

The case of *Carlill v Carbolic Smoke Ball Co* [1893] QB 256, CA provides a good example of this. You considered the *Carlill* case at **1.2.3** above. If you do not remember the facts of that case, please remind yourself of them. The Court of Appeal decided that using the smoke ball in the prescribed manner was the act of acceptance and that the company had waived the need for communication. It would not be reasonable to expect everyone who bought one of the smoke balls and started to use it to contact the company.

However, although performance of an act specified by the offeror may amount to acceptance, the offeror cannot impose a contract on the offeree by stipulating that the offeree's silence (ie doing nothing) will amount to acceptance. Suppose, for example, that the offeror says that unless they hear from the offeree by the end of the week, the offeree will be deemed to have accepted the offer. It would be unfair on the offeree if they had to go to the trouble of contacting the offeror in order to reject the offer.

The leading case on this point is *Felthouse v Bindley* (1862) 11 CB NS 869. The facts of the case were as follows.

An uncle offered to buy his nephew's horse for £30.15s. He said, 'If I hear no more about him I shall consider the horse mine at £30.15s.'

The nephew did not reply. He had previously arranged for the horse to be sold by auction, and so now instructed the auctioneer to withdraw the horse from the sale.

The auctioneer, however, sold the horse by mistake and the question before the court was whether there had been a contract between the uncle and the nephew for the sale of the horse. If so, the uncle would be entitled to sue the auctioneer in the tort of conversion (on the basis that the auctioneer had sold something that rightfully belonged to the uncle).

The court held that there was no contract between the uncle and nephew.

The court said that the uncle had no right to impose upon his nephew a sale of his horse unless the nephew wrote to him to reject the offer. Although it was clear that the nephew in his own mind intended his uncle to have the horse, he had not communicated this intention to his uncle or done anything to bind himself. For these reasons, there was no contract for the sale of the horse.

Why do you think the court has been criticised for applying the general rule, that mere silence is not consent, to the facts of *Felthouse v Bindley*? Remember that the rule is supposed to exist to protect an unwilling offeree from the need to reject offers.

The approach adopted by the court has been criticised because the nephew was not an unwilling offeree who needed the protection of the rule that mere silence is not consent. He was quite happy to sell the horse to his uncle. Also, he had demonstrated that he accepted his uncle's offer by telling the auctioneer not to include the horse in the sale.

Although the decision in *Felthouse v Bindley* has been criticised, the case is still good law as it has not been overruled.

However, it is not clear how *Felthouse v Bindley* would be applied if an offeree asked the court to uphold a contract on the basis that the offeree's silence constituted acceptance of an offer. For example, imagine in *Felthouse v Bindley* that the nephew had in fact withdrawn the horse from the sale and then the uncle had refused to pay for it. Would it not have been unreasonable for the uncle to deny the existence of a contract based on the nephew's (offeree's) silence?

The rule that silence is not acceptance of an offer exists to protect an unwilling offeree. If the offeree has been led to believe by the offeror that silence is acceptance and the offeree has acted on that belief, surely it would be reasonable for the courts to uphold a contract.

Furthermore, in *Re Selectmove* Ltd [1995] 1 WLR 474, the Court of Appeal saw no reason in principle why offerees should not bind themselves by silence (eg by saying something like 'If you don't hear from me, assume I accept your offer').

1.4.3 Acceptance by post

The general rule is that acceptance must be communicated (*Entores v Miles Far East Corp*). An exception is the postal rule, which may apply where a letter of acceptance is posted.

1.4.3.1 The postal rule

The issue was considered in *Adams v Lindsell* (1818) 1 B & Ald 681, and the rule that comes from that case is that, subject to certain limitations (see below), a letter of acceptance which is posted is complete on posting and the contract will be formed at that point. This is known as the postal rule.

In *Household Fire and Carriage Accident Insurance Co (Ltd) v Grant* (1879) 4 Ex D 216, CA, the acceptance was posted, but never arrived. The Court of Appeal (by majority) decided that the postal rule applied and the acceptance was valid on posting. It was irrelevant that the letter had somehow got lost in the post.

Thesiger LJ said:

> There is no doubt that the implication of a complete, final, and absolutely binding contract being formed as soon as the acceptance of an offer is posted, may in some cases lead to inconvenience and hardship. But such there must be at times in every view of the law. ...

> At the same time I am not prepared to admit that the implication in question will lead to any great or general inconvenience or hardship. An offeror, if he chooses, may always make the formation of the contract which he proposes dependent upon the actual communication to himself of the acceptance. If he trusts to the post he trusts to a means of communication which, as a rule, does not fail, and if no answer to his offer is received by him, and the matter is of importance to him, he can make inquiries of the person to whom his offer was addressed.

> On the other hand, if the contract is not finally concluded, except in the event of the acceptance actually reaching the offeror, the door would be opened to the perpetration of much fraud, and putting aside this consideration, considerable delay in commercial transactions, in which despatch is, as a rule, of the greatest consequence, would be occasioned; for the acceptor would never be entirely safe in acting upon his acceptance until he had received notice that his letter of acceptance had reached its destination.

1.4.3.2 Limitations to the postal rule (ie conditions for the postal rule to apply)

As mentioned above, the postal rule is subject to a number of limitations:

(a) It only applies to acceptances, and not to any other type of communication which may pass between potential contracting parties (eg the postal rule does not apply to a letter revoking an offer).

(b) It only applies where it was reasonable for the acceptance to be sent by post (eg the offer was sent by post, and/or there is no express or implied need for a prompt response). It would clearly be unreasonable to use the post in the event of a postal strike.

(c) The letter must be properly stamped, addressed and posted.

(d) The rule can always be excluded by the offeror, either expressly or by implication.

In the case of *Holwell Securities Ltd v Hughes* [1974] 1 WLR 155, CA the defendant granted the claimant an option to buy a house expressed as being 'exercisable by notice in writing to [the defendant]'. The claimant wrote to the defendant purporting to exercise the option but the letter never arrived. If the postal rule applied, there would have been a binding contract at the time of posting (irrespective of the fact the notice did not arrive (*Household Fire and Carriage Accident Insurance v Grant*)); whereas if the postal rule did not apply, there would be no contract, as acceptance had not been communicated (*Entores v Miles Far East Corp Ltd*).

Thinking back to the limitations on the postal rule, the post was clearly a reasonable method of acceptance, as notice had to be in writing and there was no urgency. But even assuming that the notice had been properly addressed and posted etc, the offer said 'notice in writing to [the defendant]', and the court held that by using the word 'notice', the offeror had impliedly excluded the postal rule. So whilst it might have been appropriate to accept by post, the acceptance actually had to arrive with the defendant to be effective. The postal rule did not apply.

So the rule does not have to be excluded expressly. It may be excluded by implication if the words used in the offer indicate that the offeror wants the acceptance to actually reach the offeror. For example, the offeror has said something like 'I need to know whether, or not, you accept by the end of the week' or 'You must tell me before the end of this month'. By saying 'need to know' or 'tell me', the offeror may be regarded as having given the impression that the acceptance must be communicated to be valid. Therefore, if the acceptance was sent by post, it would not be valid when posted, but only when it reached the offeror (and it must reach the offeror by the stipulated deadline).

It is important to remember that exclusion of the postal rule itself does not necessarily exclude use of the post as a means of acceptance. It simply means that if the post is used to communicate acceptance, the letter will not be an effective acceptance unless and until it is received. If the offeror wants to make sure that the postal rule will not operate then the offeror should make this clear in the offer, but otherwise exclusion of the postal rule may be implied.

1.4.3.3 Retraction of a postal acceptance

A final matter for consideration in relation to postal acceptance is the possibility of retraction. If the postal rule applies, and acceptance is deemed to be effective on posting, can the sender then change their mind and retract the acceptance before it comes to the attention of the offeror? One possible argument is to say that as the purpose of the postal rule is to benefit the acceptor, the rule should not be applied in any way that disadvantages them. So, if the offeror is unaware of the acceptance, why should the acceptor be prevented from retracting? Being in ignorance of the acceptance, the offeror cannot in any way have acted on it, and so cannot suffer from its withdrawal. Another possible view is that to allow retraction would be too favourable to the acceptor. The postal rule benefits the acceptor by giving them the certainty of knowing that there is a contract as soon as the acceptance is posted. It is then too late for the offeror to revoke the offer, and so why should the acceptor be able to withdraw acceptance? It seems to give the acceptor the best of both worlds as the acceptor could speculate at the expense of the offeror, and some would regard that as being grossly unfair to the offeror.

There is no English authority on retracting a postal acceptance when the postal rule applies. Such authority as there is leaves the position uncertain, so a lawyer could argue either way.

If the postal rule does not apply, retraction of an acceptance is clearly possible unless and until the acceptance is actually communicated, because until that point there will not be a binding contract (*Entores v Miles Far East Corp*).

1.4.4 Acceptance by electronic communication

Nowadays, contracts are much more likely to be made by electronic communication, such as email, than by the post. If one of these methods is used for acceptance, when is it effective?

A case which involved communication by telex is *Entores v Miles Far East Corp* [1955] 2 QB 327, CA. The claimant was a company based in London and was dealing with the defendant, an American company, through agents in Amsterdam. The claimant telexed the defendant's agents offering to buy goods. The agents accepted the offer by telex. Later a dispute arose and the claimant wanted to sue the defendant for breach of contract. To do this it was essential to know where the contract had been made: Amsterdam or London? The Court of Appeal held that the parties were effectively in the same position as if they had been in each other's presence, and accordingly acceptance took place in London where it was received.

Entores Ltd v Miles Far East Corp is authority for the fact that for an acceptance to be effective it must have been communicated, but when exactly will it be communicated? When it would be reasonable to expect the recipient to have read it, or when it is actually read by the recipient?

Entores Ltd v Miles Far East Corp was concerned with the place and not the time of communication. It provides no direct authority on the issue of exactly when a telexed acceptance takes effect. Clearly the postal rule does not apply as *Entores v Miles Far East Corp* requires the acceptance to have arrived.

At **1.3.1.1** above, you considered this issue in the context of revocation of an offer. You saw that a notice telexed during normal office hours, but not read until the next day, may be effective on receipt (*The Brimnes*). By analogy, therefore, a telexed acceptance will be effective when it would be reasonable to expect the recipient to have read it, even if it is not read until a later time.

With instantaneous methods of communication (such as email), there are bound to be occasions when the email is not read as soon as it arrives.

This situation was also considered in the case of *Brinkibon Ltd v Stahag Stahl und Stahlwarenhandelgesellschaft GmbH* [1983] 2 AC 34, where Lord Wilberforce said: 'No universal rule can cover such cases; they must be resolved by reference to the intentions of the parties, by sound business practice and in some cases by a judgment where the risks should lie.'

Acceptance – summary

- Acceptance is an unqualified expression of assent to the terms of an offer.
- The offeree cannot accept if the offer has come to an end by revocation, rejection or lapse of time.
- An acceptance should be distinguished from:
    (a) a counter offer. If the offeree introduces a new provision, it will be a counter offer which acts as an implied rejection of the offer (*Hyde v Wrench*); and

(b) a request for information (*Stevenson v McLean*). A request for information does not destroy the original offer, which can still be accepted.

Note: Sometimes there may be a clear acceptance followed by a request for information, in which case the acceptance will be valid.

- Acceptance must be communicated (*Entores v Miles Far East Corp*).
- Silence will not normally amount to acceptance (*Felthouse v Bindley*).
- The postal rule is an exception to the general rule that acceptance must be communicated. Provided certain conditions are satisfied, a letter of acceptance will be binding when it is posted (*Adams v Lindsell*). For the postal rule to apply, it must be reasonable to use the post as a means of communication, the letter must be properly posted, and the offeror must not have excluded the rule either expressly or by implication (*Holwell v Hughes*).
- In offers of a unilateral contract, the offeror will be deemed to have waived their right to have acceptance communicated, and in these cases the offeree's conduct will amount to acceptance, eg *Carlill v Carbolic Smokeball Co*.
- If an acceptance is received (eg in an email) but not read until the following day, comments made by the court in *The Brimnes* and the *Brinkibon* cases may help to determine when communication takes place.

You have now studied both offer and acceptance, which together constitute 'agreement'. At **1.5**, you will study contractual intention, but before moving on, attempt the following activity to test yourself on what you have learned so far in terms of the agreement aspect of a contract.

ACTIVITY 1 Offer and acceptance

PART 1 – Offer

Please tick the appropriate box to say whether the statement is true or false and make a note of the name of any relevant case. If you think the statement is false, please make a note of the reason for your answer.

Statement	True	False/reason
1. A person makes an offer if they intend to be bound as soon as it is accepted.		
2. The court applies a predominantly subjective test to decide whether a person has made an offer.		
3. A self-service display in a shop is usually an offer.		
4. An advert in a newspaper is usually an invitation to treat.		
5. An advertisement of a reward is generally regarded as an offer.		
6. A bilateral contract is a promise in return for an act.		
7. An offer can usually be revoked at any time before acceptance.		
8. Revocation of an offer must be communicated by the offeror.		
9. If you make a counter offer, you can still accept the offer which was made to you.		
10. If you make a request for information, you can still accept the offer which was made to you.		

COMMENT

Statement	True	False/reason
1. A person makes an offer if they intend to be bound as soon as it is accepted.	√	
2. The court applies a predominantly subjective test to decide whether a person has made an offer.		√ The court applies a predominantly objective test and asks whether a reasonable person would regard the statement as an offer (*Smith v Hughes* and *The Leonidas*).
3. A self-service display in a shop is usually an offer.		√ A self-service display is usually an invitation to treat (*Pharmaceutical Society of Great Britain v Boots Cash Chemists*).
4. An advert in a newspaper is usually an invitation to treat.	√ *Partridge v Crittenden*	
5. An advertisement of a reward is generally regarded as an offer.	√ *Williams v Carwardine; R v Clarke*	
6. A bilateral contract is a promise in return for an act.		√ A bilateral contract is where one party makes a promise in return for a promise from the other side. It is a unilateral contract where a promise is made in return for an act.
7. An offer can usually be revoked at any time before acceptance.	√ *Routledge v Grant*	
8. Revocation of an offer must be communicated by the offeror.		√ Revocation must be communicated (*Byrne v Van Tienhoven*) but it can be communicated by a reliable third party (*Dickinson v Dodds*).
9. If you make a counter offer, you can still accept the offer which was made to you.		√ A counter offer destroys the original offer (*Hyde v Wrench*).
10. If you make a request for information, you can still accept the offer which was made to you.	√ *Stevenson v McLean*	

PART 2 – Acceptance

Please tick the appropriate box to indicate whether the statement is true or false and make a note of the name of any relevant case. If you think the statement is false, please make a note of the reason for your answer.

Statement	True	False/reason
1. Acceptance is an unqualified assent to the terms of the offer.		
2. The general rule is that acceptance must be communicated and is effective when and where it is received.		
3. Provided a letter of acceptance is posted, the postal rule will automatically apply.		

Statement	True	False/reason
4. The postal rule may apply even if the letter of acceptance is lost or delayed in the post.		
5. The postal rule cannot be excluded by the offeror.		
6. You can accept an offer even if you do not know about the offer.		
7. The offeree's motive for accepting is irrelevant.		
8. An attempt to introduce new terms is not acceptance but a counter offer.		

COMMENT

Statement	True	False/reason
1. Acceptance is an unqualified assent to the terms of the offer.	√	
2. The general rule is that acceptance must be communicated and is effective when and where it is received.	√ *Entores v Miles Far East Corp*	
3. Provided a letter of acceptance is posted, the postal rule will automatically apply.		√ The postal rule in *Adams v Lindsell* will only apply if it is reasonable to use the post; the postal rule has not been excluded by the offeror; and the letter has been properly posted.
4. The postal rule may apply even if the letter of acceptance is lost or delayed in the post.	√ *Household Fire and Carriage Accident Insurance v Grant*	
5. The postal rule cannot be excluded by the offeror.		√ *Holwell Securities v Hughes*: the postal rule can be excluded either expressly or by implication, eg if the circumstances make it clear that the parties only intended acceptance to be effective when communicated.
6. You can accept an offer even if you do not know about the offer.		√ *R v Clarke*: you must know about the offer when you accept.
7. The offeree's motive for accepting is irrelevant.	√ *Williams v Carwardine*	
8. An attempt to introduce new terms is not acceptance but a counter offer.	√ *Hyde v Wrench*	

1.5 Intention to create legal relations

In this final section of **Chapter 1**, you will be considering another essential element of a legally binding contract, namely the parties' intention to create legal relations. (You will look at the other constituent of a legally enforceable contract (ie consideration) in **Chapter 2**.)

For the courts to treat an agreement as binding, the parties themselves must have intended it to be legally enforceable (ie enforceable in the courts). One way to legally achieve this would be through formal requirements, for example, for the law to insist that, to be legally enforceable, an agreement must be in writing and specifically state that it is intended to have legal effect. Generally, however, the English law of contract does not require formalities. Oral agreements are enforceable and no specific forms of words are required. Given that formalities are not usually required, how are those agreements which are intended to be legally binding to be distinguished from those which are not? As the evidence of the parties themselves is likely to be unreliable, as each party will have their own interests to serve, the courts have evolved another way of deciding the issue.

With regard to intention to create legal relations, English contract law operates on the basis of rebuttable presumptions, which differ according to whether the agreement is to be regarded as 'domestic' or 'commercial'. This means that the courts make certain presumptions about domestic agreements (ie agreements between family members and/or friends) and commercial agreements.

With commercial agreements, there is a very strong presumption that the parties intended their agreement to have legal consequences; whereas with domestic agreements (ie agreements reached between family members or friends), the presumption is that the parties did not intend to create legal relations. For example, if you agreed with your partner that you would clean the car if they would put out the recycling bins, neither of you would intend that agreement to have legal consequences if one of you did not do what you had agreed to do. But what if there was a lot of money at stake, eg a joint business adventure or the purchase of a property? Then the parties may well be taken as having intended to create legal relations.

We will now look at these two categories in a bit more detail.

1.5.1 Domestic and social agreements

For domestic and social agreements (eg an agreement between family members), the presumption is that there is no intention to create legal relations unless the facts show otherwise. The leading case in this category is *Balfour v Balfour* [1919] 2 KB 571, CA which involved an agreement made between a husband and wife.

Atkin LJ commented that agreements between spouses 'are not sued upon, not because the parties are reluctant to enforce their legal rights when the agreement is broken, but because the parties in the inception of the arrangement, never intended that they should be sued upon'.

The policy reason in the judgment of Atkin LJ is the need to prevent the court being inundated with claims. He said: 'All I can say is that the small courts of this country would have to be multiplied one hundredfold if these arrangements were held to result in legal obligations.'

If the couple had been separated, the likelihood is that they would have been bargaining at arm's length. They would not have been prepared to rely on honourable understandings and accordingly would have intended the agreement to have legal effect. Authority for this proposition is *Merritt v Merritt* [1970] 1 WLR 1211, CA. The husband had left the wife and was living with another woman. He signed a written agreement to the effect that he would pay his wife £40 a month and, in consideration of her repaying the mortgage on the jointly owned matrimonial home, he would transfer it to her sole ownership. The couple clearly had not wanted to leave anything to chance. It was a formal agreement which they obviously intended to be legally binding.

1.5.2 Commercial agreements

If the agreement is not a 'domestic' one, it will be regarded as 'commercial'. Here there is a strong presumption the parties intended the agreement to be legally binding. Again, it is a rebuttable presumption, but whereas in relation to domestic agreements, the onus of rebutting the presumption is not heavy, the same cannot be said for commercial agreements. This is illustrated by the decision in *Edwards v Skyways* [1964] 1 WLR 349.

An airline pilot was made redundant and as part of their redundancy package was offered and accepted a certain 'ex gratia' payment. The employer then refused to make the payment on the basis that there was no intention to be legally bound.

The subject of the agreement obviously related to business matters, and accordingly there would be a presumption that the parties intended the agreement to be legally binding. As to what was meant by 'ex gratia', the judge said the words simply indicated that the employer did not admit any pre-existing liability on its part to make the payment: 'The words did not mean, to put it another way, that the promise, when accepted, should have no binding effect at law.' Accordingly, it was held that the employer had not rebutted the presumption in order to establish there was in fact no intention to be bound.

So in a commercial context, very clear words are needed to rebut the presumption of an intention to create legal relations.

A case where the presumption was rebutted is *Rose and Frank Co v Crompton Bros* [1925] AC 445, HL, in which the agreement between the two companies included an 'Honourable Pledge Clause'. The clause specifically stated that it was not entered into as a 'formal or legal agreement' but was only a definite expression and record of the intention of the parties. The parties 'honourably pledged' themselves to the agreement in the confidence 'that it will be carried through by each of the ... parties with mutual loyalty and friendly co-operation'. The Court of Appeal regarded this as clear evidence that the parties did not intend the agreement to be legally binding, and this was accepted by the House of Lords.

Intention to create legal relations – summary

In social and domestic situations, there is a presumption that the parties did not intend to create legal relations (*Balfour v Balfour*) which may be rebutted on the facts (eg if there is a lot of money at stake). Conversely, in a commercial context, there is a very strong presumption of contractual intention (*Edwards v Skyways*) which is difficult to rebut.

You have now studied agreement (ie offer and acceptance) and contractual intention and should be in a position to attempt a problem question on formation – see **Activity 2** below. In **Chapter 2** you will be introduced to the third essential constituent for a legally binding contract, ie consideration.

ACTIVITY 2 Problem question on formation

Please read the suggested structure for answering offer and acceptance questions which is set out below. Then using that structure, have a go at answering the short problem question.

Offer and acceptance questions – suggested structure

1. Identify who is seeking to show a contract exists and state the elements needed to form a contract. [Where there is more than one character then deal with each one separately and consider events in chronological order.]

2. Is a party making an offer or invitation to treat? Define offer and identify offer on the facts.

3. Has an offer been accepted? Define acceptance and apply to the facts.

    (a) Must be complete acceptance of all the terms – you may sometimes need to consider whether there is a counter offer or request for information and discuss the effects of these.

    (b) General rule – acceptance must be communicated. What does this mean? Does an exception apply, eg the postal rule?

Agreement and Contractual Intention

4. Has the offer been revoked? State and apply the rules relating to revocation.
5. Conclusion.

NB This is a very basic structure – sometimes an offer and acceptance question may involve other elements, eg contractual intention, which you will need to discuss.

Question

Recently Paul moved into a new house. He decided to have a conservatory built and on Monday 14 April he discussed his plans for the conservatory with John, who was in the building trade. John said he could do the work for £5,000 but that he needed to know for sure by 28 April.

On 15 April Paul sent a letter to John saying that he would like him to build the conservatory for £5,000. He added that he hoped John would be able to complete the work by the beginning of June.

Paul's letter to John was delayed in the post and only arrived at John's house on 28 April. In the meantime, on 18 April, Paul received a letter from John saying he was unable to do the building work.

John is refusing to do the work.

Advise Paul, explaining his legal position.

COMMENT

Paul and John

If Paul wishes to take any action against John, he must first establish that a contract exists between them. For a contract, there must be agreement, contractual intention and consideration. As the problem is set in a commercial context, contractual intention will be presumed (*Edwards v Skyways*). The real issue here is whether or not the parties reached an agreement.

Agreement

There must be an offer by one party which is accepted by the other. If a person makes an offer then they intend to be bound straight away by an acceptance without further negotiation. If a person makes an invitation to treat, there is no such intention.

The 'acceptance' of an invitation to treat will not result in a contract.

Here John probably made an offer to do the work for £5,000 as it seems he intended to be bound without further negotiation. [If an invitation to treat – then Paul would be making the offer on 15 April which John has not accepted.]

Has Paul accepted John's offer?

Paul sent a letter of acceptance on 15 April. For an acceptance to be valid, there must be a clear acceptance of all the terms of the offer without qualification or addition.

If Paul is adding a new term (ie the need to complete the work by the start of June), this will amount to a counter offer and will destroy the original offer – *Hyde v Wrench*. If the letter is merely a request for information (ie asking if the work will be done by June), it will not destroy the offer but neither will it amount to an acceptance – *Stevenson v McLean*. Here Paul does not seem to be adding a new term as he agreed the price and simply said that he hoped it would be finished by the beginning of June. He may be deemed to have accepted the offer and just queried the completion date.

This is not just a request for information as in *Stevenson v McLean* because there seems to be prior acceptance which will take priority.

Acceptance must be communicated and is usually only valid when it reaches the offeror – *Entores v Miles Far East Corp*. An exception is if the postal rule applies, when the acceptance will be valid when posted – *Adams v Lindsell*. If this rule applies then the letter will be valid on posting even if it is lost or delayed in the post – *Household Fire and Carriage Accident Insurance v Grant*.

For the postal rule to apply, it must be reasonable to use the post as a method of communication – this seems to be so here since John did not indicate he wanted a quick acceptance, and there is no mention of a postal strike or delays in the post.

For the postal rule to apply, the letter must have been properly posted.

Also, the offeror must not have excluded the rule, expressly or by implication – *Holwell Securities v Hughes*. In the case of *Holwell*, the offeror said he wanted 'notice in writing'. The Court of Appeal held that the word 'notice' indicated that the offeror wanted to receive the acceptance and that he had impliedly excluded the postal rule. Here John did say he needed to know for sure by 28 April, which suggests he wanted acceptance to actually reach him by then. The court may well treat this in the same way as the words 'notice in writing to [the defendant]' in *Holwell* and decide that the postal rule has been impliedly excluded.

Also, it was said in *Holwell* that the rule should not apply if it would produce manifest absurdity and inconvenience.

If the rule does apply, Paul's acceptance would be valid on 15 April.

If the court decides that John has excluded the rule, then Paul's acceptance can only be valid when it is communicated.

John has sent a letter revoking his offer, and we must now consider if this is a valid revocation.

Revocation

John has tried to revoke his offer. Any offer may be revoked at any time before acceptance – even if the offeror (John) says he will keep the offer open (provided the offeree has not given consideration to keep the offer open) – *Routledge v Grant*. However, it is not effective until communicated to the offeree – *Byrne v Van Tienhoven*.

If the postal rule applies, Paul's letter of acceptance will be valid when posted on 15 April, which was before he received John's revocation. In this case there will be a contract.

If the postal rule does not apply, the revocation will be effective on 18 April and there will not be a contract.

Conclusion

It seems that the postal rule may have been excluded, and if so there is no contract. If the postal rule has not been excluded then there is a contract, and Paul should find out how much it will cost for someone else to do the work and, if for more than £5,000, he could sue John for damages for breach of contract for the difference. When assessing damages, the general aim of the court is to put the innocent party in the position they would have been if the contract had been properly performed. (You will be considering damages in detail in **Chapter 4**.)

SUMMARY

- If you are advising a client on a contractual issue (eg alleged breach of contract), you must be satisfied that there was a contract in the first place. For there to be a legally binding contract, there must be agreement (ie offer and acceptance), contractual intention and consideration. Without any one of these elements, it will not be possible to enforce a contract, for example by seeking damages for breach.

- In this first chapter you have studied what constitutes a valid offer and the various ways in which it can be accepted. You have seen the practical and commercial importance of being able to identify if, and when, parties have reached an agreement (eg in the context of auctions, tenders and the battle of the forms). You have also looked at the presumptions which govern contractual intention and how, and to what extent, they may be rebutted. Remember, in a commercial context it is very difficult to rebut the presumption that the parties did intend their agreement to have legal consequences. The process of step-by-step analysis is central to 'thinking as a lawyer'.

2 Consideration, Privity, Agency and Capacity

LEARNING OUTCOMES

When you have completed this chapter, you should be able to:

- explain and discuss in depth consideration and how it impacts in particular on the formation and variation of contracts;
- appreciate the basic concepts of privity and agency and how they impact on the formation of contracts;
- apply core legal principles to advise on issues relating to capacity.

In **Chapter 1** you considered two of the essential constituents of a legally enforceable contract, namely agreement (which manifests itself in terms of offer and acceptance) and contractual intention. Indeed, in many countries, this is all that is required to create a legally binding contract, but in English law there is an additional requirement, ie 'consideration'. In this chapter you will look at what is meant by 'consideration' and circumstances in which it may become an issue.

2.1 What is consideration?

The need for consideration is the idea that, in order to be able to hold the other party to a promise, you must have agreed to provide 'something in return' for that promise: it is this 'something in return' that lawyers call 'consideration'.

The 'something in return' may be a promise (called executory consideration) or an act (executed consideration). Bilateral contracts by their nature involve an exchange of promises; whereas a unilateral contract comprises a promise in return for an act (**Chapter 1**).

So in order to sue for breach of a promise, a party must be able to show they gave consideration for that promise.

2.1.1 Definitions of consideration

- An often quoted definition of consideration is that contained in *Currie v Misa* (1875) LR 10 Ex 153 which refers to benefit and detriment:

    A valuable consideration, in the sense of the law, may consist either in some right, interest, profit or benefit accruing to the party or some forbearance, detriment, loss or responsibility, given, suffered or undertaken by the other.

In other words, what is provided by way of consideration should either be a benefit to the person receiving it, or a detriment to the person giving it. Often both will be present.

For example, if Adam sells his car to Daryl for £9,000, Adam is suffering a detriment by transferring ownership of his car and that is clearly a benefit to Daryl. Conversely, Daryl is suffering a detriment by paying Adam £9,000 for the car and Adam is gaining that benefit. So it will be in many cases that there is both benefit and detriment, but the presence of one or other is enough. For example, suppose that Adam had agreed to transfer the car to Daryl if Daryl paid the price to a particular charity. In that case, Daryl's consideration in paying £9,000 to the charity is a detriment to him but not a personal benefit to Adam.

- As well as thinking of consideration in terms of benefit and detriment, it is also possible to think of consideration as the price one party pays for the other party's promise, ie what one party does or promises to do for the other party's promise.

Sir Frederick Pollock defined consideration as 'an act or forbearance of one party, or the promise thereof, is the price for which the promise of the other is bought' (*Pollock on Contracts*, 8th edn, p 175).

This definition highlights the fact that a promise to do something may be consideration. Thus, if I promise to sell you my car for £10,000 and to deliver it to you next Saturday, and in return you promise to pay me on delivery, there will be a binding contract immediately. If either of us defaults on, or before, next Saturday, that person will be liable for breach of contract. For example, if next Thursday I tell you that I have decided to keep my car, you will be entitled to sue me for breach, and if it will cost you more than £10,000 to buy a similar car, you will be entitled to damages. (Damages are dealt with in **Chapter 4**.)

2.2 Adequacy and sufficiency

An often quoted phrase is 'consideration need not be adequate, but must be sufficient'.

- 'Consideration need not be adequate' means that the consideration does not have to adequately reflect the value of the promise in return for which it is given.
- 'Consideration must be sufficient' means that the consideration must have some value in the eyes of the law.

For example, payment of £1 would be good consideration for an Aston Martin car. £1 would be sufficient because it is of some value. The fact that it is not equivalent in value to the car (ie not adequate consideration) does not matter.

But what if someone promised you their Aston Martin if you would fetch it from the garage; would that be a binding contract, or a conditional gift? According to Cheshire, Fifoot & Furmston (*Law of Contract*, 17th edn, p 121), the requirement for you to fetch the car is not the price for the promise, but the condition required to trigger the promisor's generosity. So it is a conditional gift and not a contract of sale.

The fact that consideration must have some value has traditionally been interpreted to mean that it must have some economic value, albeit nominal. Nowadays, however, the need for 'economic value' does not seem to be a strict one.

In *Chappell & Co Ltd v Nestlé Co Ltd* [1960] AC 87, HL, Lord Somervell said:

> A contracting party can stipulate for what consideration he chooses. A peppercorn does not cease to be good consideration if it is established that the promisee does not like pepper and will throw away the corn.

In *Chappell v Nestlé* the claimants owned the copyright in a piece of music, 'Rockin Shoes'. Nestlé arranged for copies of this tune to be made into records, and it offered these records to the public for 1s.6d. plus three wrappers from their 6d chocolate bars. The issue before the court involved copyright. The House of Lords had to decide whether the three wrappers were part of the consideration given for the record. The House of Lords held by a majority that the wrappers were part of the consideration.

Lord Reid said:

> ... the main intention of the offer was to induce people ... to buy (or perhaps get others to buy), chocolate which otherwise would not have been bought. The requirement that wrappers should be sent was of great importance to the Nestlé Co; there would have been no point in their simply offering records for 1s.6d. each ... It is a perfectly good contract if a person accepts an offer to supply goods if he (a) does something of value to the supplier and (b) pays money; the consideration is both (a) and (b).

Viscount Simonds and Lord Keith of Avonholme dissented. They regarded the requirement for the chocolate wrappers as merely a condition which had to be satisfied in order to qualify to buy the record at a discounted price. Hence their conclusion that the wrappers did not form part of the consideration.

What about giving up, or promising to give up, a liberty such as the right to swear or moan? Do you think that should be sufficient to amount to consideration?

In *White v Bluett* (1853) 23 LJ Ex 36, a father promised not to enforce a debt against his son, on condition that the son stopped moaning about the distribution of his father's property. The court decided that the son had not provided consideration for the father's promise.

The public policy reason behind the decision is that to allow such a promise to amount to consideration might open the floodgates to litigation. There have to be limits on the types of promises that will be enforced by the courts.

Also, remember that the parties must intend to create legal relations for the agreement to be binding. If you feel that the argument about not opening the floodgates to litigation is rather a weak one, this approach can be supported by the fact that the parties may not have intended the promise to be legally binding when it was made.

In *Hamer v Sidway* (1891) 27 NE 256, the question before the court was whether William Story was contractually bound to pay his nephew $5,000 on his 21st birthday. On 20 March 1859, William had promised his nephew that if he would stop drinking alcohol, smoking, swearing and gambling until he was 21 years of age, William would pay him $5,000. His nephew agreed and 'in all things fully performed his part of the said agreement'.

Bearing in mind that prior to the agreement, the nephew had occasionally drunk alcohol, smoked etc and that he had a legal right to do so, do you think that by refraining from such activities he had provided consideration for William's promise?

It was argued that there was no consideration as the promise to stop smoking, drinking, etc did not in fact harm his nephew, but actually benefited him, and that William gained no personal benefit from the promise.

The court dismissed this argument. The nephew had a legal right to do all the things he abstained from doing. He had abandoned that right in consideration of the promise of $5,000 and the court was not prepared to speculate on the effort which had been required to give up the various activities.

As *Hamer v Sidway* is an American case which may not be followed in England, as a matter of authority, there is no conflict between *Hamer v Sidway* and *White v Bluett*. However, it is worth considering why the claim in *White v Bluett* failed and the claim in *Hamer v Sidway* succeeded. Could the court's perception of whether the nephew's, or son's, forbearance was sufficient to amount to consideration have been influenced by the nature of the conduct forgone?

We are now going to look in detail at a number of situations where the act or promise may not constitute consideration so that no contract is formed. We shall look first at past consideration and then at performance of existing duties.

2.3 Past consideration

The need for an exchange and something given in return explains why performance of a gratuitous act or promise is not deemed to be consideration for a later promise of payment. What was done or promised was not done or promised in return for anything at all. It had been gratuitous.

Example

As a favour, Helen looks after Carl's cat while Carl is on holiday. When Carl returns he promises to give Helen £30. Helen would not be able to enforce that promise because she did not look after Carl's cat in return for payment. Carl promised £30 afterwards. She had looked after the cat purely and simply as a favour.

2.3.1 Past consideration will not be sufficient

Authority for the principle that past consideration is no consideration is found in *Roscorla v Thomas* [1842] QB 234. Roscorla bought a horse from the defendant. Afterwards, the defendant assured Roscorla that the horse was 'sound and free from vice'. This proved to be untrue, and Roscorla sued the defendant for breach of contract. The assurance was held to be unenforceable as Roscorla had not given any consideration for it. Roscorla had not bought the horse in exchange for the defendant's promise. Roscorla had already bought the horse.

2.3.2 Exception to the rule that past consideration will not be sufficient

Occasionally, a past act will be good consideration. The following *three conditions* must be satisfied:

(a) The act must have been done at the promisor's request. This derives from the case of *Lampleigh v Brathwait* (1615) Hob 105, where the defendant had asked the claimant to seek a royal pardon for the defendant, in relation to a crime which the defendant had committed. The claimant made considerable efforts to do this and the defendant later promised the claimant £100 for doing it. The promise was held to be enforceable.

(b) The parties must have understood from the outset that the act was to be rewarded in some way. The case of *Re Casey's Patents, Stewart v Casey* [1892] 1 Ch 104 made it clear that this second condition also had to be satisfied.

(c) The payment, or conferment of other benefit, must have been legally enforceable had it been promised in advance. In other words, the usual requirements for a binding contract apply. If there is an issue here, it will usually be with contractual intention (which we looked at in **Chapter 1**).

In *Re Casey's Patents, Stewart v Casey* the defendants had asked the claimant (Casey) to manage certain patents for them, which the claimant did. The defendants later promised Casey a one-third share of the patents for the work.

The court held that it must always have been assumed that Casey's work would be paid for in some way; the defendants' promise simply crystallised that reasonable expectation. Thus Casey was entitled to the agreed sum.

If the subsequent promise had not been made, the claimant would have been entitled in restitution to a reasonable sum for what they had done. (We shall be looking at restitution later in **Chapter 4**.)

Past consideration - summary

A past act will not normally amount to sufficient consideration for a later promise (*Roscorla v Thomas*).

For a past act to amount to consideration for a later promise of payment or other reward, the following *three* conditions must be satisfied:

- the act must have been done at the promisor's request (ie at the request of the person who later promises payment) (*Lampleigh v Brathwait*); and
- there must have been a mutual understanding from the outset that the act would be rewarded in some way (*Re Casey's Patents*); and
- had the promise of payment/reward been made in advance it would have been legally enforceable, ie all the requirements for a binding contract are satisfied.

2.4 Performance of existing duties

Can the performance of an act which the promisee is already under a legal obligation to carry out amount to sufficient consideration? There are three types of existing duty, namely:

- duty imposed by law/public duty;
- contractual obligation owed to a third party;
- contractual obligation owed to the other contracting party.

We shall consider each of them in turn.

2.4.1 Existing duty imposed by law

As a general rule, the performance of an existing duty imposed by law is not sufficient consideration in exchange for a promise of payment.

In *Collins v Godefroy* (1831) 1 B & Ad 950 the question arose as to whether someone who had been ordered to attend court as a witness (and therefore had a legal duty to attend) could enforce a promise of payment made by the person on whose behalf the testimony was to be given. Such a promise was held to be unenforceable on the basis that there was no consideration for it.

Denning LJ took a different view in *Ward v Byham* [1956] 1 WLR 496, CA. In this case, the father of an illegitimate child promised to pay the mother an allowance if the child was 'well looked after and happy'. The mother had a duty imposed by law to support the child. The Court of Appeal had to decide if the mother had given any consideration in exchange for the father's promise. Denning LJ decided that she had and commented, *obiter*:

> I have always thought that a promise to perform an existing duty should be regarded as good consideration because it is a benefit to the person to whom it is given.

Note, however, that in *Ward v Byham* the other two judges found consideration on the basis that the mother had in fact exceeded her legal duty by promising to keep the child well looked after and happy.

To a large extent, the rule against using a legal duty as consideration seems couched in public policy. In a case such as *Collins v Godefroy*, it would clearly be against the public interest to allow the promise of payment to be enforced. However, in *Ward v Byham* there is nothing contrary to public policy in allowing the mother to enforce the allowance which she had been promised by the father.

Furthermore, in a later case of *Williams v Williams* [1957] 1 All ER 305, Denning LJ said:

> a promise to perform an existing duty is, I think, sufficient consideration to support a promise, so long as there is nothing in the transaction which is contrary to public policy.

As a general rule, then, performance of a duty imposed by law is not sufficient consideration. But what if someone exceeds an existing public duty? Will that be consideration for a promise of payment?

In *Glasbrook Bros Ltd v Glamorgan County Council* [1925] AC 270, the owners of a mine, during a coal strike, sought assistance from the police in protecting those workers who had continuing responsibility to maintain the mine. The police reasonably suggested a mobile force, but the owners insisted that officers must be billeted at the premises, and they agreed to pay the council for this service. Later, however, the owners denied any legal obligation to pay, on the basis that the police had merely been carrying out their legal obligation to keep the peace.

The House of Lords held that the police had provided protection over and above what they reasonably considered necessary for the safety of the workmen at the mine. In other words, they had exceeded their public duty, and this was consideration for the agreed sum.

Viscount Cave LC said:

> If in the judgment of the police authorities, formed reasonably and in good faith, the garrison was necessary for the protection of life and property, then they were not entitled to make a charge for it ...; but if they thought the garrison a superfluity ... then in my opinion they were entitled to treat the garrison duty as a special duty and charge for it ...

2.4.2 Existing contractual duty owed to a third party

If a person is already bound to perform a particular act under a contract, it seems that the performance of this act can amount to sufficient consideration for a separate contract with someone else. For example, consider the following set of facts.

- Arcos Ltd enters into a contract with Berry plc whereby Arcos agrees to sell and deliver 6,000 widgets to Berry by 30 April.
- Berry plans to use these widgets in manufacturing goods which it has already contracted to supply to Collins Ltd. Collins therefore has a vested interest in Arcos delivering the goods on time to Berry.
- Collins contacts Arcos and promises to pay Arcos £1,000 if the goods are delivered to Berry on time.
- Arcos delivers the goods to Berry on time.

- The question is, if Collins then refuses to pay Arcos the £1,000, can Arcos enforce the promise? What consideration has Arcos provided in exchange for the promise?
- It seems that Arcos has provided sufficient consideration by delivering the goods to Berry on time. The fact that Arcos had a contractual duty to do this in its contract with Berry does not prevent it using the same act as consideration for a contract with a different party.

Authority for this is *Scotson v Pegg* (1861) 6 H & N 3295, in which a promise to deliver a cargo of coal to the defendant was held to be consideration even though the claimant was already contractually bound to a third party to make such a delivery.

2.4.3 Existing contractual duty owed to the other party

Imagine that you and I have a contract, and I then promise you additional payment for performance of the same contract: am I bound by that promise? What extra benefit am I getting, or what additional detriment is there to you, in performing what you were contractually bound to do in any event? On the face of it, none, in which case my promise would be unenforceable for want of consideration. This view is supported by the decision in *Stilk v Myrick* (1809) 2 Camp 317.

This case established the basic rule that simply performing an existing contractual duty owed to the other party will not be sufficient consideration in exchange for a promise by the other party to pay more money.

Stilk v Myrick was an action for seaman's wages on a return voyage from London to the Baltic. At Cronstadt, two of the 11-man crew deserted, and the captain promised to split the wages of the deserters equally among the rest of the crew if they would work the ship home. They did so, but the captain did not pay them the extra money. The court held that the captain's promise was unenforceable for want of consideration.

If you exceed a contractual obligation which you owed me, that clearly will be consideration as you will have conferred an extra benefit on me (and probably suffered additional detriment). Authority for this is *Hartley v Ponsonby* (1857) 7 E1 & B1 872. The facts of the case were similar to those of *Stilk v Myrick*, in that it involved members of a ship's crew who deserted. Whereas in *Stilk v Myrick* it was only two out of the 11-man crew, in *Hartley v Ponsonby* it was almost half of the crew, and of those left only a few were able seamen. This made continuation of the voyage exceptionally hazardous for the remaining crew. On that basis they were not bound by the terms of the original contract to proceed with the voyage. By agreeing to continue the voyage, the remaining crew had given good consideration for the promise of extra payment.

So looking at the facts of *Stilk v Myrick* and *Hartley v Ponsonby*, it would seem to be a question of fact and degree. Surely the remaining sailors in *Stilk v Myrick* had had to put in extra effort to work the ship home: just not as much as in *Hartley v Ponsonby*.

Looking at cases that went before *Stilk v Myrick* and those that have come after it, the decision is perhaps best explained not in terms of consideration, but in terms of public policy.

Lord Ellenborough in *Stilk v Myrick* had referred to an earlier case of *Harris v Watson* (1791) Peak 102 (which involved very similar facts) which had been decided on public policy grounds. Lord Ellenborough preferred the view that the agreement was unenforceable as the sailors had given no consideration for the captain's promise, but in *Harris v Watson* Lord Kenyon CJ had said:

> If this action was to be supported, it would materially affect the navigation of this kingdom. It has been long since determined, that when the freight is lost the wages are lost. This rule was founded on a principle of policy, for if sailors were in all events to have their wages, and in times of danger entitled to insist on an extra charge on such a promise as this, they would in many cases suffer a ship to sink, unless the captain would pay an extravagant demand they might think proper to make.

This policy argument is now greatly reduced in importance. Since the 1970s, the courts have recognised that threats of economic pressure may amount to duress. Any promise which has been induced by economic duress may be avoided on that ground (and money paid in pursuance of it may be recovered). You will study economic duress in detail in **Chapter 7**.

The decision in *Stilk v Myrick* was accepted and applied almost without question until the decision of the Court of Appeal in *Williams v Roffey Bros & Nicholls (Contractors) Ltd* [1991] 1 QB 1.

Williams v Roffey Bros concerned a contract to refurbish a block of flats. The defendants were the main contractors, and they subcontracted the carpentry work to the claimants for £20,000. Part way through the work the claimants realised they had underestimated the cost and told the defendants of their financial difficulty. The defendants (mindful of the fact that if the work was not completed on time the defendants would be liable to pay compensation under the main contract) promised to pay the claimants extra money (ie £575 per flat) to complete on time. On this basis the claimants continued to work on the flats but in the event were not paid the extra money promised by the defendants and sued. The main issue before the Court of Appeal was what, if any, consideration the claimants had given in return for the promise of additional money. Whilst it was conceded by the defendants that they had secured practical benefits (ie avoiding liability under the compensation clause in the main contract and the cost and expense of finding other carpenters to finish the job), the defendants argued that there was no legal benefit.

In his judgment Glidewell LJ said:

> There is ... another legal concept of relatively recent development which is relevant, namely that of economic duress. Clearly, if a subcontractor has agreed to undertake work at a fixed price, and before he has completed the work declines to continue with it unless the contractor agrees to pay an increased price, the subcontractor may be held guilty of securing the contractor's promise by taking unfair advantage of the difficulties he will cause if he does not complete the work. In such a case an agreement to pay an increased price may well be voidable because it was entered into under duress ....
>
> [T]he present state of the law on this subject can be expressed in the following propositions
>
> ... (i) if A has entered into a contract with B to do work for, or to supply goods or services to, B in return for payment by B; and (ii) at some stage before A has completely performed his obligations under the contract B has reason to doubt whether A will ... complete his side of the bargain; and (iii) B thereupon promises A an additional payment in return for A's promise to perform his contractual obligations on time; and (iv) as a result of giving his promise B obtains in practice a benefit, or obviates a disbenefit, and (v) B's promise is not given as a result of economic duress or fraud on the part of A then (vi) the benefit to B is capable of being consideration for B's promise, so that the promise will be legally binding.
>
> As I have said [counsel for the defendants] accepts that in the present case by promising to pay the extra £10,300 his client secured benefits. There is no finding, and no suggestion, that in this case the promise was given as a result of fraud or duress. If it be objected that the propositions above contravene the principle in *Stilk v Myrick*, I answer that in my view they do not; they refine, and limit the application of that principle, but they leave the principle unscathed ...

Consideration, Privity, Agency and Capacity

The defendants had secured practical benefits (or otherwise obviated disbenefits). For example, they did not have to find new sub-contractors to replace the claimants and had avoided liability under the compensation clause. There was no detriment to the claimants, but if you think back to the definition of consideration (at **2.1**), it is not essential for there to be both benefit and detriment.

According to Glidewell LJ, the decision leaves intact the principle in *Stilk v Myrick*. It simply refines and limits the application of the principle, so where a promisor secures no practical or other benefit from performance of the contract by the other party, it will not be good consideration for the promise of extra payment.

Despite their Lordships' view that the decision in *Williams v Roffey Bros* leaves the principle in *Stilk v Myrick* intact, it is difficult to reconcile the two cases. In *Stilk v Myrick*, did the captain not secure practical benefits as a result of his promise? For example, he did not have to seek a replacement crew and he avoided delays. The main reason for distinguishing *Stilk v Myrick* seems to have been related to the alternative public policy basis for the decision referred to above (ie the need to protect against extortion). The court in *Williams v Roffey Bros* clearly regarded it as significant that there was no evidence of duress or fraud. Indeed, it was the defendants who had suggested the increased payment. If there had been economic duress then the variation could have been set aside/avoided (see **Chapter 7**).

Whenever a contract for services is abandoned, the innocent party will have to find someone else to complete the work. For example, as mentioned above, the captain in *Stilk v Myrick* secured the practical benefit of not having to find a replacement crew and yet there was, apparently, no consideration for his promise of extra payment. It may be argued that the decision in *Williams v Roffey Bros* suggests that there must be some extra benefit to the promisor and, to that extent, avoidance of having to pay compensation under the main contract was significant.

The decision in *Williams v Roffey Bros* has been welcomed as one which reflects the practicalities of business life as it enables contracts to be modified when unexpected difficulties arise. It can be said to be in the public interest for the parties to negotiate and

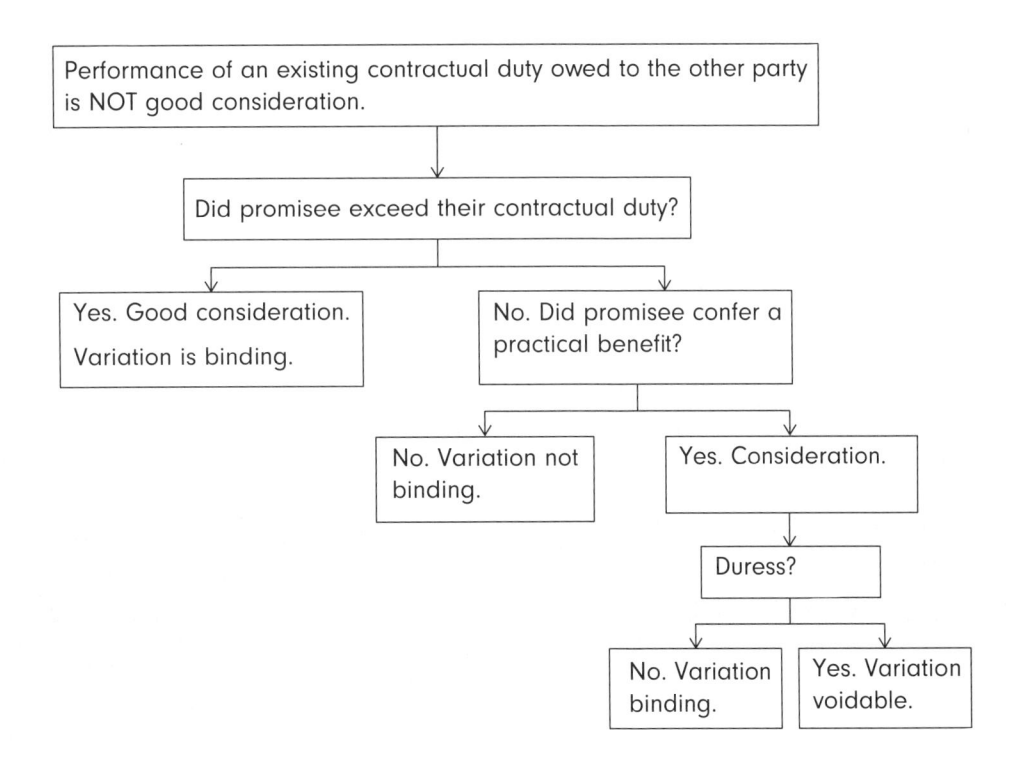

Figure 2.1 Alteration promises to pay more

```
┌─────────────────────────────────────────────────────────────┐
│ Performance of an existing contractual duty owed to the      │
│ other party is NOT good consideration.                       │
└─────────────────────────────────────────────────────────────┘
                              │
                              ▼
              ┌──────────────────────────────────┐
              │ Did promisee exceed their         │
              │ contractual duty?                 │
              └──────────────────────────────────┘
                    │                    │
                    ▼                    ▼
    ┌──────────────────────────┐  ┌──────────────────────────┐
    │ Yes. Good consideration. │  │ No. Did promisee confer a│
    │ Variation is binding.    │  │ practical benefit?        │
    └──────────────────────────┘  └──────────────────────────┘
                                       │              │
                                       ▼              ▼
                          ┌───────────────────┐  ┌──────────────────┐
                          │ No. Variation not │  │ Yes.             │
                          │ binding.          │  │ Consideration.   │
                          └───────────────────┘  └──────────────────┘
                                                          │
                                                          ▼
                                                   ┌──────────┐
                                                   │ Duress?  │
                                                   └──────────┘
                                                    │        │
                                                    ▼        ▼
                                         ┌─────────────┐ ┌──────────────┐
                                         │ No.         │ │ Yes.         │
                                         │ Variation   │ │ Variation    │
                                         │ binding.    │ │ voidable.    │
                                         └─────────────┘ └──────────────┘
```

resolve their problems. However, it could be argued that *Williams v Roffey Bros* has made it too easy for contractual obligations to be modified.

From a practical point of view, though, the thing to remember is that performance of an existing contractual duty owed to the other party may be consideration. It depends on whether, or not, the conditions laid down in *Williams v Roffey Bros* are satisfied.

Performance of existing duty – summary

- Performance of an existing public duty will not amount to consideration (*Collins v Godefroy*). If the claimant exceeds their public duty, this will usually be consideration (*Glasbrook Bros v Glamorgan CC*).
- Performance of an existing contractual duty owed to a third party will amount to consideration (*Scotson v Pegg*).
- Performance of an existing contractual duty owed to the other contracting party will not normally amount to consideration (*Stilk v Myrick*). If the claimant exceeds their existing contractual duty, this will usually be consideration (*Hartley v Ponsonby*).
- The rule in *Stilk v Myrick* was modified in *Williams v Roffey Bros*. This case provided that performance of an existing duty owed to the other party will be consideration, provided the other party receives a practical or commercial benefit. So practical benefit per se may be consideration, but if the promise to pay more was only made under duress, the variation may be avoided (see **Chapter 7**).

2.5 Part payment of undisputed debts

We have seen that performance of an existing contractual obligation owed to the other contracting party has not traditionally been regarded as consideration (*Stilk v Myrick*). Related to this rule is the principle that part payment of a debt is not usually consideration for a promise by the creditor to forgo the balance due. The debtor is already bound to pay the full amount of an undisputed debt, so by paying less they will not usually provide consideration for the creditor's promise to accept part payment and forgo the balance.

This rule on part payment of debts is to be found in *Pinnel's Case* (1602) 5 Co Rep 117a, as confirmed by the House of Lords in *Foakes v Beer* (1884) 9 App Cas 605.

The rule stated in *Pinnel's Case* was only *obiter* and so consequently, in strict legal terms, the House of Lords in *Foakes v Beer* was not bound by the rule. But as the Earl of Selborne LC commented in *Foakes v Beer*:

> The doctrine [ie the rule] ... may have been criticised ... But it has never been judicially overruled; on the contrary, I think it has always ... been accepted as law. If so, I cannot think that your lordships would do right if you were now to reverse as erroneous, a judgment of the Court of Appeal, proceeding up to a doctrine which has been accepted as part of the law of England for 280 years ...

A common law exception to the general rule that part payment of a debt is not consideration for a promise to forgo the balance is where the debtor can show that they gave something different for the creditor's agreement to accept the lesser sum in settlement. For example, if the debtor provides, or promises to provide, goods instead of cash or if they pay early. Lord Coke in *Pinnel's Case* stated:

> ... the gift of a horse, hawk or robe, etc in satisfaction is good for it shall be intended that a horse, hawk or robe, etc, might be more beneficial to the plaintiff than the money ... or otherwise, the plaintiff would not have accepted it in satisfaction.

Equally, if the creditor accepts payment of a lesser sum early, they presumably do so because they regard it as being more beneficial than receiving the full amount on the due date. In fact, this is what happened in *Pinnel's Case*, ie the debtor had paid early and had thereby provided consideration to discharge the whole debt.

The value of the goods or early payment received by the creditor in satisfaction is irrelevant. Remember that 'consideration need not be adequate' – *Chappell v Nestlé* – ie it need not be of equivalent value.

Another common law exception to the principle that part payment of a debt is not good consideration for a promise to forgo the balance is part payment of a debt by a third party. This is because it would be a fraud on the person who paid part of a debt in discharge of the whole, if an action could then be brought for the balance of the debt.

In the absence of a common law exception, the equitable doctrine of promissory estoppel may provide a defence to a claim brought under *Foakes v Beer*.

2.5.1 Promissory estoppel

Under this doctrine, a creditor may be prevented ('estopped') from going back on a promise to accept part payment (even if the promise is not supported by consideration) if in all the circumstances it would be unfair for the creditor to do so.

Promissory estoppel is simply the idea that:

- if you have made a promise not to enforce your legal rights; and
- the promisee has relied on that promise, even though they have not provided anything in return; then
- if you try to enforce your legal rights you will be 'estopped' (prevented from going back on your promise) if it would be inequitable (unfair) in all the circumstances to do so.

The doctrine of promissory estoppel is founded on the judgment of Denning J in the well-known case of *Central London Property Trust v High Trees House* [1947] KB 130 (generally referred to as '*High Trees*'). The basic facts of the case were as follows:

- Lease entered into in 1937 – annual ground rent of £2,500 (payable quarterly).
- January 1940 – agreement by landlord to accept £1,250 per annum (due to very low level of letting, arising from wartime conditions).
- The defendants paid the reduced rent throughout the war.
- By June 1945 all the flats were fully let.
- In 1946 the landlord sought to recover back rent for the last two quarters of 1945 and full rent for the future.

So there were basically three 'periods' considered by the court:

Period 1   unclaimed rent from the beginning of the war until the flats were fully let.

Period 2   unclaimed rent for last two quarters of 1945 after the war had ended.

Period 3   claiming reinstatement of full rent for the future.

The court said *obiter* that the unclaimed rent for period 1 (the war period) was not recoverable, but it held that as the concession had come to an end by early 1945, the unclaimed rent for the other two periods when the war had ended was recoverable.

So promissory estoppel may apply to prevent the enforcement of strict legal rights in circumstances where it would be unfair (inequitable) to do so.

We will now examine the four conditions which must be satisfied for promissory estoppel to apply.

2.5.2 Conditions for promissory estoppel to apply

2.5.2.1 There must be a clear promise to waive a strict legal right

The promise may be by words or implied by conduct. In the *High Trees* case, the landlord expressly promised to reduce the rent.

2.5.2.2 The promisee must act on the promise – what does this mean?

In the *High Trees* case, the act in reliance was payment of half rent. The promisee did not thereby suffer a detriment. It seemed to be enough that the promisee had altered their position in some way as a result of the promise.

In *WJ Alan & Co v El Nasr* [1972] 2 All ER 127, Lord Denning said (*obiter*):

> I know that it has been suggested in some quarters that there must be detriment. But I can find no support for it in the authorities cited by the judge. The nearest approach to it is ... that the other must have been led 'to alter his position' which was adopted by Lord Hodson in *Emanual Ajayi v RT Briscoe (Nigeria) Ltd* [1964] 3 All ER 556. But that only means that he must have been led to act differently from what he would otherwise have done. And if you study the cases in which the doctrine has been applied, you will see that all that is required is that one should have 'acted on the belief induced by the other party'.

Therefore, it seems there does not have to be detrimental reliance by the promisee.

2.5.2.3 Promissory estoppel can only be used as a defence; it cannot give rise to a cause of action

The authority for the rule that promissory estoppel can only be used as a defence is *Combe v Combe* [1951] 1 All ER 62. Here, a husband and wife were in the process of obtaining a divorce. The husband promised that he would pay the wife £100 a year as permanent maintenance. The husband did not pay, and the wife brought an action based on the husband's promise to make the payments. At first instance, the judge held that the wife could enforce the payments relying on promissory estoppel. However, the Court of Appeal reversed the decision, making it clear that the doctrine could only be used as a defence and not a cause of action.

2.5.2.4 It must be inequitable for the promisor to go back on their promise

An authority for this is the case of *D&C Builders v Rees* [1966] 2 QB 617. In this case, the defendants owed the claimants £482. The claimants were in financial difficulties and the defendants offered £300 in full settlement, indicating that if the claimants did not accept then they would not get any payment at all. The claimants accepted because they felt that they had no choice, but then sued for the balance.

Lord Denning MR said that the defendants could not rely on promissory estoppel. It was not inequitable for the claimants to go back on their promise since it had not been freely given.

It seems clear that when the court looks at whether it is inequitable for the promisor to go back on the promise, it will consider all of the circumstances of the case including the behaviour of the parties.

2.5.3 The effect of the doctrine of promissory estoppel

You have seen that there are four conditions that must be satisfied for the doctrine of promissory estoppel to apply.

Assuming all four conditions are satisfied, what effect will the doctrine have? Will the promisor's rights be extinguished completely, or will they be suspended for a time? It seems that the doctrine will generally operate to suspend legal rights, but it may extinguish them depending on what would be equitable and/or possible on the particular facts.

Cases on promissory estoppel may involve continuing obligations such as payment of rent or may involve a one-off debt. We will consider each in turn.

2.5.3.1 Promissory estoppel and continuing obligations

An example of a case involving continuing obligations is the *High Trees* case. In this sort of situation, where the promisor agrees to accept reduced rent, the promisor will generally be able to give reasonable notice and claim full rent for the future, but they will not be able to claim the full amount of rent for the period before the notice expires (although this does depend on what was agreed).

In the case of *Tool Metal Manufacturing Co v Tungsten Electric Co Ltd* [1955] 1 WLR 761, Lord Tucker made it clear that notice may not always be necessary. He said:

> There are some cases where the period of suspension clearly terminates on the happening of a certain event or the cessation of a previously existing state of affairs or on the lapse of a reasonable period thereafter. In such cases no intimation or notice of any kind may be necessary. But in other cases where there is nothing to fix the end of the period which may be dependent on the will of the person who has given or made the concession, equity will no doubt require some notice or intimation together with a reasonable period for readjustment before the grantor is allowed to enforce his strict rights.

Therefore, the court will consider whether the promise was clearly intended to last only until a particular event happened or a particular situation came to an end (such as war-time conditions in the *High Trees* case). If so, it may be that the promisor is able to resume the right to the full amount of rent (or other form of continuing payment) from that point. If not, then it is likely that the promisor can give reasonable notice and resume full rights when the notice expires. What will amount to reasonable notice will be a question of fact and equity in each case. The notice does not have to be in any particular form.

Also, it seems that if the promisee cannot be returned to their original position then the promisor's rights may be extinguished completely. In the Privy Council case of *Emanual Ajayi v RT Briscoe (Nigeria) Ltd* [1964] 3All ER 556, Lord Hodson said:

> ... the promisor can resile from his promise on giving reasonable notice, which need not be formal notice ... The promise only becomes final and irrevocable if the promisee cannot resume his position.

2.5.3.2 Promissory estoppel and one-off debts

The effect of promissory estoppel in relation to promises to waive full payment of one-off debts is unclear. This is because all the cases in which promissory estoppel has been applied concern continuing obligations (eg rental payments).

In *D & C Builders v Rees* it seems that Denning LJ would have been happy to apply promissory estoppel to a debt, but only if the debtor had acted equitably. He said:

> ... we can now say that, when a creditor and debtor enter on a course of negotiation, which leads the debtor to suppose that, on payment of a lesser sum, the creditor will not enforce payment of the balance and on the faith thereof the debtor pays the lesser sum and the creditor accepts it in satisfaction; then the creditor will not be allowed to enforce payment of the balance when it would be inequitable to do so.

It is difficult to reconcile this approach with the principle in *Foakes v Beer* whereby a creditor can go back on a promise to accept a smaller sum and sue for the balance of the debt. The difficulty is that *Foakes v Beer* is a House of Lords decision and the principle established in that case cannot, as a matter of precedent, be overturned by a lower court.

It may be possible to reconcile *Foakes v Beer* with *High Trees* on the basis that promissory estoppel will usually just suspend the creditor's right to the balance of the debt, and the creditor may resume that right by giving reasonable notice. However, the doctrine may extinguish the creditor's right to the balance of the debt in circumstances where the debtor cannot resume their original position, or it would otherwise be inequitable to allow the creditor to go back on the promise.

2.5.4 Review of promissory estoppel

Because the doctrine of promissory estoppel is vague and controversial, it has generated much debate over the years and consequently lends itself very well to essay questions which test critical evaluation as well as relevant legal knowledge. A sample essay question on the topic is set out in the following activity.

ACTIVITY 1 Essay question

Prepare a plan for answering the following question. The structure may consist simply of headings showing the issues you would consider and the order in which you would deal with them.

Start first by reading the instructions in bold. Note exactly what you are being asked and make sure you address all aspects of the instructions. Then 'unpick' the quotation by identifying key words and phrases that you might critically evaluate in your essay.

> The harshness of the common law has been relieved. Equity has stretched out a merciful hand to help the debtor ... It is worth noting that the principle may be applied, not only so as to suspend strict legal rights, but also so as to preclude the enforcement of them. (Lord Denning in *D & C Builders v Rees* (1966))

Discuss this statement with reference to consideration and the doctrine of promissory estoppel. It has been suggested that the doctrine should be extended so that, for example, it could be used to found a cause of action in certain situations. What are your views on this?

COMMENT

The question is in two parts:

- First, you are asked to discuss Lord Denning's statement.
- Secondly, you are asked to express your views on whether the doctrine should be extended.

You should make sure that you deal with both parts, although the bulk of your answer will be on the first part.

Read the quotation carefully. It starts by saying: 'The harshness of the common law has been relieved.'

You should therefore deal with this by explaining what is the common law rule (ie the rule in *Foakes v Beer*) and why it can be harsh.

The quotation then says: 'Equity has stretched out a merciful hand to help the debtor.' Again you need to explain this – which means explaining the doctrine of promissory estoppel.

Finally, Lord Denning says that the principle may be applied not only so as to suspend strict legal rights, but also so as to preclude the enforcement of them. You need to discuss this. You should explain what Denning's views are by examining the *High Trees* case and the case of *D & C Builders v Rees*.

You should try to come to some sort of conclusion as to the accuracy of the quotation.

A structure for this essay might look like this:

1. Introduction – statement of what is to be discussed, ie:
   - the statement by Denning; and
   - views as to extension of the doctrine.

2. The common law:
   - Define consideration.
   - Explain the rule in *Foakes v Beer* and the common law exception (*Pinnel's Case*). Explain why the common law can have harsh results.

3. Promissory estoppel – explain the doctrine, ie:
   - introduced by Denning in *High Trees* – obiter;
   - must be clear promise;
   - can only be used as a defence (*Combe v Combe*);
   - promisee must act on the promise – explain;
   - must be inequitable for the promisor to go back on the promise – explain what this means and illustrate with facts of *D & C Builders v Rees*.

     Assuming the conditions are satisfied, how does the doctrine operate? Does it merely suspend rights or does it extinguish them?
   - Denning's views – eg in *High Trees* and *D & C Builders*.

4. Possible conclusion – doctrine normally only suspends. Promisor can give reasonable notice and resume full rights.

   However, in 'ongoing payments' situations, eg rent, the doctrine may extinguish the right to claim the balance of past instalments, although the promisor may be able to give reasonable notice and receive in full future instalments.

5. Views on extension:
   - one possibility is to allow doctrine to be used to bring action;
   - radical step – would it mean abolition of consideration?
   - own personal views.

6. Overall conclusion.

Promissory estoppel – summary

Set out below is a summary of promissory estoppel.

Figure 2.2 Summary

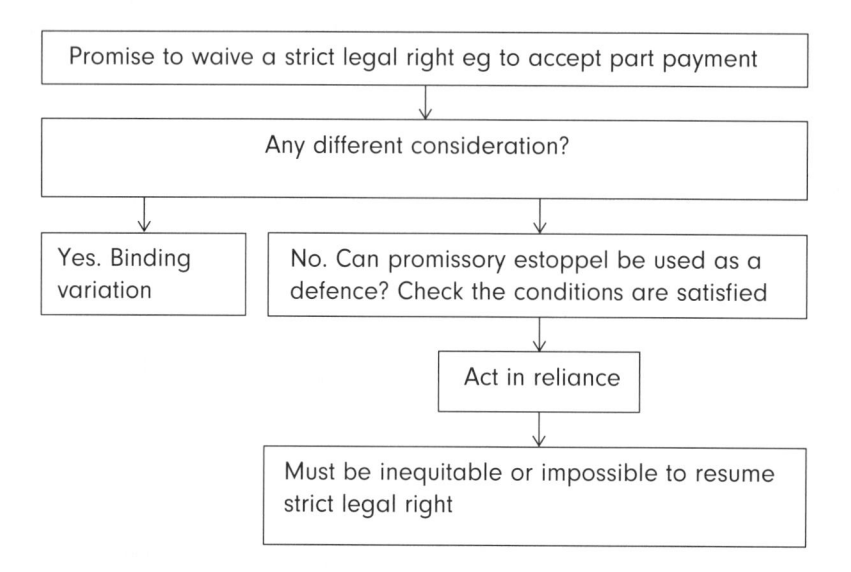

```
┌─────────────────────────────────────────────────────────┐
│ Promise to waive a strict legal right eg to accept part │
│ payment                                                  │
└─────────────────────────────────────────────────────────┘
                              ↓
┌─────────────────────────────────────────────────────────┐
│ Any different consideration?                            │
└─────────────────────────────────────────────────────────┘
           ↓                              ↓
┌──────────────────┐    ┌────────────────────────────────────┐
│ Yes. Binding     │    │ No. Can promissory estoppel be used │
│ variation        │    │ as a defence? Check the conditions  │
│                  │    │ are satisfied                       │
└──────────────────┘    └────────────────────────────────────┘
                                          ↓
                        ┌────────────────────────────────┐
                        │ Act in reliance                │
                        └────────────────────────────────┘
                                          ↓
                        ┌────────────────────────────────────┐
                        │ Must be inequitable or impossible  │
                        │ to resume strict legal right       │
                        └────────────────────────────────────┘
```

Promissory estoppel – checklist

Whenever you come across a situation where promissory estoppel may be relevant, you must consider the following issues:

- Has there been a promise to waive a strict legal right?
- Promissory estoppel can only be used as a defence when the other party is seeking to enforce a strict legal right which they had promised to waive.
- Did the promisee act in reliance on the promise to waive the strict legal right? It need not be detrimental reliance.
- It must be inequitable for the promisor to go back on their promise. Look at all the circumstances. Would it be equitable for the promisor to renege on their promise and enforce their strict legal right?
- If the above four conditions are satisfied then promissory estoppel applies, but does it operate to suspend or extinguish the legal right? In relation to ongoing payments, the legal right is usually just suspended and can be resumed only by giving reasonable notice. The right to past payments is usually extinguished. In relation to one-off debts, the position is uncertain. At the end of the day, the question may well be determined by what would be fair on the particular facts.

You should appreciate that the scope of the doctrine of promissory estoppel is vague and that aspects of it are uncertain (eg the effect of promissory estoppel on one-off debts (see above)). It is because of this uncertainty that solicitors will tend to advise clients to plead promissory estoppel only as a last resort.

2.6 Performance of existing contractual duty owed to other party and part payment of debt: can the legal principles be reconciled?

We have looked at the relationship between *Foakes v Beer* and *High Trees*; now let us consider for a moment what, if any, relationship there is between the decision in *Foakes v Beer* and that in *Williams v Roffey Bros*. If you remember, *Williams v Roffey* is authority for the principle that performance of an existing contractual duty owed to the other party may be consideration for a promise of extra money if it confers a practical benefit on the promisor and there is no economic duress or fraud.

In *Re Selectmove* [1995] 1 WLR 474, CA, counsel for the debtor argued that the principle in *Williams v Roffey* should be extended to part payment of a debt. Counsel argued that if part payment of a debt confers a practical benefit and is freely accepted (ie there is no duress or fraud), then the practical benefit should be consideration. Whilst the Court of Appeal had some sympathy with the argument, it said *obiter* that it was constrained by precedent as *Foakes v Beer* was a House of Lords decision. Peter Gibson LJ said:

> I see the force of the argument, but the difficulty that I feel with it is that if the principle in *Williams v Roffey Bros and Nicholls (Contractors) Ltd* is to be extended to an obligation to make payment, it would in effect leave the principle in *Foakes v Beer* without any application. When a creditor and a debtor who are at arm's length reach agreement on the payment of a debt by instalments to accommodate the debtor, the creditor will no doubt always see a practical benefit to himself in so doing. *Foakes v Beer* was not even referred to in *Williams v Roffey Bros and Nicholls (Contractors) Ltd*, and it is in my judgment impossible, consistently with the doctrine of precedent for this court to extend the principle of Williams' case to any circumstances governed by the principle of *Foakes v Beer*. If that extension is to be made, it must be by the House of Lords or ... by Parliament.

The Supreme Court in *Rock Advertising Ltd v MWB Business Exchange Centres Ltd* [2018] UKSC 24 did not have to consider the point but commented that any decision would involve a re-examination of the decision in *Foakes v Beer*, and as such should be before an enlarged panel of the court and in a case where the decision would be more than *obiter*.

The following table sums up and compares the rules and case law on promises to pay more money for the performance of an existing contractual obligation and promises to accept less money in full satisfaction of a debt.

Table 2.1 Summary and comparison of rules on 'upward' and 'downward' variations

Rule in *Stilk v Myrick*	Rule in *Foakes v Beer*
• If there is a contract between A and B and A agrees to pay B *more* money if B will *complete* B's obligations then you should consider the rule in *Stilk v Myrick*. **Here A is agreeing to pay more money to B.** • The rule in *Stilk v Myrick* provides that performance of an existing contractual duty owed to the other party is not sufficient consideration for a promise to pay more.	• If there is a contract between A and B and A has fully performed A's obligations and agrees to accept a reduced payment from B, you should consider the rule in *Foakes v Beer*. **Here A is agreeing to accept less money from B.** • The rule in *Foakes v Beer* provides that partial payment of a debt is not sufficient consideration for a promise by a creditor to forgo the balance.

(Continued)

Table 2.1 (*Continued*)

Rule in *Stilk v Myrick*	Rule in *Foakes v Beer*
APPLICATION • First state the rule and then consider whether B is simply performing B's existing obligations or whether B has done something extra in return for A's promise to pay more. • If B has done something extra then B can rely on *Hartley v Ponsonby* and the extra will amount to sufficient consideration. In this case you need not discuss *Williams v Roffey*. • If B has not done something extra then you should consider whether the *Williams v Roffey* exception applies.	**APPLICATION** • First state the rule and then consider whether any of the common law exceptions apply. For example, did the debtor pay early (as in *Pinnel's Case*)? If so, the debtor can rely on the exception in *Pinnel's Case* and will have provided sufficient consideration. In this case you will not need to discuss promissory estoppel. • If B cannot rely on a common law exception then you should consider promissory estoppel *in detail*. Always start by defining the doctrine and then go through it in detail.

2.7 Doctrine of privity of contract

In this paragraph we are going to consider the doctrine of privity of contract; identify why reform was necessary; and look at the key provisions in the Contracts (Rights of Third Parties) Act 1999.

The requirement that to sue for breach of a particular promise you must have given consideration to the defaulting party for that promise necessarily means that only a contracting party (ie someone who is privy to the contract) can sue for breach of contract, or otherwise be liable for breach. This general rule is referred to as privity of contract, ie only the actual parties to a contract are bound by it and therefore have rights and obligations under it.

This rule of privity effectively meant that third parties could neither sue nor be sued on a contract. As far as contractual obligations go, no one has ever really questioned the rule, but what about benefits under a contract? What if a contract has been made for the benefit of a third party? The privity rule meant that the third party still had no rights under the contract. This is illustrated by the old case of *Tweddle v Atkinson* (1861) 1 B & S 393. The claimant was engaged to be married and his father and future father-in-law made a contract providing that each of them would give a certain sum of money to the claimant. Even though the contract expressly provided that the claimant was to be entitled to enforce it, the court held that he could not do so.

It is this aspect of the rule that has been criticised and, needless to say, ways around it have emerged over the years. The main exception was introduced by the Contracts (Rights of Third Parties) Act 1999, which we look at next.

The 1999 Act applies to contracts entered into on and after 1 May 2000. Section 1 of the Act allows a third party to enforce a contract term if either:

- the contract expressly provides that they may; or
- the term purports to confer a benefit on them (unless it appears that the parties did not intend the term to be enforceable by the third party).

In either case, the third party must be identified by name, as a member of a class (eg 'employees') or answering to a particular description.

This Act explains why, in the run up to Christmas, shops will often ask if you would like a gift receipt for goods you are buying. If you say you are buying the goods for a friend or family member, you thereby confer direct contractual rights on the recipient so if something happens to be wrong with the goods, the recipient (rather than you) can take them back to the shop and seek a remedy. We will be looking at remedies under contracts for the sale of goods in **Chapter 3**.

The Act also extends to the benefit of exemption clauses, which we will also be looking at in **Chapter 3**.

2.8 Agency

2.8.1 What is agency?

Agency is the relationship which arises where someone (the agent) acts on behalf of another (the principal) and has power to affect the principal's legal position with regard to a third party. Examples of agents include:

- travel agents;
- insurance brokers;
- ticket agents;
- shop assistants; and
- auctioneers.

Note, however, that lots of persons who get called 'agents' may not be agents in the strict legal sense. For example, estate agents do not normally contract to sell property on behalf of their clients – they only tend to have authority to advertise the property for sale and facilitate the reaching of an agreement. So be aware that the commercial use of the word 'agent' is not always the same as the legal use of it.

2.8.2 How is agency created?

In order to create a binding contract between a principal and a third party, an agent must generally have authority.

2.8.2.1 Actual authority

The simplest way in which agency can be created is by the principal giving the required authority to the agent to contract on its behalf. So, agency normally arises by express appointment, ie the principal will expressly appoint someone to act as their agent to do specific thing(s).

When agency arises in this way, the agent is said to have actual authority. Actual authority can be granted expressly or it can be implied. For example, an agent may have express authority to sell particular goods, but also implied actual authority to do things usually carried out by sellers of such goods, eg to advertise them and receive payment for them.

But sometimes agents purport to act for their principals in circumstances where they do not have actual authority. This may happen for a variety of reasons – because agents do not always do exactly as they are told; because they are unsure of the extent of their authority; or even because, although they *did* have authority, it has been *revoked* in some way, eg because the principal has become ill or died.

Nonetheless, there are some circumstances where the law regards the acts of the agent as binding on the principal, despite the lack of actual authority. The third party, who has entered into a contract with the principal, may claim there is a binding agreement, and the principal may argue to the contrary, because the purported agent had no actual authority to contract on the principal's behalf.

2.8.2.2 Apparent authority

Here the agent does not have actual authority from the principal. But the agent could still be able to form a binding contract because he has a different form of authority – one which has been made apparent to the third party by the principal. It is not sufficient that the so-called 'agent' appears to be authorised. The appearance of authority must be created by the principal, and this representation must have been intended to be and in fact was acted upon by the other party.

So, for apparent (or what is sometimes called ostensible) authority to arise, the following three conditions must be satisfied:

- at some stage the principal must have represented (by words or conduct) that the agent had authority;
- the third party must rely on this representation, believing that the agent has authority; and
- the third party must alter their position eg by entering into a contract.

> ⭐ **Example**
>
> *When Paul started up a business manufacturing wooden toys (including traditional rocking horses), he employed Abba Ltd as his selling agent for the toys. Paul agreed not to supply customers direct.*
>
> *He instructed Abba Ltd to sell the rocking horses for at least £500 each. Nigel approached Paul direct to buy a rocking horse. Paul referred Nigel to Abba Ltd telling him that he had to deal through Paul's agent, Abba Ltd. Abba Ltd contracted to sell a rocking horse to Nigel for £400. Paul refuses to sell for that amount.*
>
> *But is Paul legally obliged to sell it to Nigel for £400? This hinges on whether Abba Ltd was authorised to enter into the contract with Nigel on Paul's behalf and so bind Paul. Provided Abba Ltd had authority, Abba Ltd would acquire no rights or liabilities under the contract. The contract would be between Paul and Nigel.*
>
> *Authority may be actual or apparent. Abba Ltd had express actual authority to sell the rocking horses but for at least £500 each. Abba Ltd exceeded its authority and so had no express authority to do the deal.*
>
> *As Paul told Nigel to deal through Abba Ltd and did not mention any express limitation on Abba's authority, Nigel would think Abba Ltd had authority to sell him a rocking horse for £400, ie Abba Ltd had apparent authority. Paul would be estopped from denying, as against Nigel, that Abba Ltd had authority to sell the rocking horse for £400.*
>
> *Consequently, Paul is bound to sell the horse to Nigel for £400; otherwise he will be in breach of contract. Abba Ltd has no rights or liabilities under the contract of sale, but it will be liable to Paul for breach of the agency agreement.*

If you look at the Specimen Standard Conditions of Sale (**Reading 1** of the **Appendix**), you will see that it is specifically stated at clause 2.2 that 'The Seller's sales representatives do not have authority to do any of the following things on behalf of the Seller: ...' You will now appreciate the reason behind this, ie it is to stop a customer claiming that a sales representative had apparent/ostensible authority (even though the agent may not have had actual authority) to bind the seller.

2.8.3 Effects of agency

2.8.3.1 Authorised agent

An authorised agent has no rights (or indeed obligations) under the resulting contract. The agent is authorised to enter the contract on behalf of someone else (called the principal) and the resulting contract is between the principal and other party. The agent simply drops out of the picture.

> ⭐ *Example*
>
> *Jackson's Store appoints Sara to act as its agent to buy goods. Sara, purporting to act on behalf of Jackson's Store, enters into a contract with Lewis to buy a consignment of goods for £5,000. They agree that payment will be two weeks after delivery. Lewis delivers but Jackson's Store does not pay.*
>
> *Lewis would not be able to sue Sara for the money. Provided Sara had authority of some sort (ie either actual or apparent/ostensible) then the rights and obligations under the contract belong to and bind the principal (Jackson's Store) and the third party (Lewis). It is as if the contract had been made between the principal and the third party.*

2.8.3.2 Unauthorised agent

But what about a situation where the agent purported to contract on another's behalf but did not in fact have any sort of authority?

- The principal cannot sue the third party or be sued by the third party (because the agent did not have authority to bind the principal).
- The agent cannot be sued on the contract as the agent was purporting to contract on another's behalf. The third party never thought there was a contract with the agent.
- The third party may sue the agent in deceit, where the agent knew they had no authority, or for breach of implied warranty of authority (eg, where the agent's authority had been terminated without the agent's knowledge). In *Collen v Wright* (1857) 8 E & B 647 an agent purporting to act on behalf of a named principal agreed to lease the principal's farm to the plaintiff. Both the plaintiff and the agent believed the agent had authority to make the lease, but that was not the case. The plaintiff's action against the principal failed, but the court inferred from the circumstances a separate and independent contract by which the agent promised that they had authority and in consideration of that promise the plaintiff agreed to take a lease of the farm.

We have now considered the effects of a disclosed agency (ie where the agent is purporting to act as an agent). Where the agent has some form of authority, they are in a position to bind the principal to a contract with a third party. Where the disclosed agent does not have authority, the agent cannot bind the principal to a deal and, as the agent was purporting to act on behalf of someone else, the agent will not be personally liable on the deal (although the agent may be liable for example in the tort of deceit).

In *Re Selectmove* (which we discussed in **Chapter 1** in the context of acceptance by silence and earlier in this chapter in the context of part payment of a debt), the actual decision of the Court of Appeal was based purely on agency. The representative of the creditor had no authority (express or otherwise) to bind the creditor to the proposed arrangement to pay the debt by instalments.

2.9 Capacity

This section is intended to provide you with an introduction to some of the basic legal principles governing capacity (ie the legal power to make a contract). Earlier we considered the doctrine of privity and the importance of identifying the parties to a contract. The general rule, remember, is that only parties to a contract can sue or be sued on it. Occasionally, though, a contract will not bind a party because the party lacked the necessary capacity or power to make a contract.

The main categories of people whose power, or capacity, to enter contracts is limited by law are minors (persons under the age of 18) and people with a mental incapacity.

Also, it goes without saying that a contracting party should be a person recognised as such by the law. Persons in law, however, are not confined to individuals. A lot of contracts are entered into by, or on behalf of, organisations such as companies and local authorities. Such bodies are generally called corporations, and the capacity of a corporation depends on the type of corporation.

2.9.1 Minors

The basic common law principle is that minors are not bound by contracts they have entered into – the other party is bound and can be sued, but not the minor. As with all general principles, though, there are exceptions. Contracts for 'necessaries' bind minors. 'Necessaries' include not just the supply of necessary goods and services, but also contracts of service for a minor's benefit.

'Necessaries' are defined under the Sale of Goods Act 1979 as goods 'suitable to the condition in life of the minor and to his actual requirements at the time of sale and delivery'. 'Necessaries' therefore extend beyond the absolute essentials (such as food and clothing). What is 'necessary' for a particular minor will depend to an extent on their social status *and* their actual requirements at the time of purchase.

> ⭐ *Example*
>
> A bespoke tailor shop supplies an expensive blazer to a 16-year-old boy, Michael, who comes from a wealthy family. The contract might be binding on Michael. It will depend on whether, or not, he already has an adequate supply of blazers and the like.

Minors are also bound by contracts of service which are on the whole beneficial to them. Generally, this means contracts of employment under which a minor gains training and experience (eg an apprenticeship) as long as, on balance, the contract is more favourable than not to the minor.

This point is illustrated by *Proform Sports Management Ltd v Proactive Sports Management* [2006] EWHC 2903 (Ch) (aka the 'Wayne Rooney case'). When Wayne Rooney, aged 15 years, was playing for Everton FC, he entered into a two-year contract with Proform to act as his agent. Before the end of the two years, he terminated the contract. The court held that he was entitled to do so as the contract with Proform (unlike the contract with Everton FC) was not a contract for necessaries.

2.9.2 Mental incapacity

This category covers persons suffering from mental impairment and those who are drunk when the contract is made. Generally, contracts made with someone in either state will be valid unless, at the time the contract was made, the person was incapable of understanding the nature of the transaction *and* the other party knew that to be the case. In such instances, the contract will be 'voidable', which means it is binding unless, and until, the person suffering from the mental impairment or inebriation rescinds it (ie sets aside the contract). We will be considering voidable contracts in **Chapters 6** and **7**.

> ⭐ *Example*
>
> An elderly gentleman, Jack, entered into a contract with Hansaj. Unknown to Hansaj, Jack was suffering from senile dementia.
>
> Jack now wants to get out of the contract. Advise Jack.
>
> Even if Jack did not understand the nature of the deal he had struck, he would be bound by it as Hansaj was unaware of Jack's mental incapacity.

The final type of legal 'person' that may lack capacity is a corporation, which we are going to look at next.

2.9.3 Corporations

If two or more people form themselves into an association for the purpose of some concerted enterprise (eg on the formation of a club or a trading company), the association is in some cases regarded by the law as being an independent person called a corporation. A corporation is treated by the law as having a separate legal identity from the person, or persons, who constitute it. Note, however, that not all associations are corporations; it depends on whether or not the association has been incorporated in law. An unincorporated association, such as a club, is not a competent contracting party. If a contract is made on its behalf, no individual member can be sued on it except the person who actually made it and any other member who authorised them to do so.

The three main types of corporation are:

- registered companies;
- statutory corporations; and
- limited liability partnerships.

2.9.3.1 Registered companies

Most corporations are registered under the Companies Act (CA) 2006. Section 31 of the CA 2006 allows a company to carry on whatever activity it wants (within the law, of course). Further, s 39 of the CA 2006 effectively abolishes the 'ultra vires' doctrine with regard to third parties dealing with the company. In other words, s 39 provides that an act undertaken by the company with an outsider (such as entering a contract) cannot be challenged if it is beyond the powers granted in the company's constitution. Both the company and the other party to the transaction are bound by the act. This is backed up by s 40(1), which states that the powers of the directors to bind a company (eg by entering a contract) are deemed to be free of any limitation under the company's constitution in favour of a person dealing with the company in good faith. Notwithstanding that, parties looking to enter into a contract with a company are still best advised to check the company's capacity.

2.9.3.2 Statutory corporations

These corporations (as their name suggests) are created by statute. They include local authorities. The statute creating each corporation will set out the purposes for which the corporation may enter contracts. Any contract entered outside of the stated powers will be declared ultra vires and therefore void, ie as if there had never been a contract. We will look at void contracts in **Chapter 8**.

Contract

2.9.3.3 Limited liability partnerships

These were created by the Limited Liability Partnerships Act 2000 and benefit from unlimited capacity.

ACTIVITY 2 Consideration

Please tick the appropriate box to indicate whether the statement is true or false and please give the name of any relevant case. If you think the statement is false, please give a reason for your answer.

Statement	True	False/reason
1. Consideration must be a benefit to the person who receives it and a detriment to the person giving it.		
2. Consideration must be both sufficient and adequate.		
3. X finds and returns Y's mobile phone. Y promises to pay X £10 but then does not do so. Y says Y did not ask X to find it. X has given valid consideration for Y's promise.		
4. Past consideration is sufficient consideration if the act is performed at the promisor's request or the parties understand that the act will be rewarded.		
5. Performance of a contractual obligation owed to the other contracting party may be sufficient consideration for a promise of more money if the party promising to pay obtains a practical benefit.		
6. The basic rule is that payment of a lesser sum on the due date is not good consideration for a promise to forgo the balance.		
7. To rely on the doctrine of promissory estoppel it is not necessary to have acted equitably in obtaining the promise.		
8. Promissory estoppel provides a shield not a sword.		

COMMENT

Statement	True	False/reason
1. Consideration must be a benefit to the person who receives it and a detriment to the person giving it.		√ *Currie v Misa*: it may be either a benefit or a detriment; it need not be both.
2. Consideration must be sufficient and adequate.		√ It must be sufficient. It does not have to adequately reflect the value of the promise given in exchange: *Chappell v Nestlé*.
3. X finds and returns Y's mobile phone. Y promises to pay X £10 but then does not do so. Y says Y did not ask X to find it. X has given valid consideration for Y's promise.		√ X's consideration is past. X found and returned the mobile phone before the promise of payment was made. Past consideration is usually insufficient consideration (*Roscorla v Thomas*). (The exception does not apply as X did not act at Y's request.)

Consideration, Privity, Agency and Capacity

Statement	True	False/reason
4. Past consideration is sufficient consideration if the act is performed at the promisor's request or the parties understand that the act will be rewarded.		√ Three conditions, must be fulfilled: *Lampleigh v Brathwait, Re Casey's Patents*. The two stated opposite, and the fact that had the promise been made in advance it would have been legally enforceable.
5. Performance of a contractual obligation owed to the other contracting party may be sufficient consideration for a promise of more money if the party promising to pay obtains a practical benefit.	√ *Williams v Roffey Bros*. If there was economic duress, the promise to pay more may be set aside	
6. The basic rule is that payment of a lesser sum on the due date is not good consideration for a promise to forgo the balance.	√ *Pinnel's Case; Foakes v Beer*	
7. To rely on the doctrine of promissory estoppel it is not necessary to have acted equitably in obtaining the promise.		√ You must act equitably to rely on an equitable doctrine. If you seek equitable relief you must have clean hands (*D & C Builders v Rees*).
8. Promissory estoppel provides a shield not a sword.	√ *Combe v Combe*	

ACTIVITY 3 Agency

In the questions listed below there are three statements. Only one of them is accurate. In each case, tick the statement which you consider to be accurate:

1. If an agent with express authority makes a contract with a third party on behalf of the principal then:
    1.1 If the principal defaults the third party can sue the agent.
    1.2 If the third party defaults the agent can sue the third party.
    1.3 If the principal defaults the third party can sue the principal.

2. 2.1 Apparent or ostensible authority is where the agent holds itself out as having authority and the third party alters its position in reliance.
    2.2 Where a principal represents (by words or conduct) that an agent has authority the principal may be estopped from denying the agent's authority.
    2.3 An agent will have apparent or ostensible authority provided the third party believes the agent has authority.

3. Hamil has been Ella's agent for 10 years. Ella terminates the agency, but Hamil then negotiates a contract with Ben who thinks that Hamil is still Ella's agent.
    3.1 Ella is not bound by the contract as she terminated the agency.
    3.2 Ella is bound by the contract as Hamil has actual authority.
    3.3 Ella is bound by the contract as Hamil has apparent authority.

COMMENT

1. Answer 1.3. Provided the agent has authority, the contract is between the principal and the third party and the agent 'drops out' of the picture.

2. Answer 2.2. The representation must come from the principal. Where an agent wrongly holds itself out as having authority, the agent will either be liable in the tort of deceit (if the agent was lying) or otherwise for breach of an implied warranty of authority.

3. Answer 3.3. Hamil has no actual authority (as Ella terminated his authority), but by not telling Ben (and other potential customers), Ella will be estopped from denying Hamil's apparent authority.

SUMMARY

- If you are advising a client on an alleged breach of contract, it is first of all essential to check that the agreement between the parties is legally binding. One of the things you will be checking is that the claimant gave consideration for the contractual promise which has allegedly been breached.

- In this chapter you have looked at what constitutes good consideration in the eyes of the law, and as you will appreciate from the many cases you have studied it is not always clear-cut. It is also apparent from the case law how consideration is far more likely to create problems when it comes to varying contractual terms, rather than at the formation stage. Just as you need agreement, contractual intention and consideration to create a binding contract, the same is true if a variation of a contract is to be legally binding. For example, you have looked at the extent to which performance of existing duties and part payment of a debt may constitute good consideration in the context of contractual variations.

- You have also been introduced to the doctrine of privity of contract and the main exception to it, namely the Contracts (Rights of Third Parties) Act 1999. You will look at this Act again in **Chapter 3** in the context of exemption clauses. Then you studied (albeit in overview) the law governing agency. Agency is particularly important in a commercial context, and remember that the effect of agency depends primarily on whether the agent had authority and whether the agency was disclosed.

- You also considered capacity. As a general rule, minors are not bound by contracts unless it is a contract for 'necessaries'. Even if a minor is not bound by a contract through lack of capacity, the other party will be bound by it. Persons with a mental disability or intoxicated persons will not be bound by a contract if they did not comprehend the nature of the deal *and* the other party was aware of that. Corporations have different levels of contracting ability, eg a statutory corporation will not be bound by contracts which are outside its statutory powers, whilst limited liability partnerships have unlimited capacity.

3 Contents of a Contract

LEARNING OUTCOMES

When you have completed this chapter, you should be able to:

- understand the difference between express and implied terms, how they are classified and the link with remedies for breach of contract;
- explain the ways in which terms may be implied into a contract with particular emphasis on terms implied by the Sale of Goods Act 1979, the Supply of Goods and Services Act 1982 and the Consumer Rights Act 2015;
- explain and discuss in depth the role of common law and statute in regulating exemption clauses in both business and consumer contracts;
- use a structured and analytical approach to advise a client on the effect of an exemption clause.

In **Chapters 1** and **2** you looked at the elements needed to form a contract: agreement, consideration and contractual intention. In this chapter, we are going to look at the contents of the contract. The contents of a contract are its terms. The terms determine the extent of the parties' obligations. Knowing the extent of the parties' obligations is important if things start to go wrong.

For example, suppose you want to arrange a short holiday in Cornwall. You find a suitable hotel and book five nights' accommodation. The hotel confirms your booking, but when you arrive you are told that the hotel has been overbooked and there is only a room available for two nights. To make matters worse, you had booked a room with a sea view but are given a room facing a busy main road with no hint of the sea in sight. The hotel will have broken terms of the contract (to provide you with five nights' accommodation and a room with a sea view). You will probably try to resolve the situation by negotiating with the hotel, but if this fails you can sue for breach of contract. The usual remedy is monetary compensation, which lawyers call damages. We will look at remedies for breach of contract in detail in **Chapter 4**.

In this chapter, we are going to consider the following:

- express terms;
- implied terms;
- exemption clauses (ie contract terms which exclude or restrict a party's liability for breach of contract or in some way limit the rights and remedies available to a party).

3.1 Identifying the express terms of the contract

The express terms of the contract are terms specifically agreed by the parties. They may be in writing or oral, but clearly it would be better to have all the terms included in a written contract for evidential reasons. In general, parties are free to agree to any terms they choose, although there are some restrictions which we will consider later.

> *Example*
>
> *Ashtons Ltd (a company of painters and decorators) enters into a contract with Jaswinder to paint her café for the sum of £2,000. Ashtons Ltd will supply the paint in ice blue for the doors and white for all other woodwork. Ashtons states that it will use a base coat followed by two topcoats.*
>
> *The express terms are:*
>
> *(a) Ashtons Ltd will paint Jaswinder's café*
>
> *(b) Price £2,000*
>
> *(c) Ashtons Ltd to supply paint*
>
> *(d) Paint to be ice blue for doors and white for all other woodwork*
>
> *(e) Ashtons Ltd will use a base coat and two topcoats.*

In the above case, it was reasonably easy to identify the express terms. Sometimes, however, there can be difficulty establishing what the parties have agreed. For example, the parties may disagree about whether statements made during negotiations are terms of the contract or representations. We shall be looking at the difference between terms and representations, and at the guidelines used by the court to determine whether a particular statement is a term or representation, in **Chapter 6**.

Also, in order to be terms, statements (whether oral or in writing) must be incorporated into the contract. We shall be looking at how statements can be incorporated later in this chapter when we deal with exemption clauses.

3.2 Implied terms

Implied terms are not expressly created by the parties but are implied (ie read) into the contract. Sometimes this may be done by a court in the course of litigation and sometimes it may be done by particular pieces of legislation. We shall look at the various ways in which terms are implied into contracts in a moment. First of all, though, why do you think terms may be implied into a contract?

One reason is that the parties may not expressly agree all the terms of their contract, maybe because they share the same background (eg they both work in the same line of business) and, because of this common background, they make certain assumptions which they do not bother to spell out in their contract because these points seem so obvious to them.

Also, if the parties have had previous consistent dealings, they may assume that their latest contract will contain the same provisions. We shall look at these possibilities in detail later on in this chapter.

It could be that the parties have not considered a particular point at all. However, a court will not imply a term into a contract just because the parties have been careless and forgot to deal with it.

Lastly, a term may be implied in order to protect one of the parties. This sort of term is usually implied by statute. For example, if you buy a tin of beans from a supermarket, you will not have a discussion with the supermarket about the quality of the beans. You will not have agreed on an express term about the quality of the beans. However, it would seem only fair that you should have some rights against the supermarket if you opened the tin and found the contents were mouldy. Therefore, a term is implied into the contract by statute that the goods are of satisfactory quality. If they are not, then the supermarket will be in breach of contract. We shall look at a number of statutory implied terms later in this chapter.

We will now consider situations where terms may be implied, starting with terms implied by the courts and then going on to terms implied by statute.

3.2.1 Terms implied by the courts

3.2.1.1 Terms implied by local custom or trade usage

We have seen one reason why the parties may not expressly agree all the terms of their contract, which is because they form the contract against a background of common assumptions based on what usually happens in that locality or in that line of business. Certain points seem so obvious that the parties do not bother to make express provision. If there is a disagreement about the provisions of the contract, a court may imply a term based on local custom or trade usage. For example, in *Hutton v Warren* (1836) 1 M & W 466 an outgoing tenant farmer was entitled to an allowance for seed used and work done in the last year of the tenancy even though the lease was silent on this point. This term was implied into the contract because it was customary in the locality for this allowance to be given and there was nothing in the lease to suggest that this custom should not be followed.

However, it would not have been possible to imply the term into the lease if the lease had contained a provision which contradicted the custom. The court would consider that the parties had thought about the local custom but decided to do something different.

The approach would be the same if the court was asked to imply a term based on trade usage. It would not do so if there was a provision in the contract which contradicted the trade usage.

3.2.1.2 Terms implied by a previous course of dealings between the parties

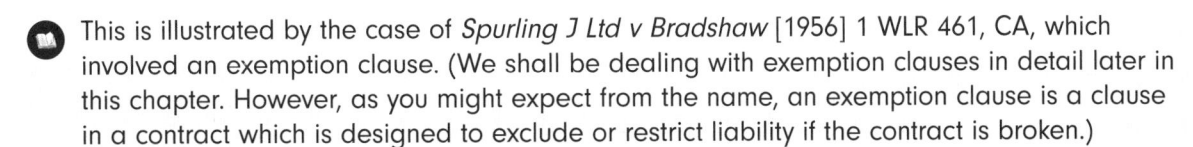

This is illustrated by the case of *Spurling J Ltd v Bradshaw* [1956] 1 WLR 461, CA, which involved an exemption clause. (We shall be dealing with exemption clauses in detail later in this chapter. However, as you might expect from the name, an exemption clause is a clause in a contract which is designed to exclude or restrict liability if the contract is broken.)

In *Spurling v Bradshaw*, Bradshaw delivered barrels of juice to the claimants for storage. As on all of the many previous occasions when they had had dealings, Bradshaw was later sent a receipt for the barrels and the receipt included an exemption clause.

When Bradshaw collected the barrels, they were empty. Bradshaw consequently refused to pay the storage charges and was sued. He counter-claimed for negligence and the claimants relied on the exemption clause as a defence.

The court held that although the exemption clause was included in a post-contractual document (ie a receipt), it was nevertheless a term of the contract. It was incorporated in the contract by the parties' previous consistent course of dealing.

This principle is not confined to exemption clauses. It could be used to imply other terms where the parties have had previous consistent dealings.

3.2.1.3 Terms implied by the courts to reflect the presumed intention of the parties

There are two tests that have been devised by the courts to imply terms into a contract based on the presumed intentions of the parties. These tests are known as the 'business efficacy' and 'officious bystander' tests.

The 'business efficacy' test was established in *The Moorcock* (1889) 14 PD 64, CA. The defendant owned a wharf on the River Thames and agreed to allow the claimants to moor their ship at the wharf. Both parties knew that the Thames was a tidal river and that the ship would rest on the riverbed at low tide. The ship was damaged due to a ridge of hard ground beneath the mud of the riverbed. There was no express term of the contract dealing with this. However, the Court of Appeal felt that the parties must have contracted on the basis that the wharf owner had taken reasonable care to see whether the berth was safe and implied a term into the contract on this basis. The reason for this is that it was necessary to give business efficacy to the contract (ie so that the contract made business sense). The court would not imply a term making an absolute guarantee that the berth was safe as that would be wider than necessary to give business efficacy to the contract.

The idea behind the decision in *The Moorcock* is that the court should consider whether a term is necessary to make the contract work commercially. It is not enough that the term would be a reasonable one to imply in the sense that it would improve the contract. The fact that the business efficacy test was supposed to be a stringent one was emphasised by the court in *Shirlaw v Southern Foundries Ltd* [1939] 2 KB 206, CA. In this case MacKinnon LJ explored the principle on which the decision in *The Moorcock* rests.

He suggested that a term could only be implied if the point was so obvious that it went without saying that was what the parties intended. He described this as an 'officious bystander test'. Suppose the parties are negotiating their agreement and a bystander suggests a term to include, then, if the response of both parties would be a common, 'Oh, of course', the test would be passed and the court would imply the term into the contract.

There are not many situations where both parties would react in this way. Very often, one of the parties would have reservations about the proposed term because it would impose additional obligations on them.

3.2.1.4 Terms implied by the courts because of the type of contract

Where a contract is of a kind which frequently occurs, the court may identify provisions which are typical of that kind of contract and say that these provisions will be implied terms unless the parties make contrary provision. Examples of contracts which frequently occur include tenancy agreements and employment contracts. (Also, contracts for the sale of goods are very common contracts but terms are implied into sale of goods contracts by statute rather than the common law. We shall look at statutory implied terms later on in this chapter.)

The case of *Liverpool City Council v Irwin and Another* [1977] AC 239, HL involved a tenancy agreement of flats in a tower block owned by the local authority. Owing to vandalism, the lifts were regularly out of action, the stairs were often unlit and the rubbish chutes were often blocked. The tenants withheld rent in protest. The agreement did not contain any provision about repair and maintenance of the lifts, stairs or rubbish chutes. The House of Lords had to decide whether there was any implied duty on the landlord to repair and maintain these common parts

Lord Wilberforce said that a test of necessity should be applied bearing in mind the nature of this particular contract. Accordingly, the House of Lords did not imply an absolute obligation to repair as Lord Wilberforce said that this would go beyond what was necessary in the circumstances. Instead, a term was implied that the landlord should take reasonable care to keep the common parts in reasonable repair.

The House of Lords went on to find that the landlord was not in breach of the term implied as reasonable care had been taken.

Implied terms – summary

We have now considered the various grounds the court can use to imply terms into contracts. We have seen that terms may be implied:

- by custom or trade usage;
- by a previous course of dealings between the parties;
- for business efficacy;
- because of the type of contract.

We shall now go on to consider some terms that have been implied into contracts by statute.

3.2.2 Terms implied by statute

We are going to look at terms implied by the Sale of Goods Act (SGA) 1979, the Supply of Goods and Services Act (SGSA) 1982 and the Consumer Rights Act (CRA) 2015. These Acts cover contracts for the sale of goods and contracts for the supply of services and work and materials.

The SGA 1979 and the SGSA 1982 have been amended on a number of occasions, most recently by the CRA 2015.

3.2.2.1 The Sale of Goods Act 1979

As the name of the Sale of Goods Act 1979 suggests, this statute implies terms into contracts for the sale of goods, but not into all contracts for the sale of goods. Since the CRA 2015 came into force, the SGA 1979 no longer applies to contracts for the sale of goods made between a trader and a consumer. In CRA 2015, a 'trader' is defined as 'a person acting for purposes relating to that person's trade, business, craft or profession, whether acting personally or through another person acting in the trader's name or on the trader's behalf'. A 'consumer' is defined as 'an individual acting for purposes that are wholly or mainly outside that individual's trade, business, craft or profession'. So the SGA 1979 now only applies to contracts for the sale of goods which are made business-to-business, consumer-to-consumer or consumer-to-business.

Terms implied by the Sale of Goods Act 1979

If you look at **Reading 3** of the **Appendix** you will see that the SGA 1979 says that some of the implied terms are conditions. A condition is a major term of the contract, as opposed to a warranty which is a minor term. The distinction is important for the remedies which will be available to the innocent party if the term is broken. We will be looking at the classification of terms later in this chapter.

For the moment, please read the extracts from ss 13 and 14 of the SGA 1979 set out in **Reading 3** in the **Appendix** and then consider the example below.

Example

The owner of a public house, Gary, is on the internet looking to buy a large smart screen TV to mount on a wall in the bar so that customers can watch live sports coverage. He finds a suitable TV on the Supatelly company website. It is priced at £1,200. There is a description underneath the picture of the TV, stating its screen size and resolution, the inputs it can take and other details. Gary likes what he reads and orders one. He clicks on the 'I agree to Supatelly's terms and conditions' button, puts in his credit card details and in due course the new TV arrives.

So let's see what Gary agreed (expressly and impliedly) with Supatelly.

The express terms will be for the sale of the specified TV at the price of £1,200; together with the standard Supatelly terms and conditions to which Gary gave his agreement online.

What about the terms that will be implied into his contract by the SGA 1979?

Section 13(1) implies a term commonly referred to as 'correspondence with description'. The idea here is that if the TV has been sold 'by description' – as is likely to be the case here where the goods are described as having certain characteristics and specifications – then the buyer is entitled to something that corresponds with that description.

Section 14 implies two further terms into Gary's contract with Supatelly: s 14(2) implies a term that the goods will be of satisfactory quality, and s 14(3) implies a term that the goods will be fit for purpose.

Having seen how the terms implied by ss 13 and 14 of the SGA 1979 work, we shall now consider them in more detail.

Section 14 – Satisfactory quality and reasonable fitness for purpose

We will look first at s 14 and begin by drawing together some of the points which arose.

- The implied terms of satisfactory quality (s 14(2)) and reasonable fitness for the buyer's purpose (s 14(3)) apply only if the seller sells in the course of a business to a commercial buyer.

- Section 14(3) refers to the buyer's purpose being made known to the seller expressly or by implication. If you intend to use goods just for their normal purpose, you do not have to tell the seller what this is. It is made known by implication. Therefore, in the example above, Gary did not have to tell Supatelly the intended purpose for the TV.

  However, if you have a special or unusual purpose in mind, then to get the benefit of s 14(3) you should tell the seller what this is. Remember, though, that it must be reasonable for the buyer to rely on the seller's skill and judgement.

- It is important to note that liability for breach of s 14(2) and 14(3) is strict, ie the buyer does not have to prove that the seller is at fault. This means, for example, that it is no defence for the seller to say that the seller did not know and could not have known that the goods were defective.

Suppose a shop buys goods from a wholesaler and then discovers that they are faulty due to a manufacturing defect. The wholesaler may well be in breach of both s 14(2) and s 14(3) of the SGA 1979 even though it was not in any way at fault. The wholesaler will have bought the goods from the manufacturer and the same terms will have been implied into that contract. So the wholesaler will, in turn, be able to sue the manufacturer for breach of the terms implied by s 14(2) and s 14(3).

Section 13 – Sale of goods by description

The second implied term that we need to consider in a little more detail is the term implied by s 13 of the SGA 1979.

- Section 13 says that where there is a contract for the sale of goods by description, there is an implied condition that the goods will correspond with that description.
- This term will be implied whether the seller is a business or a private individual, unlike the terms implied by s 14(2) and 14(3) where the seller must sell in the course of a business.
- The question is: when will a contract for the sale of goods be a sale by description? In the case of *Harlingdon & Leinster Enterprises Ltd v Christopher Hull Fine Art Ltd* [1991] 1 QB 564 the Court of Appeal made it clear that in order for s 13 to apply, the buyer must rely on the description. Therefore, in order to identify a sale by description, you should ask whether the buyer relied on the seller's description and whether this was reasonable.
- There will clearly be a sale by description where the buyer does not see the goods but relies on a description, eg on a website as in the Example above.
- There can also be a sale by description even where the buyer has seen the goods and examined them, provided the buyer has reasonably relied on the description. For example, in the case of *Beale v Taylor* [1967] 3 All ER 253, the defendant advertised a car for sale, describing it as a 1961 model. In fact, the car was made up of two halves of different cars welded together. One half dated from 1961, the other was older. The court decided that there had been a sale by description even though the buyer had inspected the car.
- Liability for breach of the term implied by s 13 is strict, ie the buyer does not have to prove that the seller is at fault.

Having considered the terms implied by s 13 and s 14 of the SGA 1979, we shall now have a look at some of the remedies which may be available if one of these terms is broken.

Remedies for breach of terms implied by s 13 and s 14 of the Sale of Goods Act 1979

Remedies for breach of contract generally (including breach of implied terms) will be considered in detail in **Chapter 4**. However, the SGA 1979 (as amended) provides some basic rights and remedies which apply if there is a breach of one of the terms implied by the Act. So we are going to consider these basic rights and remedies now, as you will probably find it more convenient to deal with all issues arising under the Act in one place. We shall also come back to this later in **Chapter 4**, so you should not worry about the detail at this stage.

If one of the terms implied by s 13 or s 14 is broken then normally the buyer can terminate the contract and reject the goods even if the breach is minor. This means that the buyer is not obliged to perform any further obligations under the contract and can recover money paid, but the buyer must return the goods to the seller. The buyer can also sue for damages if there is any further loss. Alternatively, the buyer may affirm the contract, keep the goods and just sue for damages for any loss suffered.

By way of example, imagine Tom, a decorator, buys a van for his business from a dealer. The van turns out to be defective. If the van is not of satisfactory quality, the dealer will have broken the term implied by s 14(2) of the SGA 1979. Potentially, Tom could terminate the contract, return the van to the dealer and get his money back. Tom could also claim damages if he has suffered other loss.

The right to terminate the contract and reject the goods will be lost in the following circumstances:

- First of all, the right to reject the goods is lost where the buyer has accepted the goods. This is covered by s 11(4) and s 35 of the 1979 Act. Section 11(4) provides that the buyer cannot reject the goods if the buyer has accepted them. Section 35 sets out situations when the buyer will be deemed to have accepted the goods.

  The most common situation where the buyer is deemed to have accepted the goods is where the buyer retains the goods beyond a reasonable time without intimating rejection. What is a reasonable time is a question of fact in each case. In deciding this, the court must consider whether the buyer has had a reasonable opportunity in commercial terms to examine the goods to see whether they are in conformity with the contract. The nature of the goods and their complexity will be relevant. It seems that time starts to run from the date of delivery. The buyer is allowed a reasonable time to try out the goods in general terms.

- Secondly, the right to reject the goods for breach of s 13 and s 14 will be lost if the breach is so slight that it would be unreasonable for the buyer to reject them (SGA 1979, 15A). So, for example, if you buy something for your business and the goods are usable but very slightly defective, you will not be able to reject the goods for breach of s 14(2) and s 14(3). Your remedy will be restricted to damages.

  It is up to the seller to show that the breach is so slight that rejection of the goods would be unreasonable.

SGA 1979 implied terms – summary

We have now considered the terms implied into a sale of goods contract by ss 13 and 14(2) and (3) of the Sale of Goods Act 1979, and the remedies available if one of these implied terms is broken.

- *Section 13*   Where there is a contract for the sale of goods by description, s 13 implies a condition that the goods will correspond with their description.

- *Section 14(2)*   Where the seller is selling in the course of a business, s 14(2) implies a condition that the goods supplied will be of satisfactory quality.

- *Section 14(3)*   Where the seller is selling in the course of a business and the buyer expressly or by implication makes known any particular purpose for which the goods are being bought, s 14(3) implies a condition that the goods supplied are reasonably fit for that purpose (except where it is not reasonable of the buyer to rely on the seller's skill or judgement).

- *Remedies*

    (a) Reject goods and recover money. Not available if:
    - (i) breach is so slight it would be unreasonable to reject; or
    - (ii) the buyer has accepted goods, eg by keeping the goods beyond a reasonable time without intimating rejection.

    (b) The buyer may also be able to claim damages. The remedy of damages is dealt with in **Chapter 4**.

We shall now go on to consider terms implied by the Supply of Goods and Services Act 1982.

3.2.2.2 Supply of Goods and Services Act 1982

In broad terms, the Supply of Goods and Services Act (SGSA) 1982 implies terms into contracts for services, and contracts for work and materials that are not made between a trader and consumer. Terms are now implied into contracts between traders and consumers by the Consumer Rights Act 2015.

A service contract is one where the supplier is simply contracting to provide a service. Examples of service contracts governed by the SGSA 1982 are commercial cleaning contracts and commercial courier services.

Work and materials contracts are contracts which are predominantly for work, but which necessarily involve the supply of goods. Examples of work and materials contracts governed by the SGSA 1982 are contracts to build office blocks or a sports stadium and contracts for garages to service commercial vehicles. The SGSA 1982 implies terms into these contracts in relation to both the work carried out and the materials (goods) supplied (see **Reading 4** in the Appendix).

Table 3.1 Supply of Goods and Services Act 1982 implied terms

Sale of Goods and Services Act 1982	Type of business-to-business contract	Condition	Innominate term
2(1) In a contract for the transfer of goods, there is an implied condition on the part of the transferor that he has a right to transfer the property [ownership] in the goods.	Work and materials	√	
3 Where there is a supply of goods by description, there is an implied term that the goods will correspond with that description.	Work and materials	√	
4(2) Where goods are supplied in the course of a business, it is an implied term that the goods will be of satisfactory quality.	Work and materials	√	
4(5) Where goods are supplied in the course of a business, and the buyer makes known to the supplier the buyer's purpose for the goods (either expressly or impliedly) and reasonably relies on the supplier's skill/knowledge, there is an implied term that the goods will be fit for that purpose.	Work and materials	√	
13 Where work or a service is done in the course of a business, there is an implied term that it will be carried out with reasonable care and skill.	Work and materials and service contracts		√
14 Where work or a service is done in the course of a business and no time for performance has been agreed, it is implied that the work will be done within a reasonable time.	Work and materials and service contracts		√
15 If a price for work or a service has not been fixed, there is an implied term that a reasonable sum will be charged.	Work and materials and service contracts		√

Contract

Note

- Section 4(2) and s 4(5) only apply where goods are supplied in the course of a business.
- The terms implied by ss 3 and 4 are described as conditions.
- Sections 13–15 do not impose strict liability and are innominate terms.
- The terms implied by ss 14 and 15 only apply in the absence of express agreement to the contrary.
- If the contract is just for the supply of a service, only ss 13, 14 and 15 need to be considered.
- Where the contract is to supply both goods and services, you have to consider ss 13, 14 and 15 for the service and also ss 3 and 4 for the goods.

⭐ Examples

Situation	Application of 1982 Act
1. Srinath has just had a new conservatory built on the back of his wine bar by 'Glasshouses'. He has paid the firm £15,000, which is the price they agreed. He now thinks he has been overcharged. Will s 15 of the SGSA 1982 help him?	Section 15 will not help Srinath with his claim that he has been overcharged as s 15 only implies a term that a reasonable price will be paid if the contract is silent and here the parties had agreed a price.
2. John runs a central heating business and he installs a new central heating system in an office building owned by Wakeford plc. Two weeks later the boiler explodes. What term(s) implied by the SGSA 1982 will have been broken in the following circumstances? (a) The boiler was defective. (b) The boiler was not defective but John had not installed it properly.	(a) If the boiler supplied by John was defective then, as he supplied it in the course of his business, he will be in breach of s 4(2), as it will not be of satisfactory quality, and s 4(5), as it will not be reasonably fit for Wakeford plc's purpose. (b) If the boiler was not defective but was not installed properly, then John will be in breach of s 13 as he will have provided a service in the course of his business without reasonable care and skill.

3.2.2.3 Consumer Rights Act 2015

One of the main aims of the Consumer Rights Act (CRA) 2015 was to consolidate and clarify the law relating to the rights of consumers and protection of their interests. Part 1 of the Act deals with 'Consumer contracts for goods, digital content and services'. Here, we will be focusing on:

- some of the main terms implied into consumer contracts for the supply of goods and contracts for services; and
- the consumer's rights to enforce those terms.

Later in the chapter, we shall be looking at the extent to which liability for breach of the relevant implied terms may be excluded or restricted.

Sales contracts

The CRA 2015 applies only to 'sales contracts' made between a trader and consumer (s 5). 'Sales contracts' not only include straightforward contracts for the sale of goods but also any contract where goods are supplied and paid for as part of the contract, eg a work and materials contract (such as a building contract). The CRA 2015 defines a 'trader' as 'a person acting for purposes relating to that person's trade, business, craft or profession, whether acting personally or through another person acting in the trader's name or on the trader's behalf', and a 'consumer' is defined as 'an individual acting for purposes that are wholly or mainly outside that individual's trade, business, craft or profession' (s 2).

Terms implied into sales contracts

If you look at **Reading 2** in the **Appendix**, you will see that the CRA 2015 implies terms into sales contracts which largely reflect those implied by ss 13 and 14 of the SGA 1979 and ss 3 and 4 of the SGSA 1982. Section 9 of the CRA 2015 implies a term that goods will be of satisfactory quality, s 10 implies a term that goods will be reasonably fit for their particular purpose, and s 11 implies a term that goods will be as described.

Note, however, that the CRA 2015 does not pre-classify these terms as 'conditions'; instead it presents them as 'statutory rights' – statutory rights which are of fundamental importance to the consumer. On that basis, it should be the case that these terms are conditions. You will be looking at the significance of terms being 'conditions' of the contract later in this chapter.

Consumer's rights to enforce terms about goods

These are set out in s 19 of the CRA 2015, and, broadly speaking, if the goods do not conform to the contract because of a breach of ss 9–11, the consumer's rights are as follows:

(a) the short-term right to reject and get a full refund (ss 20 and 22);

(b) the right to repair or replacement (if appropriate) (s 23); and

(c) the right to a price reduction or the final right to reject and get a partial refund to reflect the consumer's use of the goods (ss 20 and 24).

Basically, this is a pecking order of remedies. If the short-term right to reject has been lost, then consider whether it is appropriate/reasonable to get the goods repaired or replaced; if not, then the consumer may be entitled to an appropriate price reduction or to reject the goods and get a partial refund of the price.

Unless the parties have expressly agreed otherwise, the time limit for the short-term right to reject non-perishable goods is 30 days after they have been bought, delivered and, where appropriate, installed. With perishable goods, the time limit is no longer than the goods could reasonably be expected to last.

For the purposes of the other rights, if goods do not conform to the contract at any time within six months of the date of delivery, they will be taken as not having conformed to the contract on that day. The only exceptions to this are in relation to perishable goods and where it can be proved that the goods did conform with the contract on the day (but this may be very difficult to establish).

Services contracts

The CRA 2015 basically applies to any contract for a trader to supply a service/work to a consumer. So it will cover straightforward service contracts (eg a dry cleaning contract) and also work and materials contracts.

Terms implied into services contracts

If you look at **Reading 2** in the **Appendix**, you will see that the terms implied by ss 49, 51 and 52 are very similar to the terms implied by ss 13–15 of the SGSA 1982:

- s 49 implies a term that the service/work will be carried out with reasonable care and skill;

- s 51 implies a term, where no price has been fixed, that a reasonable price will be paid for the service/work; and
- s 52 implies a term, where no time for performance has been fixed, that the service/work will be performed within a reasonable time.

As with the terms implied in relation to goods, these terms are again presented by the CRA 2015 as 'statutory rights', although, as you will see later, there is some (albeit limited) scope to restrict the trader's liability.

Consumer's rights to enforce terms about services

Very simply, s 54 of the CRA 2015 provides that where a service/work does not conform to the contract because of either breach of an express term relating to the performance of the service/work or breach of the implied term to exercise reasonable care and skill (s 49), the consumer has the right to require repeat performance (where reasonable) or to a price reduction. In relation to a breach of the implied term as to performance within a reasonable time (s 52), the consumer simply has the right to an appropriate price reduction.

⭐ Examples

Situation	Term broken	Remedy/remedies
Jenny decided to have a conservatory built at the back of her house and contracted with Windows Ltd for them to build it. Two days after the conservatory was completed, it became apparent that some of the double-glazed window panels were defective and were getting misted up. When she pointed this out to Windows Ltd, they said it was not their fault as it was a manufacturing defect.	This is a goods and services contract within the CRA 2015 as made between a trader and consumer. There is a breach by Windows Ltd of the implied terms as to satisfactory quality and fitness for purpose – ss 9 and 10. Liability is strict, so it is no excuse that the fault is due to a manufacturing defect.	Exercise short-term right to reject the faulty window panels but might be more practical to go for replacement window panels. Repair or a price reduction would not seem to be appropriate or desirable.
Patrick employed John, a local builder, to supply and lay a grey Indian stone patio at the back of his house. In the event John laid brown Indian stone and did not lay it properly as the surface was not level.	This is also a goods and services contract governed by the CRA 2015. Brown instead of grey stone is breach of an express term and also s 11 of the CRA 2015 (the implied term that goods will correspond with their description). In practice it would be better to sue for breach of s 11 (a statutory right). Not laying the patio properly would be breach of s 49 of the CRA 2015 – the implied term to exercise reasonable care and skill.	Exercise the short-term right to reject but again might be more appropriate to claim replacement stones that conform to the contract description. Patrick could require repeat performance in preference to a price reduction (which is unlikely to be desirable).

Figure 3.1 Contract terms

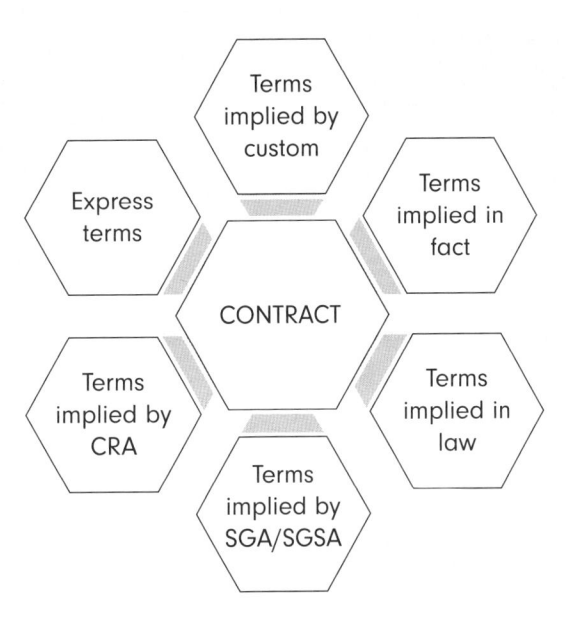

[Diagram: Central hexagon labeled "CONTRACT" surrounded by six hexagons labeled: Terms implied by custom, Terms implied in fact, Terms implied in law, Terms implied by SGA/SGSA, Terms implied by CRA, Express terms.]

3.3 Classification of terms

We are now going to look at how terms of a contract are classified and the importance of that classification. All terms which impose contractual obligations on a party, whether express or implied, will be conditions, warranties or innominate terms.

As you will see, the distinction between conditions, warranties and innominate terms is important because of the link with remedies. Essentially, breach of any term gives the other party the right to claim damages, whereas breach of some terms normally gives the other party the right to terminate the future performance of the contract, ie the non-defaulting party does not have to perform future obligations or accept any further performance from the party in breach. In addition to this, the party terminating can claim damages if there is additional loss. We shall look at remedies in detail in **Chapter 4.**

We shall first consider the difference between conditions and warranties.

3.3.1 Conditions and warranties: the traditional approach

Traditionally, the court would classify a term as either a condition or a warranty.

3.3.1.1 Difference between a condition and a warranty

A condition is a major term or, as some writers say, a term going to the root of the contract. A warranty is a minor, less important, term. To decide whether a term in a contract is a condition or a warranty, the court applies an objective test. Would a reasonable person think the parties intended the term to be a condition or a warranty?

In applying this test, the court will look at the circumstances surrounding the making of the contract, the contract as a whole, and it will take into account whether the parties have described the term as a condition or a warranty in the contract. The emphasis, therefore, is on deciding the importance of the term which has been broken at the time the contract was made, rather than looking at the effects of the breach and the loss or damage which has resulted from the breach.

3.3.1.2 Effect if term is a condition or a warranty

If the court decides that the term is a condition, and the contract has not been fully performed, the innocent party will usually have the option of terminating the future performance of the contract, as well as obtaining damages for any additional loss suffered. This is so, even if they have only suffered minor loss or damage.

If the court decides the term is a warranty, the innocent party cannot terminate the contract but can only sue for damages for loss suffered. This applies even if the innocent party has suffered serious loss or damage. You may find this surprising, and you will see later on in this chapter that this approach has been criticised.

As we said above, the court will take into account whether the parties have described a particular term as a condition or a warranty. The use of the word 'condition' raises a presumption that it is used in the legal sense, but this may be rebutted from evidence of the contract as a whole.

In the case of *Schuler v Wickman Machine Tool Sales Ltd* [1974] AC 235, HL, the parties had described a particular term as a 'condition', but the House of Lords decided that the parties had not intended to use the word in its strict legal sense.

The term the court was considering stated that, over a long period, one of two named representatives from Wickman would visit six other firms every week. There was no provision to substitute other representatives to cover illness, and neither was there provision for the six firms saying a visit was not convenient. If the term was a condition, failure to make a single visit would entitle Schuler to terminate the contract. The court thought this was such an unreasonable result that it was unlikely to be what the parties had intended, despite the fact that the term was called a condition in the contract.

3.3.1.3 Advantages and disadvantages of classifying terms as conditions and warranties

The advantage of the traditional classification into conditions and warranties is that it helps to promote certainty. If a term is clearly a condition, both parties know from the outset that if the term is broken and the contract has not been fully performed, the innocent party may terminate. Conversely, if the term is a warranty, both parties know from the outset that if the term is broken the innocent party cannot terminate.

(There are special rules in the SGA 1979 and CRA 2015 which apply to sale of goods contracts. You considered these earlier in this chapter and we shall be reviewing them later in **Chapter 4**.)

However, classifying terms as either conditions or warranties can lead to unfairness. A party may use a breach of condition as an excuse to end the contract even where the breach is fairly minor. It also means that if a term is a warranty, the innocent party cannot terminate even if the breach is major: the only remedy will be damages. Therefore, classifying terms without looking at the consequences of the breach can lead to unfairness and lacks flexibility.

For these reasons, another approach to the classification of contractual terms has developed. We shall look at this next.

3.3.2 Innominate terms: a more recent approach

Instead of classifying all terms of the contract as conditions or warranties, a second approach to classification is to say that a term is innominate, ie neither a condition nor a warranty. You may also see innominate terms referred to as intermediate terms.

These terms were first recognised by Diplock LJ in *Hong Kong Fir Shipping Co Ltd v Kawasaki Kisen Kaisha Ltd* [1962] 2 QB 26, CA.

The defendants agreed to hire a ship from the claimants for 24 months. A term of the contract provided that the ship was 'fitted in every way for ordinary cargo service', ie that the ship was seaworthy. In fact the engines were old and the engine room staff inefficient, with the result that the ship was in port for repairs for 20 weeks.

The defendants terminated the contract, ie refused to carry on with it. The claimants sued, claiming that the defendants were in breach of contract.

The judge at first instance found that the ship was unseaworthy but that the defendants were not entitled to terminate the contract. The defendants appealed to the Court of Appeal.

Diplock LJ suggested that the test which should be used to decide whether the innocent party could terminate the contract was to ask whether the event which had occurred, ie the breach of contract, had deprived the innocent party of substantially the whole benefit of the contract. This meant that you would look at the effect of the breach to decide the remedies available to the innocent party.

He did not think that the test he suggested should be used in all cases. He said that the parties might expressly agree when the innocent party could terminate, or the situation might be governed by statute. Also, he thought it was still appropriate to classify terms as conditions or warranties if the term was very simple, in the sense that you could say that breach of the term would always deprive the innocent party of substantially the whole benefit of the contract (a condition) or that the breach would never have this effect (a warranty).

Diplock LJ thought that many terms were too complex to be classified as conditions or warranties. These terms were complex in the sense that some breaches would, and others would not, deprive the innocent party of substantially the whole benefit of the contract. You could not say in advance what the effect of the breach would be. You had to wait until the breach of contract occurred and then look at the effect of the breach. (Terms that are not classified as either conditions or warranties are referred to as innominate or intermediate terms.)

In the *Hong Kong Fir Shipping* case, the defendants who had hired the ship were not entitled to terminate the contract. The time lost repairing the ship was not sufficient to deprive the defendants of substantially the whole benefit of the contract of hire.

We have seen that in the *Hong Kong Fir Shipping* case, Diplock LJ suggested that not all terms should be classified as conditions or warranties. Some terms should be classified as innominate or intermediate terms, in which case it is necessary to wait until the breach of contract has occurred to decide whether the innocent party should be allowed to terminate the future performance of the contract. If the breach deprives the innocent party of substantially the whole benefit of the contract, they can terminate, but not otherwise.

3.3.3 Which approach should the court adopt?

The two approaches to the classification of contractual terms exist side by side. This means that, subject to some restrictions (see below), it is up to the court to decide whether to adopt the traditional approach and classify terms as conditions or warranties, or to adopt the approach described by Lord Diplock LJ in the *Hong Kong Fir Shipping* case and classify terms as innominate.

There are some restrictions on the court. For example, you have seen that the parties may make it clear in their contract that a particular term is a condition or a warranty. Also, a statute may express a particular term to be a condition or a warranty, eg the terms implied by s 13 and s 14 of the SGA 1979 are conditions; the term implied by s 13 of the SGSA 1982 is simply described as a term and so is treated as innominate.

Contract

Figure 3.2 Classification of terms

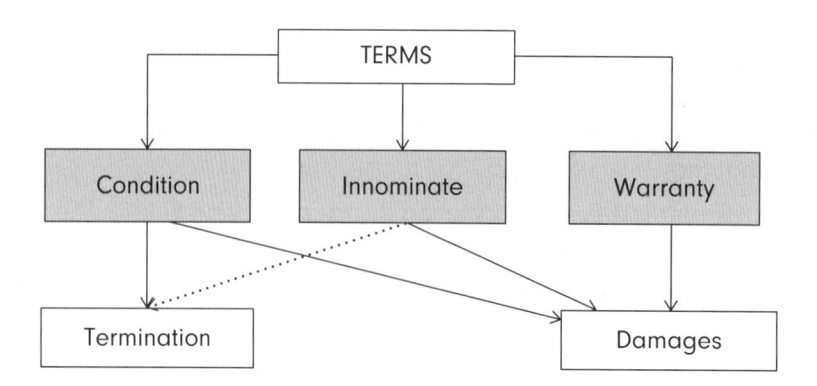

```
                    TERMS
         ┌────────────┼────────────┐
         ▼            ▼            ▼
    Condition    Innominate     Warranty
         │   ╲    ╱    ╲      ╱    │
         ▼    ╲  ╱      ╲    ╱     ▼
    Termination              Damages
```

3.4 Exemption clauses

3.4.1 What are exemption clauses?

Before we begin to study the rules which apply, we need to consider what exemption clauses are designed to do and when they might occur.

An exemption clause is a clause which seeks to exclude liability completely or to limit liability if a breach of contract occurs or a tort is committed.

Note that a clause which seeks to limit liability is often referred to as a limitation clause, eg a clause on a dry-cleaning ticket which says that liability for loss or damage is limited to the value of the garment.

A clause which attempts to restrict or limit a party's remedies for breach of contract is also an exemption clause, eg a sale of goods contract may provide that the seller will be liable only if the buyer notifies the seller of defects within two weeks of delivery. This is an exemption clause because it is saying that if the buyer does not notify the seller within the time limit, the seller will not be liable.

In this textbook we use the phrase 'exemption clauses' to include 'limitation clauses'.

Have a look at the Specimen Conditions of Sale (**Reading 1** in the **Appendix**) and see if you can spot the exemption clauses there.

How many did you find? Clause 4.3 is purporting to exclude liability for non-delivery in certain circumstances. Clause 4.6 states that the seller will not be liable for any loss caused by delay in delivering goods, and it also restricts the buyer's remedies if there is such delay.

Clause 5 is also an exemption clause which excludes liability if goods are defective unless the buyer gives notice within a specified time. You will notice that clause 5.3 limits the buyer's remedies.

Finally, did you spot clause 8 which, although headed 'Limitation of Liability', is really a mixture of exclusion and limitation clauses.

3.4.2 Establishing liability

For an exemption clause to be relevant, a breach of contract or a tort must have been committed. For example, imagine you have had an extension added to your house and it collapses. You want to sue the builder. The builder may be liable to you for breach of contract because the builder did not do the work with reasonable care and skill. This would be a breach of the term implied into the contract by s 49 of the CRA 2015 which we looked at earlier in this chapter. Suppose that there is an exemption clause in the contract which excludes the builder's liability for defective work. In this situation it would be important to know whether the builder can rely on the clause. If the builder can rely on it, you would not be able to obtain damages to compensate you for the loss you have suffered.

There are both common law and statutory rules governing exemption clauses. We start by examining the common law.

3.4.3 Common law rules on exemption clauses

3.4.3.1 Incorporation into the contract

We saw earlier in this chapter that in order to amount to a term, a provision must be part of the contract, ie it must be incorporated into the contract.

There are three main ways in which a provision may be incorporated, namely:

- by signature;
- by notice;
- by consistent course of dealings between the parties.

The rules on incorporation apply to all terms of a contract, but most of the case law on this concerns exemption clauses and so we are going to consider the rules of incorporation in the context of exemption clauses.

Incorporation by signature

The basic rule is that if you sign a contractual document then the clauses in that document will normally be incorporated as part of the contract. This is so even if you did not read the clauses. This principle is illustrated by *L'Estrange v Graucob Ltd* [1934] 2 KB 394. Here the exemption clause was in 'regrettably small' print but was legible, and the court therefore found that the clause was incorporated into the contract because the contract had been signed.

- Note that it is not necessary for the party relying on the clause to have signed the document. Only the claimant must have signed it.
- Note also that the document must be a contractual document, that is the sort of document which people in general might assume contained some terms of the contract, eg a holiday booking form. We shall look at this in more detail when we deal with the second method of incorporating an exemption clause into a contract.

There are three situations where an exemption clause will not be incorporated into the contract even if the innocent party has signed the document containing the clause:

(a) The exemption clause is illegible. We have seen in the *L'Estrange v Graucob* case that, although the print was 'regrettably small', it was still legible.

(b) The exemption clause will not be incorporated if the effect of the clause has been described inaccurately (ie misrepresented) and the innocent party has reasonably relied on the inaccurate description in entering the contract.

For example, in *Curtis v Chemical Cleaning & Dyeing Co* [1951] 1 KB 805, CA, the claimant took a wedding dress, trimmed with beads and sequins, to the defendant's shop for cleaning. The assistant asked the claimant to sign a receipt. The claimant asked why, and the assistant said that the receipt exempted the defendant from liability for damage to the beads and sequins. The claimant signed. In fact, the receipt exempted the defendant from liability for any damage however caused. When the dress was returned, it was stained. The court held that the defendant could not rely on the clause as its effects had been misrepresented to the claimant.

Please note that the subject of misrepresentation is a large area of law in its own right, and we look at this in full in **Chapter 6**.

(c) The clause is unusual and onerous and is not fairly and reasonably drawn to the attention of the other party.

Contract

> In *Blu-Sky Solutions Ltd v Be Caring Ltd* [2021] EWHC 2619 (Comm), the Order Form stated *'orders and contracts are subject to and incorporate our standard terms and conditions by signing this document I agree I have logged on to the Blu Sky website at www.bluskysolutions.co.uk, have read agree and fully understand all terms and conditions regarding the contract ... and am bound by the same'*. Although Be Caring did not review the terms of the order form or log on to Blu-Sky's website as indicated to read the terms and conditions, they did return a signed Order Form. The terms and conditions, which were not labelled as such on their face, totalled just over a page of detailed text in closely spaced small type and with no separate clause headings. Among the terms and conditions were some particularly onerous clauses relating to cancellation, and Blu-Sky sought to rely on those clauses when Be Caring purported to cancel. The court found that the relevant clauses had not been fairly and reasonably brought to Be Caring's attention and therefore had not been incorporated and could not be relied upon. Although the Order Form did refer to Blu-Sky's terms and conditions, it did not explain their purpose or give any warning that they imposed potentially substantial obligations. Blu-Sky had made no attempt to highlight the relevant clauses; instead they were concealed in the middle of a myriad of small print.

Incorporation by notice

So far, we have looked at incorporation by signature. However, not all exemption clauses are contained in signed documents. We now go on to consider the conditions which must be satisfied in order for a clause contained in an unsigned document (eg a ticket) or on a notice (eg a notice in a car park) to be incorporated.

The document containing the clause must be contractual in nature

The first thing to bear in mind is that the document containing the clause must be contractual in nature. The question you could ask yourself is whether it is the sort of document which a reasonable person might expect to contain some terms of the contract.

In *Chapelton v Barry Urban District Council* [1940] 1 KB 532, the court decided that a deck chair ticket was not contractual in nature as a reasonable person would regard it as a mere receipt to show that the claimant had paid for the chair. It was not regarded as a document which might contain terms on which the claimant had hired the chair.

Note that this case does not prevent all tickets from being contractual documents: it depends on whether a reasonable person would expect a particular kind of ticket to include terms of a contract. Many tickets, for example railway tickets, would normally be regarded as contractual in nature.

The innocent party must either know of the clause, or the party relying on the clause must have taken reasonable steps to bring it to the other's notice before the contract is finalised

This point was made in *Parker v South Eastern Railway* (1877) 2 CPD 416, CA. Here the Court of Appeal said that it was not necessary for the innocent party to know about the clause provided that the party seeking to rely on it had taken reasonable steps to draw the clause to the other's attention.

What factors do you think a court might take into account when deciding whether reasonable steps have been taken? A court will take into account factors such as:

(a) the position of the clause on the document (eg if it is on the back, are there words on the front, such as 'For conditions see over' or 'Please turn over', drawing attention to the back?);

(b) the prominence of the clause on the document; and

(c) the type and nature of clause, eg is the clause particularly unusual or onerous?

In cases where certain exemption clauses are expected, simply handing the document over will be enough to amount to reasonable steps. In fact the document itself may not contain the exemption clause. The document may simply refer to another document where the clause can be found. For example, a railway ticket usually just says 'Subject to the current National Rail Conditions of Carriage' and goes on to say that these are available at ticket offices. Usual exemption clauses that you might expect to find in a rail travel contract would probably be regarded as validly incorporated.

However, some exemption clauses may be regarded as particularly onerous or unusual in which case they need to be drawn to the other party's attention in the most explicit way.

In *Spurling Ltd v Bradshaw* [1956] 1 WLR 461, CA, Lord Denning MR said that in order to give sufficient notice of an onerous or unusual clause, it would be necessary for the clause to be 'printed in red ink with a red hand pointing to it or something equally startling'.

You can see, therefore, that what constitutes reasonable steps will depend on the nature of the clause. More needs to be done to draw an unusual or onerous clause to the attention of the other party.

This approach is not restricted to exemption clauses but applies to other clauses which are onerous or unusual, as illustrated by *Interfoto Picture Library Ltd v Stiletto Visual Programmes Ltd* [1989] QB 433, CA.

The claimants ran a photographic transparency lending library. The defendants asked if the claimants had any transparencies of the 1950s. The claimants delivered 47 transparencies together with a delivery note containing various conditions. Condition 2 stated that all transparencies had to be returned by March 19, and if not there would be a fine of £5 per transparency per day plus VAT. The defendants did not notice this. The defendants returned the transparencies 14 days late. The claimants claimed £3,783.

The Court of Appeal first decided that the contract had been formed after the transparencies and delivery note were delivered. The court then went on to consider whether the claimants had taken reasonable steps to bring the clause in the delivery note to the defendants' attention.

Dillon LJ held as follows:

> Condition 2 of these conditions is in my judgment a very onerous clause. The defendants could not conceivably have known if their attention was not drawn to the clause that the plaintiffs were proposing to charge a 'holding fee' for the retention of the transparencies at such a very high and exorbitant rate.

> At the time of the ticket cases in the last century it was notorious that people hardly ever troubled to read printed conditions on a ticket or delivery note or similar document. That remains the case now. In the intervening years the printed conditions have tended to become more and more complicated and more and more one-sided in favour of the party who is imposing them, but the other parties, if they notice that there are printed conditions at all, generally still tend to assume that such conditions are only concerned with ancillary matters of form and are not of importance. In the ticket cases the courts held that the common law required that reasonable steps be taken to draw the other parties' attention to the printed conditions or they would not be part of the contract. It is, in my judgment, a logical development of the common law into modern conditions that it should be held,

as it was in *Thornton v Shoe Lane Parking Ltd,* that, if one condition in a set of printed conditions is particularly onerous or unusual, the party seeking to enforce it must show that that particular condition was fairly brought to the attention of the other party.

In the present case, nothing whatever was done by the plaintiffs to draw the defendants' attention particularly to condition 2; it was merely one of four columns' width of conditions printed across the foot of the delivery note. Consequently condition 2 never, in my judgment, became part of the contract between the parties.

The *Interfoto* decision can be criticised on the basis that the defendants were in business and should have been capable of reading the conditions at the foot of the delivery note. It can be argued that if they did not do so, they should be taken as accepting the risk that the conditions might be disadvantageous to them.

The timing of reasonable steps

We have seen that the party seeking to rely on the exemption clause must have taken reasonable steps to bring it to the attention of the other party. Generally, these steps must be taken before the contract is finalised. This is because a party should have the opportunity of seeing all the terms of the contract before entering into it.

This is illustrated by the case of *Olley v Marlborough Court Ltd* [1949] 1 KB 532. The claimant made a contract for the use of a hotel room at the reception desk. In the hotel bedroom there was a notice exempting the hotel from liability for any items which were lost or stolen. It was held that this came too late to be incorporated in the contract. The position might have been different if the claimant had been a regular user of the hotel, and therefore as a result of a previous consistent 'course of dealing' could be said to have prior notice of the clause.

So far, we have seen that reasonable steps must be taken to draw the exemption clause to the other party's attention before the contract is finalised. However, the exemption clause may still be incorporated even if the steps are only taken after the contract is finalised if there has been a consistent course of dealings between the parties. We consider this next.

Incorporation by a previous consistent course of dealing

In order for a clause to be incorporated on this basis, the dealings must be both consistent and amount to a 'course' of dealings, ie a sufficient number of regular dealings (as in *Spurling v Bradshaw,* which we looked at in **3.2.1.2** above). An exemption clause was also incorporated on this basis in *Kendall (Henry) & Sons v Lillico & Sons Ltd* [1969] AC 31, HL, where two businesses had dealt with each other three or four times a month for three years. After each contract was made, a 'sold note' would be sent to the buyer. The note contained exemption clauses. The court decided that the clauses were incorporated in the latest contract because of the previous consistent course of dealings. The recipient had had plenty of opportunity to read the clauses.

By contrast, in the case of *Hollier v Rambler Motors* [1972] 2 QB 71, CA, the claimant had had a car serviced by the defendant's garage only three or four times over five years. This did not amount to a course of dealing.

Even if there is a course of dealings, a clause will not be incorporated unless the dealings are consistent. In the case of *McCutcheon v David MacBrayne Ltd* [1964] 1 WLR 125, HL, although the parties had dealt with each other many times, sometimes the document containing the exemption clause had been signed and sometimes it had not. The House of Lords decided that the exemption clause had not been incorporated as the dealings had not been consistent.

Incorporation – summary

We have now looked at the first common law rule which applies to exemption clauses, that is the clause must be incorporated into the contract. As we have seen, a clause may be incorporated:

- by signature;
- by notice; or
- by consistent course of dealings between the parties.

The other common law rule which applies to exemption clauses is the principle that the wording of the clause must cover the breach of contract and the loss or damage which has occurred. We consider this next.

3.4.3.2 Construction (or interpretation) of exemption clauses

Even if an exemption clause is incorporated into a contract, the party in breach will not be able to rely on it unless, as a matter of construction, the clause covers the breach of contract and loss or damage which has occurred. For example, if you saw a notice in a hair salon stating that the salon would not be liable for damage to your clothing caused by products used on your hair, you would not expect the clause to protect the salon if the hair stylist dyed your hair the wrong colour, or if an assistant spilt coffee on your suit. The clause is not worded to cover these events.

Before the Unfair Contract Terms Act 1977, the court had no power to declare a clause invalid on the basis that it was unreasonable. Provided the clause was incorporated into the contract and was properly worded to cover the breach and loss that had occurred then the clause would be valid. Because of this, the courts would very often adopt a strained and restrictive approach when interpreting an exemption clause in order to protect the weaker party.

We shall now have a look at some of the principles which the court adopts when interpreting an exemption clause.

The *contra proferentem* rule

If a party tries to rely on a clause which is ambiguous or unclear, the court will interpret the clause against the defaulting party. This is known as the *contra proferentem* rule. The party seeking to rely on the clause is sometimes referred to as the *proferens* and the clause is construed against (*contra*) this person. The *contra proferentem* rule applies to any clause which is unclear or ambiguous, not just to an exemption clause.

In *Houghton v Trafalgar Insurance* [1954] 1 QB 247, a five-seater car was involved in an accident whilst carrying six people. The insurance company wanted to rely on a clause in the insurance policy which exempted it from liability if the car was carrying an 'excessive load'. The court decided that the clause did not cover a situation where the car was carrying too many people. The clause was ambiguous as the word 'load' is usually applied to goods, not to people, and so the insurance company could not rely on the exemption clause.

Exemption clauses and negligence

If an exemption clause is intended to cover liability for the tort of negligence or a negligent breach of contract, the clause must be carefully worded. The following guidelines were suggested in *Canada Steamship Lines v The King* [1952] AC 192:

- If the clause expressly exempts a party from liability for negligence (ie the word 'negligence' or a synonym is used) then it will be effective.
- If there is no express reference to negligence, the court must decide whether the words are wide enough to exclude liability for negligence, eg if a clause stated that a party

73

would not be liable 'for any damage howsoever caused', the phrase 'howsoever caused' would normally include liability for negligence.

- Even if this is so, the defendant is still not necessarily entitled to rely on the clause. This is because the court must then ask if the clause could cover liability other than negligence, eg strict liability, where proof of fault is not required. If such liability does exist, then the court may well decide that the clause should be restricted to this other liability and does not cover negligence.

However, it seems that in commercial cases the courts may take a more relaxed approach here. In *Monarch Airlines Ltd v London Luton Airport Ltd* [1997] CLC 698, the claimant's aeroplane was damaged by a loose paving block at the defendant's airport. A clause in the contract stated that the defendant would not be liable 'for any damage to aircraft resulting from an omission, neglect or default ...'.

The court decided that those words were clear enough to cover negligence. The judge said that, when construing the clause, a court should not ask whether there is an alternative head of legal liability which the clause might cover and, if there is, immediately construe the clause as inapplicable to negligence. Instead, the court should look at the facts and realities of the situation at the time of the contract and ask what potential liability the parties had in mind.

Exemption clauses and very serious breaches of contract

In the past, courts were reluctant to allow a party to rely on exemption clauses where a very serious breach of contract had occurred. However, the case of *Photo Productions Ltd v Securicor Transport Ltd* [1980] AC 827, HL clarified the position and illustrates the modern approach in relation to exclusion of liability for a very serious breach of contract.

In this case the House of Lords said that where there has been a very serious or deliberate breach of contract, it is simply a matter of construction whether the exemption clause covers the breach. If the clause is clearly worded, it may cover the breach which has occurred even if that breach is very serious or deliberate.

Limitation clauses

Although the rules of construction which we have considered above apply to both exclusion and limitation clauses, limitation clauses are sometimes less strictly construed than clauses completely excluding liability. The reason for this is that it is highly improbable that one party intended to release the other completely from all liability for breach, but a party might well agree to the other limiting liability in some way. However, it does depend on the limitation clause.

Construction – summary

We have now covered the main principles of construction. We have seen that:

- an unclear or ambiguous clause will be construed against the person seeking to rely on it under the *contra proferentem* rule (*Houghton v Trafalgar Insurance*);
- clear words are needed to exclude liability for negligence, but if the wording is clear, the word 'negligence' need not be used (*Canada Steamship*; *Monarch Airlines Ltd*);
- an exemption clause can cover a very serious or a deliberate breach of contract provided the clause is clearly worded (*Photo Productions Ltd v Securicor*).

3.4.4 Unfair Contract Terms Act 1977

Having looked at the common law rules governing exemption clauses, we now go on to consider the effect of the Unfair Contract Terms Act (UCTA) 1977.

3.4.4.1 Scope of the Act

UCTA 1977 does not apply to exemption clauses in contracts which are made trader-to-consumer as these are now governed by the CRA 2015. Subject to that, UCTA 1977 applies to any clause excluding, limiting or otherwise restricting liability, including a clause which makes liability or its enforcement subject to restrictive or onerous conditions, and a clause which subjects a person to any prejudice in consequence of pursuing a right or remedy (s 13).

Most of the key provisions (except s 6) apply only to business liability, ie liability arising from things done by a person in the course of a business or from the occupation of business premises (s 1(3)).

If UCTA 1977 does apply, it does one of two things: it either renders the exemption clause void or subjects it to a reasonableness test (the reasonableness test is dealt with in s 11 and Sch 2).

Schedule 1 contains a number of contracts to which the key provisions of UCTA 1977 do not apply. These include contracts of insurance and any contract insofar as it relates to the creation, transfer or termination of an interest in land. Remember, too, that UCTA 1977 does not apply to contracts which are made trader-to-consumer.

The 1977 Act has three main areas of operation (see **Reading 6** in the Appendix):

- Sections 6 and 7 apply to clauses which exempt liability for breaches of the terms implied by the SGA 1979 and the SGSA 1982 in relation to goods.

Table 3.2 Effect of ss 6 and 7 of UCTA 1977

SGA 1979	Effect of s 6 of UCTA 1977
• s 13 – in a sale of goods by description, a condition is implied that goods will fit the description. • s 14(2) and s 14(3) – where a seller sells goods in the course of a business, a condition is implied that the goods are of satisfactory quality and reasonably fit for any purpose made known to the seller.	A seller can exclude or restrict liability for breach of these terms provided the exemption clause satisfies the reasonableness test. (You will be considering the reasonableness test at **3.4.4.2** below.)
SGSA 1982	**Effect of s 7 of UCTA 1977**
s 3 – condition implied that goods transferred fit their description. s 4(2) and (5) – goods transferred in the course of a business: condition implied that the goods are of satisfactory quality and reasonably fit for purpose.	Liability for breach of terms implied by ss 3 and 4 can be excluded or restricted provided the clause satisfies the reasonableness test.

- Section 2 applies to clauses which exempt liability for negligence or a negligent breach of contract. An example of a negligent breach of contract is breach of the term implied into business-to-business contracts by s 13 of the Supply of Goods and Services Act 1982 that the provider of a service must exercise reasonable care and skill.

    Section 2(1) provides that a business cannot exclude or restrict its liability for negligence where it causes death or personal injury.

    Section 2(2) provides that in relation to other loss or damage (eg physical damage or loss of profit) caused by negligence, a business can exclude or restrict its liability provided the exemption clause satisfies the reasonableness test.

- Section 3 basically applies to clauses in standard form contracts which exempt liability for breaches of express term(s).

Although of much wider application, in practice, s 3 of UCTA 1977 only tends to be used where there has been breach of an express term of the contract (in relation to other breaches the 1977 Act provides equivalent or greater protection under ss 2, 6 and 7).

Section 3 of the 1977 Act applies only where a party deals on the other party's written standard terms of business (eg, the Specimen Standard Conditions of Sale, **Reading 1** in the **Appendix**). So, if there has been breach of an express contractual term and the party in breach seeks to rely on an exemption clause, the first question is whether, or not, s 3 applies. It will do if the innocent party was dealing on the defaulting party's written standard terms of business. The phrase 'written standard terms of business' is not defined in the Act.

If s 3 does not apply, a clause purporting to exclude or restrict liability for breach of an express term will be upheld provided it is valid at common law (ie, it is incorporated in the contract and as a matter of construction covers the breach and damage alleged).

Where s 3 does apply, a business can exclude or restrict its liability for breach only if the term satisfies the reasonableness test.

Summary of ss 2, 3, 6 and 7 of UCTA 1977

Exemption clause excluding or limiting liability for:

- *negligent breach of contract*, eg breach of the term implied by s 13 of the SGSA 1982 that the supplier of a service in the course of a business will exercise reasonable care and skill

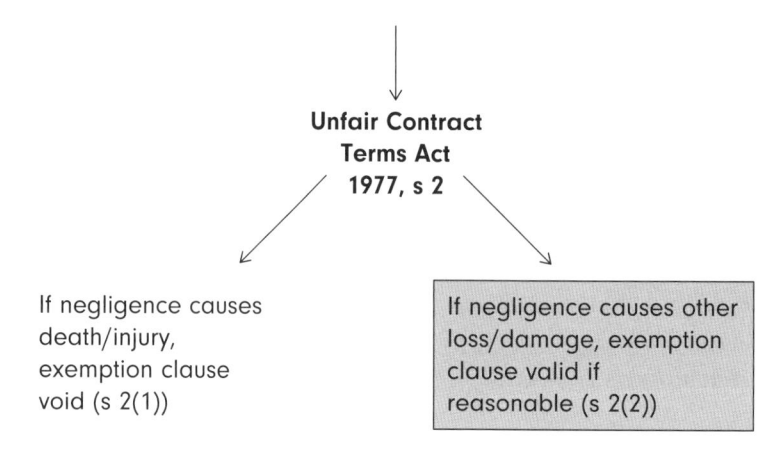

Unfair Contract Terms Act 1977, s 2

If negligence causes death/injury, exemption clause void (s 2(1))

If negligence causes other loss/damage, exemption clause valid if reasonable (s 2(2))

- *breach of express term of contract*

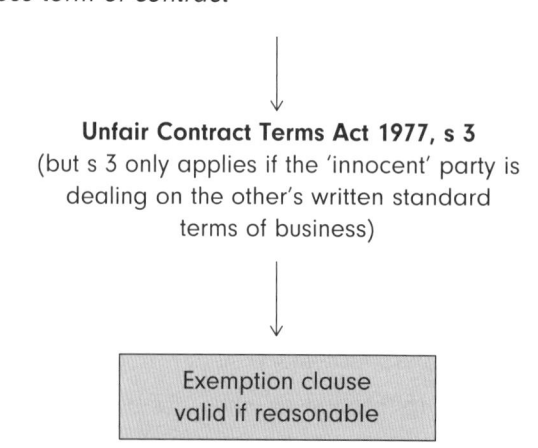

Unfair Contract Terms Act 1977, s 3
(but s 3 only applies if the 'innocent' party is dealing on the other's written standard terms of business)

Exemption clause valid if reasonable

- *breach of terms implied by ss 13 and 14 of the Sale of Goods Act 1979* (goods sold in course of a business to fit description and be of satisfactory quality/fit for purpose)

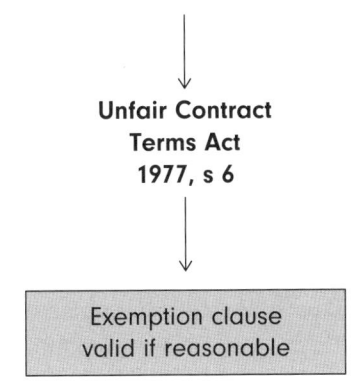

Unfair Contract Terms Act 1977, s 6

↓

Exemption clause valid if reasonable

- *breach of terms implied by ss 3 and 4 of the Supply of Goods and Services Act 1982* (goods supplied to fit description and goods supplied in course of business to be of satisfactory quality/fit for purpose)

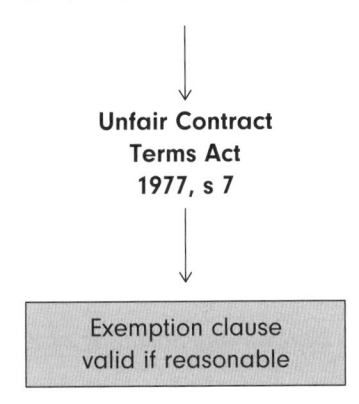

Unfair Contract Terms Act 1977, s 7

↓

Exemption clause valid if reasonable

3.4.4.2 The reasonableness test

Section 11 of UCTA 1977 sets out the reasonableness test. The exemption clause must have been a fair and reasonable one to include having regard to the circumstances which were (or ought reasonably to have been) known to the parties or within the contemplation of the parties when the contract was made (s 11(1)).

The burden of proof is on the party seeking to rely on the exemption clause to show that it is reasonable (s 11(5)).

You can see therefore that the court should ask whether the clause was a reasonable one to include taking into account factors known, or contemplated, at the time of the contract.

⭐ *Examples*

Situation	Clause more or less likely to be reasonable?
The seller is a large company that insists on selling goods on its own standard terms and conditions, which contain exemption clauses similar to those of other suppliers.	The buyer is in a weaker bargaining position than the seller, and the seller may be taking advantage of the buyer's position. That makes it *less* likely to pass the reasonableness test.

Situation	Clause more or less likely to be reasonable?
The seller agreed to reduce the price of goods if the buyer was prepared to accept the exemption clause.	The buyer has chosen to get the lower price in exchange for the exemption clause. It would be a touch harsh on the seller to deny them the benefit of the exemption clause, when in effect the seller has paid for the protection of the exemption clause by reducing the price. That all makes it *more* likely to pass the reasonableness test.
The exemption clause is set out in the small print at clause 76(3)(i)(d). Clause 76 is headed 'Other matters'.	Whether the customer knew – or even ought to have known – about the clause is relevant to determining its *reasonableness*. Here, the clause is buried in the small print and overall is less likely to be reasonable.

Whilst s 11 of UCTA 1977 itself is not very helpful, there are guidelines to assist the court, both in the 1977 Act and in case law. The guidelines in the 1977 Act are contained in Sch 2. They specifically apply when the court is considering the reasonableness test under ss 6 and 7. As these are the only guidelines in the 1977 Act, however, the court can, and does, take them into account when applying the reasonableness test in other situations.

The Sch 2 guidelines

The Sch 2 guidelines say that the court should have regard to certain matters if they appear relevant. These include the following:

(a) The relative strength of the bargaining positions of the parties

For example, if the bargaining positions of the parties are equal, it will be easier to show that the exemption clause is reasonable (*Watford Electronics v Sanderson CFL Ltd* [2001] EWCA Civ 317 and *Goodlife Foods Ltd v Hall Fire Protection Ltd* [2018] EWCA Civ 1371) than if a multinational corporation is dealing with a small trader.

Businesses negotiating contracts will very often agree on exemption clauses as a legitimate method of allocating the commercial risk between them. Risk is generally reflected in the price; so the greater the risk to the supplier, the higher the price. The following extract from Chadwick LJ's judgment in *Watford Electronics v Sanderson CFL Ltd* [2001] EWCA Civ 317, CA sums up the attitude of judges in commercial cases:

> Where experienced businessmen representing substantial companies of equal bargaining power negotiate an agreement, they may be taken to have had regard to the matters known to them. They should, in my view, be taken to be the best judge of the commercial fairness of the agreement which they have made.
>
> ... They should be taken to be the best judge on the question whether the terms of the agreement are reasonable.

(b) Did the customer receive an inducement to agree to the exemption clause, or in accepting it did the customer have an opportunity to enter a similar contract with someone else, but without having to accept a similar exemption clause?

For example, was the customer offered a lower price for accepting a contract with an exemption clause and a higher price for accepting a contract without an exemption clause? If so, this might suggest that the clause was reasonable. Also, if the customer could have gone elsewhere and avoided an exemption clause but chose not to do so, the court might feel that the customer had some good reason for accepting the contract with the clause and be reluctant to interfere with the agreement the parties had reached.

(c) Did the customer know, or ought reasonably to have known, of the existence and extent of the clause, taking into account any trade custom or previous dealings between the parties?

For example, if the clause is clearly worded and clearly set out in the document, the court might be encouraged to say that the clause is reasonable as the customer should have been aware of the existence and extent of the clause.

(d) Where the exemption clause will apply if a condition is not complied with, was it reasonable at the time of the contract to expect that compliance with the condition would be practicable?

For example, have a look at clause 5.1 in the Specimen Conditions of Sale (**Reading 1** in the **Appendix**). You will see that the seller is saying that the seller will not be liable for defects in goods unless the buyer notifies the seller of the defects within 14 days of the time when the buyer discovers, or ought to have discovered, the defect.

At the time of the contract, was it reasonable to expect that it would be practicable for the buyer to comply with this condition?

(e) Were the goods manufactured, processed or adapted to the special order of the customer?

Additional guidelines for limitation clauses

There are also additional guidelines in s 11(4) of UCTA 1977 which apply to limitation clauses. If the court is trying to decide whether a limitation clause is reasonable, s 11(4) says that the court should also have regard to:

- the resources which the defendant could expect to be available for the purpose of meeting the liability should it arise; and
- how far it was open to the defendant to cover itself by insurance.

Must the whole clause be reasonable?

It may be that the defendant is relying on just part of a much longer exemption clause. The question then is whether the whole clause has to satisfy the reasonableness test or whether the court will consider only the part on which the defendant is relying.

In the case of *Stewart Gill Ltd v Horatio Myer & Co Ltd* [1992] 1 QB 600 the Court of Appeal took the view that the court should consider the clause as a whole and not just the part relied on. Lord Donaldson MR said that, in the face of the wording of s 11 of the 1977 Act:

> The issue is whether the term [the whole term and nothing but the term] shall have been a fair and reasonable one to be included.

The Court of Appeal refused to sever the unreasonable parts of an exemption clause when assessing reasonableness. The Court took the view that the clause as a whole was unreasonable, and that it was immaterial that parts of the clause might have been reasonable had they stood on their own.

However, in the case of *Watford Electronics Ltd v Sanderson CFL Ltd* [2001] EWCA Civ 317, the Court of Appeal decided that an exemption clause could be split into two parts as the two parts served two distinct purposes. In this case the reasonableness of each part could be decided separately.

In *Goodlife Foods Ltd v Hall Fire Protection Ltd* [2018] EWCA Civ 1371, the Court of Appeal took an even more liberal approach. The defendant in that case sought to rely on a clause which excluded all liability for loss caused to '... property, goods, persons or the like, directly or indirectly resulting from our negligence ...'.

Notwithstanding the attempt to exclude liability for personal injury/death, the Court of Appeal held the clause to be reasonable and valid. There were a number of things relevant to the decision:

(a) As in *Watford Electronics v Sanderson,* the parties were of equal bargaining power.

(b) Goodlife Foods could have gone elsewhere and found a supplier who was prepared to contract on a less stringent basis.

(c) Goodlife ought reasonably to have known of the existence of the terms.

(d) Finally, Goodlife was best placed to obtain insurance.

Nevertheless, when drafting exemption clauses, it is best to be cautious. Draft for reasonableness and have several separate exemption clauses dealing with different issues rather than one long clause.

Guidelines in *Smith v Eric Bush*

We have now considered the guidelines on reasonableness in the 1977 Act. When deciding whether the reasonableness test has been passed, the court may consider factors which are not mentioned in these guidelines. For example, which party was better placed to insure against the particular risk (*Goodlife Food v Hall Fire Protection*) and, where the exemption clause is purporting to exclude liability for failure to exercise reasonable care and skill, the guidelines laid down in *Smith v Eric Bush* [1990] 1 AC 831, HL.

In *Smith v Eric Bush*, the respondent applied to a building society for a mortgage to purchase a house. The building society instructed a firm of surveyors to inspect the house. The respondent signed an application form for the survey and paid for it. The form contained a disclaimer stating that the surveyor did not accept any responsibility for the accuracy of the report. After receiving the report, the respondent bought the house. The report turned out to be inaccurate. As the respondent had not instructed the surveyor, they could not sue the surveyor for breach of contract (ie for breach of the statutory implied term that the work would be carried out with reasonable care and skill). Instead the respondent sued the surveyor in negligence. The surveyor tried to rely on the disclaimer to exempt him from liability.

Section 2(2) of UCTA 1977 applied to the disclaimer, ie the disclaimer would only be effective if it was reasonable. The House of Lords decided that the disclaimer was not reasonable and the surveyor could not rely on it.

Lord Griffiths stated that the following factors should be considered in determining whether the disclaimer was reasonable:

- Were the parties of equal bargaining power?
- In the case of advice, would it be reasonably practicable to obtain the advice from an alternative source taking into account considerations of cost and time?
- How difficult is the task being undertaken for which liability is excluded?
- What are the practical consequences of the decision on reasonableness? This must involve the sums of money potentially at stake and the ability of the parties to bear the loss involved which in turn raises the question of insurance.

The factors listed by Lord Griffiths repeat the guidelines on reasonableness in Sch 2 of the 1977 Act to the following extent:

(a) Equality of bargaining position is the same as the first guideline in Sch 2.

(b) Considering whether it would be reasonably practicable to obtain the advice from an alternative source is very similar to the second guideline in Sch 2, which refers to whether the customer had an opportunity of entering into a similar contract with other persons, but without having to accept a similar clause.

As for the other factors mentioned by Lord Griffiths (difficulty of the task and the practical consequences of the court's decision), there is no obvious overlap with the Sch 2 guidelines. These other factors are additional points the court can bear in mind where relevant.

The importance of insurance is mentioned in s 11(4) of the UCTA 1977 Act, where the reasonableness test is applied to a limitation clause.

The *Smith v Eric Bush* guidelines were considered and applied in *St Albans City and District Council v International Computers Ltd* [1995] FSR 686.

The claimant, a local authority, entered into a contract with the defendant for the supply of a computer system to be used in administering its collection of the community charge. The software contained an error so that the population figure for the area was overstated. As a result, the local authority set the community charge rate too low and therefore suffered loss. The local authority brought an action for damages, and the defendant sought to rely on a limitation clause in the contract limiting their liability to £100,000. Such limitation clauses were common in the computer industry and the local authority knew about the clause.

Scott Baker J, at first instance, held that the defendant was in breach of an express term in the contract and s 3 of UCTA 1977 was applicable in respect of the limitation clause. The claimant was not a consumer but had dealt on the defendant's written standard terms of business. Therefore, the limitation clause would only be valid if it satisfied the requirement of reasonableness.

Scott Baker J considered the provisions in s 11(4) of UCTA 1977 and the first three Sch 2 guidelines, together with the additional factors set out in *Smith v Bush* (1990). He went on to hold that the limitation clause was not reasonable and could not be relied upon. The following factors were identified as leading to the conclusion that the limitation was not reasonable:

(a) The defendant was a very substantial company and, as a wholly owned subsidiary of a multinational group, had ample resources to meet any liability.

(b) The defendant company had product liability insurance cover of £50 million and could not justify limiting liability to £100,000 which was small both in relation to the potential risk and the actual loss. The judge said that the burden of proof of reasonableness lies on the defendant, but the company called no evidence to show that it was fair and reasonable to limit their liability to £100,000. It seems also that the defendant was using out of date conditions and current ones had limitation set at £125,000.

(c) The defendant company was in a very strong bargaining position relative to the claimant since it was one of a limited number of companies capable of fulfilling the local authority's requirements. The other companies also dealt on similar standard conditions. Also, council officials are not, in the ordinary sense of the word, businesspersons and their bargaining position was therefore weaker than the defendant's.

(d) The practical consequence of a contrary finding of reasonableness would be that the loss would be borne by the local authority's population, either through increased taxation or reduced services. The defendant was covered by insurance and should carry the risk since it was the party which stood to make the profit on the contract. The practical consequences counted in favour of the local authority.

The factors above clearly pointed to the clause being unreasonable.

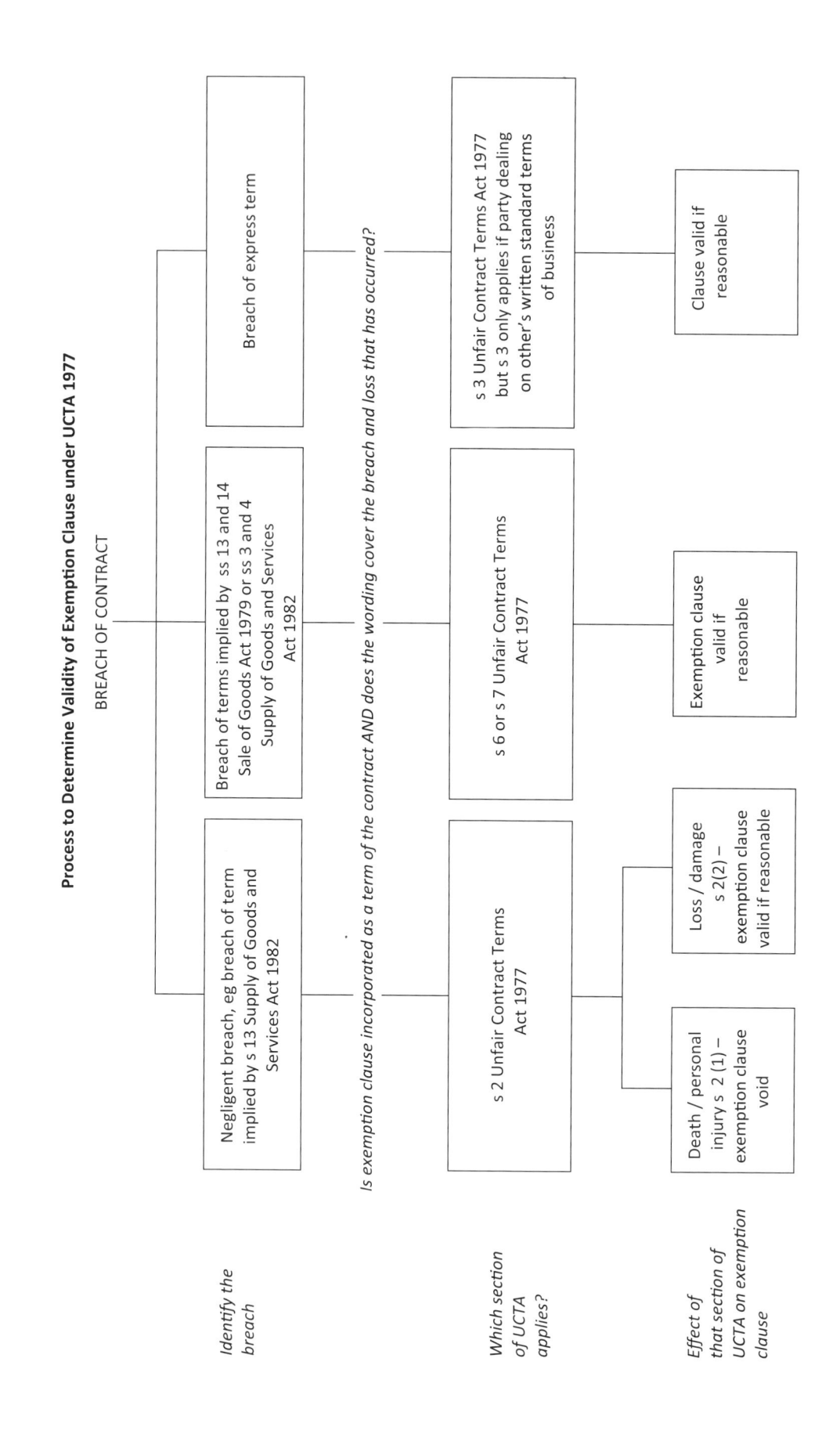

Contract

Process to Determine Validity of Exemption Clause under UCTA 1977

BREACH OF CONTRACT

Identify the breach

- Negligent breach, eg breach of term implied by s 13 Supply of Goods and Services Act 1982
- Breach of terms implied by ss 13 and 14 Sale of Goods Act 1979 or ss 3 and 4 Supply of Goods and Services Act 1982
- Breach of express term

Is exemption clause incorporated as a term of the contract AND does the wording cover the breach and loss that has occurred?

Which section of UCTA applies?

- s 2 Unfair Contract Terms Act 1977
- s 6 or s 7 Unfair Contract Terms Act 1977
- s 3 Unfair Contract Terms Act 1977 but s 3 only applies if party dealing on other's written standard terms of business

Effect of that section of UCTA on exemption clause

- Death / personal injury s 2(1) – exemption clause void
- Loss / damage s 2(2) – exemption clause valid if reasonable
- Exemption clause valid if reasonable
- Clause valid if reasonable

82

3.4.5 Consumer Rights Act 2015

Remember that the CRA 2015 consolidates consumer rights, protection and remedies in contracts made with traders. We have already looked at some of the main terms implied by the Act and the remedies for consumers if those terms are breached.

As a codifying Act, the CRA 2015 also governs the extent to which a trader may contract out of the consumer's statutory rights and remedies, and in Part 2 deals with unfair terms in contracts between a trader and consumer.

3.4.5.1 Exclusion and restriction of liability

Sales contracts

If you look at **Reading 2** in the **Appendix** you will see that s 31(1) of the CRA 2015 provides that liability for breach of s 9 (goods to be of satisfactory quality), s 10 (goods to be reasonably fit for purpose) and s 11 (goods to be as described) cannot be excluded or restricted. This includes preventing an obligation or duty arising or limiting its extent (s 31(3)).

Section 31(2) points out that this also means that a term in a sales contract is not binding on the consumer to the extent that it would:

(a) exclude or restrict a right or remedy in respect of breach of ss 9–11;

(b) make such a right or remedy or its enforcement subject to a restrictive or onerous condition;

(c) allow a trader to put a person at a disadvantage as a result of pursuing such a right or remedy; or

(d) exclude or restrict rules of evidence or procedure.

So, goods to be of satisfactory quality, fit for their particular purpose and as described are all non-excludable statutory rights which consumers should be able to enforce without restriction to attain the appropriate remedy.

Service contracts

Also set out in **Reading 2** of the **Appendix** is s 57(1), which effectively provides that a trader cannot exclude (compare restrict) liability for breach of s 49 (the implied term to perform a service with reasonable care and skill). This also includes preventing an obligation or duty arising in the first place (s 57(5)).

To illustrate how a trader might do this, let us consider for a moment a domestic decorating contract. You would expect the decorator to use dust sheets, etc to cover the carpet and furniture as part of the decorator's duty to exercise reasonable care and skill under s 49. It goes without saying. So if there were a clause in the contract which made protection of the carpets and furniture the householder's responsibility, the decorator would be redefining their implied contractual obligations; in other words, the decorator would not be liable in the first place, if they did not take reasonable care to protect the carpet, etc. It is this sort of clause at which s 57(5) is aimed.

Section 57(3) goes on to state that a trader cannot restrict liability for breach of s 49 and, where they apply, ss 51 and 52 (reasonable price and reasonable time) if it would prevent the consumer in an appropriate case from getting a refund.

Finally, s 57(4) points out that this also means that a trader cannot:

(a) exclude or restrict a right or remedy in respect of liability for breaches of ss 49–52;

(b) make such a right or remedy or its enforcement subject to a restrictive or onerous condition;

(c) put a person at a disadvantage as a result of pursuing such a right or remedy, or exclude or restrict rules of evidence or procedure.

Any clause which falls foul of s 57 will simply not bind the consumer.

3.4.5.2 Unfair terms

Very simply, an unfair term in a contract between a trader and consumer will not be binding on the consumer, and a term will be 'unfair' if, contrary to the requirement of good faith, it causes a significant imbalance in the parties' rights and obligations under the contract to the detriment of the consumer. Whether a term is fair is to be determined by taking into account the subject matter of the contract and all the circumstances at the time of the contract.

An exemption clause may be an 'unfair term' (eg a term which purports to exclude a trader's liability for death or personal injury caused by an act or omission of the trader), but many other different types of clause may be deemed 'unfair' under the CRA 2015 and therefore not bind the consumer. For example, if a sales contract requires a consumer to pay a 50% deposit and further provides that the consumer will forfeit the full deposit if the consumer does not proceed with the purchase, the latter term is likely to be deemed 'unfair'. Note, however, that a term may not be assessed for fairness to the extent that it defines the subject matter of the contract or the price. This is to stop consumers complaining that they have been overcharged. If you are interested, Sch 2 to the CRA 2015 sets out a list of contract terms which are likely to be deemed unfair, but a detailed discussion of unfair terms is beyond the scope of this textbook.

Problem question – summary

We have now looked at the common law provisions which apply to exemption clauses and at the effect of UCTA 1977 and the CRA 2015.

Whenever you are dealing with a problem involving exemption clauses, the starting point must always be to identify the type of contract. Is it a contract between a trader and consumer which is governed by the CRA 2015, or is it another type of contract governed by the SGA 1979/SGSA 1982 and UCTA 1977? Once you have identified the particular type of contract, the next thing to do is identify the particular breach(es), liability for which the supplier is purporting to exclude/limit.

3.4.6 Exemption clauses and third parties

Sometimes an exemption clause may seek to protect someone who is not a party to the contract, and we shall now go on to consider the law on this.

A third party is someone who is not a party to a contract. The general rule is that an exemption clause in a contract cannot protect a third party, as the privity rule (which you considered in **Chapter 2**) provides that only a party can rely on a clause in a contract.

A case which illustrates this is *Adler v Dickson* [1955] 1 QB 158. Mrs Adler was injured boarding a ship. Her contract was with the shipping company and contained an exemption clause. She sued the master and boatswain alleging negligence in not securing the gang plank. The court held that the master and boatswain were not protected by the exemption clause as they were not parties to the contract.

A major exception to this general rule that exemption clauses do not protect third parties is contained in the Contracts (Rights of Third Parties) Act 1999 (discussed earlier in **Chapter 2**, in the context of privity). Under this Act, a third party can acquire rights if:

- the contract expressly provides that they may acquire a benefit (s 1(1)(a)); or
- the term purports to confer a benefit on them (s 1(1)(b)).

Subsection (1)(b) does not apply, however, if on a true construction of the contract it was not intended that the term be enforceable by a third party (s 1(2)).

For a third party to enforce a term of the contract in its own right, the third party must be expressly identified in the contract by name or as a member of a class (eg 'employees') or answering a particular description.

The Act extends to the benefit of an exemption clause (s 1(6)), but it can be relied on only to the extent that the clause is valid.

Example

Jordan took his taxi cab to Car Care Ltd to be serviced. When he drove the taxi away from Car Care Ltd, the brakes failed and the taxi crashed into a tree. The taxi was damaged and Jordan was injured. Jordan has now discovered that the reason the brakes failed was negligence on the part of George, a mechanic employed by Car Care Ltd.

Clauses in the contract between Jordan and Car Care Ltd provide:

8.1 Neither Car Care Ltd nor any of its employees will be liable for loss or damage to property howsoever caused (including negligence).

8.2 Neither Car Care Ltd nor any of its employees will be liable for personal injury, unless caused by negligence.

Statements	True or false?
Jordan could sue Car Care Ltd for breach of contract.	True. Car Care Ltd is in breach of the term implied by s 13 of the SGSA 1982, ie Car Care Ltd has not provided the service with reasonable care.
If clause 8.1 is found to be incorporated into the contract and reasonable, Car Care Ltd could rely on it to protect it from liability in respect of damage to the taxi.	True. Section 2(2) of the UCTA 1977.
If clause 8.2 is found to be incorporated into the contract and reasonable, Car Care Ltd could rely on it to protect it from liability in respect of the injury.	False. As a matter of construction, the clause does not cover injury. If it did, s 2(1) of the UCTA 1977 would apply – cannot exempt liability for death or injury caused by negligence.
Jordan could sue George for breach of contract.	False. There is no contract between them.
Jordan could sue George in the tort of negligence.	True.
If clause 8.1 is incorporated into the contract and reasonable, George could rely on it to avoid liability in respect of the taxi because of the C(RTP)A 1999.	True.
George cannot rely on the clauses as he is not named in the contract.	False. George does not have to be named – he is identified as a member of a class, ie employee.

Exemption clauses – summary

We have now considered:

- express and implied terms;
- the difference between conditions, warranties and innominate terms;
- the common law rules in relation to incorporation and construction of exemption clause and other terms;

- the effect of the Unfair Contract Terms Act 1977 and the Consumer Rights Act 2015 on exemption clauses
- exemption clauses and third parties.

You have now looked at the express and implied terms of a contract, and at the common law rules and statutory restrictions on exemption clauses.

Set out below is a suggested structure to use when answering problems involving exemption clauses. It may not be necessary to consider all the points listed – this will depend on the facts of the individual problem.

Structure for problems involving exemption clauses

1. Who are the parties to the contract?
2. Start by finding a cause of action. Have any terms (express and/or implied) been breached?
3. Is the exemption clause incorporated into the contract?

    Is the clause in a signed contractual document? (If so, likely to be incorporated provided legible, not misrepresented, and not onerous unless reasonably drawn to the other party's attention.)

    If not then:

    Have reasonable steps been taken to bring the clause to the other party's attention? Consider such things as:

    - the nature of any document containing the clause
    - position of clause in document
    - prominence of clause
    - is clause unusual or onerous?

    When were the steps taken? (Must be before contract finalised unless there has been a previous consistent course of dealings.)

    If the steps were taken after the contract was finalised then consider whether there was a consistent course of dealing between the parties.

4. Does the clause cover the breach and damage alleged?

    Look carefully at the wording of the clause. If it clearly does cover the breach and damage alleged then say this – if there is doubt then state and apply any relevant rule of construction.

5. Consider the Unfair Contract Terms Act 1977 or the Consumer Rights Act 2015 (as appropriate). Which sections apply? (Remember that, in order to work out which section of UCTA 1977 or the CRA 2015 applies, you must think about the term that has been breached.)

    - What is the effect of UCTA 1977/the CRA 2015?
    - Is the reasonableness test in UCTA 1977 relevant? If so, state the test (s 11) and the relevant guidelines and apply them to the facts.

6. Remedies [You will be dealing with remedies in **Chapter 4**. We have included this here as a reminder that you would be expected to consider remedies available.]

7. Think about whether it is possible to bring an action against a person who is not a party to the contract in the tort of negligence. If so, can that person rely on the exemption clause? Consider the general privity rule and the exception contained in the Contracts (Rights of Third Parties) Act 1999.

8. Come to a conclusion. Do you think the innocent party can recover for the loss and damage they have suffered?

SUMMARY

- Whether you are drafting a contract for a client or advising a client on a possible breach of contract, you need a thorough knowledge of the rules relating to express and implied terms and the law relating to exemption clauses.

- Therefore, in this chapter you have looked at the difference between express and implied terms and the various ways in which terms might be implied into contracts. You have also dealt with the common law and statutory provisions relating to exemption clauses and seen how these provisions would apply in a number of factual scenarios.

- You have seen that the terms of a contract may be conditions, warranties or innominate terms, and that the classification is important in relation to the remedies which may be available if there is a breach of contract. This is an area which we will explore more fully in the next chapter.

4 Remedies for Breach of Contract

LEARNING OUTCOMES

When you have completed this chapter, you should be able to:

- explain, apply and discuss in depth the principles governing the availability of damages for breach of contract, including agreed damages clauses;
- identify the other remedies which may be available if there is a breach of contract and explain the legal and equitable principles which govern them.

In **Chapter 3** you studied the rules relating to terms of a contract. We are now going to look at the remedies which may be available if a term of the contract is broken. For example, suppose you decide to have a new kitchen fitted. You select the kitchen units you want from a firm of kitchen suppliers and arrange for the firm to install the units. The firm starts to fit the units, but you feel that the workmanship is not up to standard and you want to know what you can do about it. First of all, you must establish that a term of the contract has been broken. Thinking back to the terms implied by statute that you looked at in **Chapter 3**, what term has the firm most likely broken here?

The contract is one for work and materials, so you probably thought of the term implied by s 49 of the Consumer Rights Act 2015, ie the service/work must be provided with reasonable care and skill. Having established the term broken, you will then want to consider the remedies which may be available. For example, can you tell the firm to stop work and employ someone else? Can you obtain damages and, if so, how will these be assessed?

The main remedy for breach of contract is damages, but we are also going to look at the remedies of:

- action for an agreed sum;
- termination of the contract;
- specific performance and injunctions; and
- restitution.

4.1 Damages

4.1.1 Introduction

Breach of any term of the contract gives the innocent party the right to claim damages, although if the claimant has not suffered any loss, damages will be nominal only.

To recover damages, the claimant must prove that loss has been suffered as a result of the defendant's breach, and the loss or damage must not be too remote a consequence of the breach. We shall be dealing with types of loss and remoteness later in this chapter.

4.1.1.1 Compensation not punishment

The object of awarding damages is to compensate the claimant for their loss and not to punish the defendant. Although punitive or exemplary damages can be awarded in certain tort cases to punish the defendant, they cannot as a general rule be awarded in a purely contractual claim. Also, damages are based on the loss to the claimant and not on the gain to the defendant. This means that if the claimant has not suffered any loss, only nominal damages (usually about £5–£10) will be awarded.

For example, assume you agree that a decorator will paint your house for £1,000, starting in two months' time. You agree to pay on completion of the work. Before the decorator is due to start work, they tell you that they will not be doing the painting for you. The decorator has found a more lucrative job elsewhere. The decorator is clearly in breach of the contract with you. However, you find someone else who will do the job for £800, starting at the same time. It would not be in your interests to sue the decorator for breach of contract as you have not suffered any loss. Any award would be for nominal damages only.

A party should be wary of bringing a claim in these circumstances as it may result in having to pay all the costs of the proceedings. This is what happened in the commercial case of *Obagi v Stanborough (Developments) Ltd* [1993] TLR 646. The defendant was found to have broken a term of the contract which provided that the defendant must use best endeavours to obtain planning permission. However, it was shown that there was never any substantial chance of planning permission being granted and so the defendant's breach did not cause any loss to the claimant. The judge at first instance awarded nominal damages of £5 and ordered the claimant to pay the defendant's costs. This was upheld by the Court of Appeal. Therefore, it is not worth bringing a claim where only nominal damages will be awarded.

4.1.2 Assessment and measure of damages

As you have seen, the object of awarding damages in contract is to compensate the claimant for loss suffered because of the defendant's breach. The question is how can this be achieved?

The normal aim of the court in assessing damages was stated in the judgment of Parke B in *Robinson v Harman* (1848) 1 Exch 850:

> The rule at common law is that where a party sustains loss by reason of a breach of contract, he is so far as money can do it, to be placed in the same situation with respect to damages as if the contract had been performed.

The next question is how will the court measure damages in order to achieve this aim; in other words, how much is the court likely to award?

4.1.2.1 Measure of damages: expectation loss

Generally, the claimant will be able to recover for loss of the benefit which the claimant would have obtained had the contract been properly performed. Damages assessed in this way are sometimes said to be worked out on an expectation loss basis as the claimant will be compensated for their lost expectation.

Remedies for Breach of Contract

⭐ Examples

1. Ayesha sells a Ming vase to Barbara for £50,000. It is a term of the contract that the vase is Ming. In fact, the vase turns out to be a copy worth £1,000. Had it actually been Ming, it would have been worth £60,000.	The court is likely to award Barbara £59,000. If the contract had been properly performed, Barbara would have a Ming vase worth £60,000. In fact, she has a fake worth £1,000. She needs £59,000 so that she can buy an equivalent vase.
2. Carol agrees to buy goods from David at a price of £1,000, payment on delivery. Delivery to be on 1 October. David refuses to deliver. (In fact he had sold the goods to someone else for £2,000.) On 1 October Carol can buy similar goods elsewhere for £1,200.	The court is likely to award damages of £200. If the contract had been properly performed, Carol should have received the goods for £1,000. If she has to pay £1,200, she will have paid £200 more, so she needs this amount in damages. The fact that David makes a profit out of the breach is not relevant – the court will compensate Carol, not punish David.
3. Esher & Co orders goods from Fields plc at a price of £8,000 to be paid on delivery. Delivery to be 1 October. Fields plc tries to deliver on 1 October but Esher & Co refuses to accept the goods. Fields plc can sell elsewhere but only for £2,500.	The court is likely to award £5,500. If the contract had been properly performed, Fields plc would have received £8,000. Now the company can only sell for £2,500 – so it needs £5,500 to put it in the position it would have been in if the contract had been properly performed.
4. Jason, sole owner of a gardening business, agreed to cut down a tree in Carol's garden and remove all timber from the premises for £250. He agreed to do the work on 1 May. On 26 April Carol told Jason that she had changed her mind and no longer wanted him to cut down the tree. Jason could not find alternative work for 1 May. He tells you that he would have made a net profit of £220, taking into account the expenses he would have had to pay to do the job, including the fee to dispose of the timber.	The court is likely to award Jason £220. If the contract had been properly performed, Jason would have earned £250 altogether. However, in order to earn that sum, he would have had to pay out expenses amounting to £30, and these must therefore be deducted.
5. Smith is a manufacturer of cables. With his old machine: • he made £10,000 of cables per week, • he had costs of £5,000 per week (materials, labour and servicing), • giving him a profit of £5,000 per week. He recently bought a machine from Jones, which they calculated would enable him to: • make £10,000 worth of cables per week, • with costs of £4,000 per week, • giving him a profit of £6,000 per week. In the first three weeks of its operation, the machine only worked at 70% of its proper capacity because of a fault (which Jones has now rectified). As a result, Smith could only make £7,000 worth of cables per week. However, his costs were only £3,000 per week, as he used fewer materials. What can Smith claim?	Smith was £3,000 worse off using his new machine than if he had used his old one. But his complaint is not that he bought the new machine and now wishes he had not done so; his complaint is that the new machine did not work as well as it should have. What we need to find out is how much Smith has lost compared with his position if the new machine had been working properly from the start. So, what about giving him £9,000? Well, the machine may have been operating at reduced capacity for a while, but he was still making £7,000 worth of cables per week. And it is true that over three weeks, he has made £9,000 worth fewer cables than he did before. But over those three weeks, he has also saved costs of £3,000. If you awarded Smith £9,000 damages, you would actually be making him better off than

91

> if the contract had been properly performed. You would be giving him £9,000 to compensate his loss of production, but also letting him keep his £3,000 saved costs. The object is merely compensation, so he cannot have £9,000. What he should get is £6,000. Why? Well, if the contract had been performed properly, he would have been able to make £9,000 worth more of cables but would have incurred £3,000 more costs. Because of the breach, he is £6,000 worse off. Give him £6,000 and he is in the same financial position as he would have been if the contract had been properly performed. Put another way, Smith gets what he bargained for.

We have looked at scenarios where goods turn out to be fake, and where goods are not delivered or not accepted. Next, we consider the situation where goods delivered under a contract are defective or services are defectively performed. Again, when assessing damages on an expectation loss basis, the court will try to put the claimant in the position the claimant would have been in if the contract had been properly performed, but how will this be achieved?

Traditionally, the court would award either the difference in value or the cost of cure. This means that if goods are defective, the basic rule is that the amount of damages awarded will be the difference in value between the actual value of the goods and the value the goods would have had if they had not been defective.

With contracts for services, the basic rule is that the amount of damages awarded will be the cost of putting the work right, ie cost of cure. However, the court would award the cost of cure for defective goods and the difference in value for defective services if reasonable to do so.

So, at one time, it was thought that difference in value or cost of cure were the only potential awards of damages. It was one or the other. But what if neither award would compensate the claimant for their true loss as a result of the breach of contract? Is there an alternative measure that the court can award?

This was the dilemma faced by the courts in *Ruxley Electronics v Forsyth* [1996] AC 344.

Ruxley agreed to build a swimming pool for Mr Forsyth in his garden. Mr Forsyth stipulated that the deep end of the pool should be 7 feet 6 inches deep. In the event it was only 6 feet 9 inches deep. It was established there was no difference in value, but it was going to cost £21,560 to rectify the problem.

The question before the House of Lords was whether Mr Forsyth should get nothing (representing the difference in value), £21,560 (representing the cost of cure) or a sum somewhere between those two figures. The original trial judge had awarded Mr Forsyth £2,500.

Whilst cost of cure (here £21,560) is the normal measure in cases of defective work, the House of Lords did not consider it should be used where it was unreasonable in relation to the benefit to be obtained. So the House of Lords reinstated the original trial judge's award of £2,500 as representing the true loss suffered by Mr Forsyth; namely that his personal preference for a deeper pool had not been satisfied. The House of Lords referred to this loss as 'loss of amenity' and the 'consumer surplus'.

One significant aspect of the case was that it was all about a swimming pool – something meant to provide pleasure and amenity. So the loss of amenity/consumer surplus could be viewed as his 'true' loss. If the contract had been for a more mundane construction, Mr Forsyth might have received nothing, on the basis that there would have been no loss of value or amenity and that curing the defect would have been unreasonable. Conversely, if the depth of the swimming pool had been critical for some reason and consequently may well have been rebuilt, the full cost of cure (ie £21,560) may have been awarded.

4.1.2.2 Measure of damages: reliance loss

We have seen that the claimant will normally ask for damages to compensate for the benefit the claimant would have obtained if the contract had been properly performed, including loss of profits. However, sometimes loss of expectation may be too speculative, and so instead the claimant may ask for damages to cover the expenses incurred in reliance on the contract. Damages assessed in this way are sometimes said to be worked out on a reliance loss basis.

In the case of *Anglia Television v Reed* [1972] 1 QB 60, CA, Anglia engaged the defendant, an actor, to play the leading role in the production of a play for television. The defendant later refused to carry on with the contract and Anglia was forced to abandon the production as it could not get a substitute. Anglia claimed as damages all of the expenditure which they had wasted on the production, which included such things as director's fees, designer's fees and stage manager's fees. Anglia TV did not claim damages on an expectation loss basis because they did not know what profit (if any) they would have made if the contract had been properly performed by the defendant.

Counsel for the defendant argued that Anglia TV should not be able to recover expenditure incurred before the contract with the defendant was concluded on the ground that this part of the loss was too remote a consequence of the breach. (We will be looking at remoteness at **4.1.4** below.) However, the Court of Appeal disagreed and held that Anglia TV could recover all their wasted expenditure including expenditure incurred before they entered into the contract with the defendant.

Lord Denning felt that the pre-contract expenditure was not too remote because it should have been in Reed's contemplation when he entered into the contract with Anglia TV that expenditure had already been incurred and that all the expenditure would be wasted if, at the last minute, he broke his contract with them.

As we have just seen, in *Anglia TV v Reed* the claimant asked for damages on a reliance loss basis because the company did not know what profit the film would have made if the contract had been performed properly by the defendant. It will generally be for the claimant to decide whether to seek damages on an expectation or a reliance loss basis, but sometimes the court will decide that the reliance loss basis is the correct approach if the claim for damages on an expectation loss basis is too speculative.

It is important to remember that in order to obtain damages (whether on a reliance or expectation loss basis), the claimant must prove that they have suffered loss due to the defendant's breach.

> This was emphasised in the case of *Omak Maritime Ltd v Mamola Challenger Shipping Co (The Mamola Challenger)* [2010] EWHC 2026.

Omak agreed to charter a vessel from the owners for a term of five years. Omak breached the contract, and the owners (rightfully) terminated the contract. The contract required the owners to make various modifications to the vessel, and the owners had incurred expenses in preparation for these modifications. These expenses were wasted, ie they had no residual value or benefit for the owners. The owners claimed damages for the wasted expenditure.

It was found that the owners were able to re-charter the vessel at a higher rate than under the original charter, and over the five-year period they would earn more than they would have earned under the original charter.

The High Court held that the owners could not recover damages for wasted expenditure. This decision seems logical as the owners had mitigated their loss by re-chartering, and as a result they had not suffered any loss. (We will look at the mitigation rule later in this chapter.)

We shall now go on to consider the types of loss or damage for which damages may be awarded in contract.

4.1.3 Types of loss

Loss includes any harm to the person or property of the claimant and any injury to the claimant's economic position. This means that the claimant can recover for personal injury, damage to property and also loss of profit. The restrictions that apply to recovering damages for economic loss in tort do not apply to contract claims.

For example, suppose the claimant has purchased a machine for use in its business. The machine is defective and cannot be repaired. The seller has broken the term implied by s 14 of the Sale of Goods Act 1979 as the machine is not of satisfactory quality. The claimant would want to obtain damages for the cost of a new machine and for any profit it has lost due to the breakdown. Furthermore, if the defect causes the machine to catch fire and the fire damages the claimant's factory and injures the claimant, the claimant would also be able to obtain damages in respect of the damage to the factory and for the personal injury. The claimant can obtain damages for all of these losses in an action for breach of contract.

4.1.3.1 Damages for a lost opportunity

The court may award damages for a lost opportunity. In the case of *Chaplin v Hicks* [1911] 2 KB 786, the *Daily Express* ran a talent contest. The top 50 contestants had to attend an audition where 12 winners would be selected. The winners would be given theatrical engagements for three years. The claimant was one of the top 50, but the organisers failed to tell the claimant the time and place of the audition. The Court of Appeal decided that the claimant was entitled to damages to compensate for the loss of the chance of being one of the 12 winners.

A more modern example of a lost opportunity is the case of *Blackpool and Fylde Aero Club v Blackpool Borough Council* [1990] 1 WLR 1195, CA, which you looked at in **Chapter 1**. Here the Court of Appeal held that the Council had a duty to consider all properly submitted tenders. The club had properly submitted its tender but it was not considered. The club had therefore lost the opportunity of being selected for the concession to run pleasure flights.

4.1.3.2 Damages for mental distress and disappointment

Damages will not normally be awarded for distress or disappointment. A certain amount of annoyance, distress and disappointment is usually felt by the innocent party when a breach of contract occurs. However, the courts have been very reluctant to award damages for such distress in contract cases, possibly because of a fear that it would open the floodgates for such claims. Traditionally, the courts have been more willing to award damages for mental distress in tort.

The case of *Addis v Gramophone Co Ltd* [1909] AC 488, HL reflects the usual approach of the court when dealing with a claim for damages for distress in contract. The claimant was dismissed from their job and sought damages for the distress suffered because of the harsh and humiliating manner of the dismissal. The House of Lords refused to award damages for mental distress.

However, the court has awarded damages for mental distress in situations where one of main objects of the contract was to have peace of mind, eg hospitality and holiday contracts.

A case which illustrates this is *Jarvis v Swans Tours* [1973] 1 QB 233, CA.

The defendants, a firm of travel agents, advertised a 'houseparty' holiday in Switzerland. The claimant, Mr Jarvis, booked two weeks' holiday with the defendants and paid £63.45. The holiday was a catalogue of disasters. There was supposed to be a 'houseparty', but there were only 13 guests there during the first week and none during the second – apart from Mr Jarvis. The holiday failed to comply with the description in the brochure in numerous other respects. For example, the skiing was some distance away, and in the first week there were no ordinary length skis to hire, only mini skis; in the second week longer skis were available, but the boots did not fit properly and Mr Jarvis' feet became blistered so he could not continue even with the long skis. There was supposed to be a bar at the hotel, but it was in an unoccupied annex and only open for one evening. All in all, Mr Jarvis had a pretty miserable holiday and brought an action for breach of contract. The county court judge awarded £31.72 damages. Mr Jarvis appealed.

Lord Denning MR held as follows:

> The one question in the case is: what is the amount of damages? The judge seems to have taken the difference in value between what he paid for and what he got. He said that he intended to give 'the difference between the two values and no other damages' under any other head. He thought that Mr Jarvis had got half of what he paid for. So the judge gave him half the amount which he had paid, namely, £31.72. Mr Jarvis appeals to this court. He says that the damages ought to have been much more ...

> What is the right way of assessing damages? It has often been said that on a breach of contract damages cannot be given for mental distress ...

> I think that those limitations are out of date. In a proper case damages for mental distress can be recovered in contract, just as damages for shock can be recovered in tort. One such case is a contract for a holiday, or any other contract to provide entertainment and enjoyment. If the contracting party breaks his contract, damages can be given for the disappointment, the distress, the upset and frustration caused by the breach. I know that it is difficult to assess in terms of money, but it is no more difficult than the assessment which the courts have to make every day in personal injury cases for loss of amenities. Take the present case. Mr Jarvis has only a fortnight's holiday in the year. He books it far ahead, and looks forward to it all that time. He ought to be compensated for the loss of it.

> Here, Mr Jarvis's fortnight's winter holiday has been a grave disappointment. It is true that he was conveyed to Switzerland and back and had meals and a bed in the hotel. But that is not what he went for. He went to enjoy himself with all the facilities which the defendants said he would have. He is entitled to damages for the lack of those facilities, and for his loss of enjoyment. Looking at the matter quite broadly, I think the damages in this case should be the sum of £125.

So, damages for distress and disappointment can be awarded where the contract is to provide pleasure, entertainment, enjoyment or peace of mind.

In the case of *Farley v Skinner* [2001] 3 WLR 899, HL, the House of Lords made it clear that the sole object of the contract need not be to provide pleasure, enjoyment or peace of mind. It is sufficient if this is an important object of the contract. In the *Farley* case the claimant employed the defendant to survey a house the claimant was thinking of buying. The claimant particularly wanted to know if the house might be affected by aircraft noise as it was close to Gatwick airport. This was an important object of the contract. The surveyor said that it was unlikely to suffer greatly from noise. This turned out to be incorrect, and the House of Lords restored the trial judge's award of £10,000 damages for non-pecuniary loss.

Types of loss – summary

The claimant may obtain damages for various kinds of loss including:

- loss of profit;
- damage to property;
- physical injury;
- loss of opportunity; and
- mental distress and disappointment, but only in limited situations.

We have looked at how damages are assessed and at the types of loss for which the claimant might want to be compensated. However, a claimant may not be able to recover damages for all loss suffered as a result of the defendant's breach. The loss or damage must not be too remote a consequence of the breach. We now go on to consider the rule relating to remoteness.

4.1.4 The remoteness rule

A party will not be awarded damages for loss which is too remote a consequence of the breach. The remoteness rule exists because to make someone responsible for all the loss which might follow from their breach could lead to unfair results.

4.1.4.1 What is the remoteness rule?

The remoteness rule in contract was established by the case of *Hadley v Baxendale* (1854) 9 Exch 341. In this case the claimants owned a mill. The mill shaft broke and so the claimants entered into a contract with the defendants for the defendants to take the mill shaft to Greenwich where it would be used as a pattern for a new shaft. The defendants delayed and the shaft was delivered late. The mill was idle during the delay because, unbeknown to the defendants, the claimants did not have a spare mill shaft that they could use in the meantime. The claimants sued for their loss of profit caused by the delay.

Alderson B said that the damages the innocent party ought to receive in respect of a breach of contract should be such as may fairly and reasonably be considered either arising naturally (ie according to the usual course of things) from the breach of contract itself, or such as may reasonably be supposed to have been in the contemplation of both parties at the time they made the contract as the probable result of the breach because of special circumstances known to them.

The claimants in *Hadley v Baxendale* could not recover their loss of profit for the period when the mill was idle because the loss did not pass the remoteness test. The loss of profit did not arise naturally from the defendants' breach as many millers would have had a replacement shaft so the mill would not have been idle during the defendants' delay. The claimants did not tell the defendants (who were only carriers) that they did not have a replacement shaft, so the defendants did not have knowledge of the special circumstances which would have brought the loss of profit within their reasonable contemplation.

If the defendants had known that the mill would be idle then it is likely the decision would have been different and the defendants would have been liable to pay damages. The defendants would have known of special circumstances to bring the loss within their contemplation.

Therefore, the remoteness rule in contract means that the loss must have been within the reasonable contemplation of the parties at the time of the contract as being a probable result of the breach.

It is sometimes said that there are two limbs to the remoteness rule established in *Hadley v Baxendale*. Loss which arises naturally from the breach will normally be within the parties' reasonable contemplation (Limb 1). Unusual loss will be within the parties' reasonable contemplation only if the special circumstances which give rise to the loss are known to both parties at the time the contract is made (Limb 2).

The other party should be told about the special circumstances before the contract is finalised. The reason for this timing is that knowledge of special circumstances may affect the terms of the contract. The party who finds out about special circumstances may want to charge more for providing a service or insert a clause limiting liability. Knowledge which the defendant acquires after the contract is formed is therefore irrelevant to the application of the remoteness rule.

The defendant's knowledge of the claimant's business practices was considered in the case of *Balfour Beatty Construction (Scotland) Ltd v Scottish Power plc* 1994 SLT 807, HL. The House of Lords held that Scottish Power was not liable for the full loss suffered by the claimant as a result of an interruption in the electricity supply.

The interruption in electricity supply happened when the claimant was in the middle of a construction project which required a continuous pour of concrete. Because of the interruption in supply, the work already done was worthless. The defendant did not know about the need for a continuous pour, and the House of Lords stated that there was no general rule that contracting parties were presumed to have knowledge of all techniques in each other's business practices. However, the simpler the activity, the easier it would be to imply knowledge. In this case, the construction project was complicated and Scottish Power was not deemed to know about it.

The remoteness rule established by *Hadley v Baxendale* has been considered in a number of cases, and the relationship between the remoteness rule in contract and tort has also been explored. We will now consider subsequent interpretations of the rule in *Hadley v Baxendale*.

4.1.4.2 Subsequent interpretation of the remoteness rule

The Court of Appeal considered the remoteness rule in the case of *Victoria Laundry (Windsor) Ltd v Newman Industries Ltd* [1949] 2 KB 528, CA. Here the claimants were launderers and dyers. They wanted to extend their business and bought a boiler from the defendant to be delivered on 5 June. The defendant did not deliver until 8 November. The defendant knew that the claimants were launderers and dyers and that they intended to put the boiler to immediate use in their business.

The claimants claimed damages at the rate of:

- £16 per week for loss of ordinary profits, taking into account the extra customers they could have taken on had they received the boiler in time; and
- £262 per week for loss of profit on some highly lucrative dyeing contracts with the Ministry of Supply which they would have accepted had they received the boiler in time.

Asquith LJ said that the innocent party could recover for loss which at the time of the contract was reasonably foreseeable as liable to result from the breach. (The use of the phrase 'reasonably foreseeable' suggested that the test for remoteness in contract was the same as in tort. Asquith LJ's use of the phrase has been criticised and we will look at that criticism later.)

Asquith LJ identified the defendant's knowledge at the time the contract was formed as the crucial factor when deciding whether a particular type of loss was too remote. He said that the knowledge possessed by the defendant could be of two types: imputed knowledge, which everyone as a reasonable person is assumed to possess; and actual knowledge.

If the loss arises in the usual course of things under Limb 1 in *Hadley v Baxendale*, the defendant will have imputed knowledge of it (ie they will be taken to know of it) and it will not be too remote. If the loss is unusual loss under Limb 2 of *Hadley v Baxendale*, then it will be too remote unless the defendant had actual knowledge of special circumstances. Bearing this in mind, what do you think the court decided in this case?

The court decided:

- The defendant was liable for the loss of ordinary business profit. This was a reasonably foreseeable result of the late delivery as the defendant knew the nature of the claimants' business and that they intended to put the boiler to immediate use.
- The defendant was not liable for the loss of profit on the highly lucrative contracts with the Ministry of Supply. This loss of profit went beyond ordinary profit, and, as the defendant had no knowledge of these special circumstances, the loss was too remote.

The decision in *Victoria Laundry Ltd v Newman Industries Ltd* and the comments of Lord Asquith were considered by the House of Lords in *Koufos v C Czarnikow Ltd, The Heron II* [1969] 1 AC 350, HL. Here, the House of Lords, whilst approving the decision in *Victoria Laundry*, disapproved of the phrase 'reasonably foreseeable'. The House of Lords said that the test in contract is not the same as that used in tort and reinstated the phrase 'within the reasonable contemplation of the parties' used in *Hadley v Baxendale*.

In *The Heron II*, Lord Reid said that the remoteness test in tort imposes a wider liability than the test in contract. In tort, a defendant will be liable for any damage which is reasonably foreseeable, even in the most unusual case.

Can you think of a reason for having different remoteness tests in contract and tort?

In contract, you are normally aware of the identity of the other contracting party. You can therefore take steps to ensure you can recover for unusual loss by pointing out the possibility of such loss to the other party before the contract is made. In tort, there is usually no opportunity to draw to the attention of the party who injures you the possibility of unusual loss or damage.

In *The Heron II*, the House of Lords considered the degree of probability needed in order for the loss to be within the reasonable contemplation of the parties. Lord Reid said the question to ask is whether the loss in question is 'of a kind which the defendant, when he made the contract, ought to have realised was not unlikely to result from [the] breach ...'.

The relationship between the remoteness rules in contract and tort was discussed again, this time by the Court of Appeal, in *Parsons (Livestock) Ltd v Uttley Ingham Ltd* [1978] 1 QB 791.

The claimants were pig farmers. They bought a hopper from the defendants for storage of pig food. The defendants agreed to erect the hopper at the claimants' farm. The defendants forgot to unseal the ventilator at the top of the hopper, and, because of this, pig food stored in the hopper became mouldy. As a result of eating the mouldy food, many of the pigs contracted a rare infection and died. The claimants brought an action for damages for breach of contract. The judge at first instance found in favour of the claimants. The defendants appealed to the Court of Appeal.

One question the Court of Appeal had to decide was whether the illness and death of the pigs was too remote a consequence of the breach.

Lord Denning suggested (*obiter*) that the contract test of remoteness, ie reasonable contemplation, should be limited to cases of economic loss, and that where there has been physical damage (eg, as here loss of the pigs) the tort test of reasonable forseeability should apply. In this case, the defendants ought reasonably to have foreseen the possibility that the pigs might become ill and were accordingly liable to pay damages for the loss of the pigs. The other two judges reached the same conclusion on damages but gave different reasoning, with Scarman LJ stating:

> My conclusion in the present case is the same as that of Lord Denning MR but I reach it by a different route. I would dismiss the appeal. I agree with him in thinking it absurd that the test for remoteness of damage should, in principle, differ according to the legal classification of the cause of action ... I differ from him only to this extent: the cases do not, in my judgment, support a distinction in law between loss of profit and physical damage. Neither do I think it necessary to develop the law judicially by drawing such a distinction. Of course (and this is a reason for refusing to draw the distinction in law) the type of consequence, loss of profit or market or physical injury, will always be an important matter of fact in determining whether in all the circumstances the loss or injury was of a type which the parties could reasonably be supposed to have in contemplation.
>
> I would agree with Mr McGregor in his work on Damages that – 'in contract, as in tort, it should suffice that, if physical injury or damage is within the contemplation of the parties, recovery is not to be limited because the degree of physical injury or damage could not have been anticipated.'
>
> This is so, in my judgment, not because there is, or ought to be, a specific rule of law governing cases of physical injury but because it would be absurd to regulate damages in such cases on the necessity of supposing the parties had a prophetic foresight as to the exact nature of the injury that does in fact arise. It is enough if on the hypothesis predicted physical injury must have been a serious possibility. Though in loss of market or loss of profit cases the factual analysis will be very different from cases of physical injury, the same principles, in my judgment, apply. Given the situation of the parties at the time of contract, was the loss of profit, or market, a serious possibility, something that would have been in their minds had they contemplated breach?
>
> It does not matter, in my judgment, if they thought that the chance of physical injury, loss of profit, loss of market, or other loss as the case may be, was slight or that the odds were against it provided they contemplated as a serious possibility the type of consequence, not necessarily the specific consequences, that ensued upon breach. Making the assumption as to breach that the judge did, no more than common sense was needed for them to appreciate that food affected by bad storage conditions might well cause illness in the pigs fed on it.

So Scarman LJ agreed with Lord Denning in thinking it absurd that the test for remoteness of damage should in principle differ according to the legal classification of the cause of action (ie contract or tort). However, he did not think the cases supported a distinction in law between loss of profit and physical damage, and he did not think it was necessary to develop the law by drawing that distinction.

The court decided that if the defendant can contemplate the type of loss as a serious possibility, then all loss of that type is recoverable even though the extent of the loss could not have been contemplated. Therefore, in *Parsons v Uttley Ingham*, the defendants were liable for the death of a large number of the claimants' pigs as some harm to the pigs was within the reasonable contemplation of the parties as a result of the defective installation of the hopper used for storing the pigs' food. Since some harm to the pigs could be contemplated, it did not matter that the death of so many pigs was not within the contemplation of the parties.

In *Parsons v Uttley Ingham*, the court said that, if a particular type of loss is within the parties' contemplation as a serious possibility, then all loss of that type is recoverable even if more serious than could be contemplated. Although the *Parsons* case involved physical injury, Scarman LJ said that the same principles applied in loss of profit cases.

In *Victoria Laundry v Newman Industries*, the claimants recovered for their normal business profits but not for the profit on the highly lucrative dyeing contracts. To reconcile this decision with *Parsons v Uttley Ingham*, the normal business profits and the profit on the highly lucrative contracts would have to be treated as different types of loss.

The problem of distinguishing between different types of loss was recognised by Stuart-Smith LJ in *Brown v KMR Services Ltd* [1995] 4 All ER 598, CA. The claimant had been underwriting as a Lloyd's name and brought proceedings against the claimant's former agent, alleging the agent had acted negligently and in breach of contract in failing to warn the claimant of the dangers of joining high-risk syndicates. The claimant wanted damages for the loss suffered.

The Court of Appeal held that, in this case, the underwriting losses, although of far greater magnitude than contemplated, were nevertheless of the same type as ones that were contemplated and so were not too remote.

Stuart-Smith LJ said, *obiter*, that although in practice it may be difficult to categorise loss into types or kinds, especially where financial loss is involved, he did not see any difficulty in holding that loss of ordinary business profits is different in kind from that flowing from a particular contract which gives rise to very high profits. It is clear from this that *Victoria Laundry* might well be decided in the same way if the facts were to occur today.

Remoteness – summary

Looking at all of the cases that you have considered so far, can you draw the key points together in order to formulate a test for remoteness?

You could say that loss will not be too remote a consequence of the breach if it is of a kind which would have been within the reasonable contemplation of the parties at the time the contract was made as being not unlikely to result.

The remoteness rule was considered by the House of Lords more recently in *Transfield Shipping Inc v Mercator Shipping Inc (The Achilleas)* [2008] UKHL 48. The defendant had chartered a ship from the claimant but was late returning the ship to the claimant. This amounted to a breach of contract. Because of the breach, the claimant had lost the opportunity to re-charter the ship at a very lucrative rate, although it was able to re-charter at a lower rate. The problem arose because, at that time, the market rate for chartering such vessels was fluctuating wildly.

Essentially the House of Lords had to decide whether the claimant could recover damages in respect of the extra profit it would have earned on the lucrative lost charter.

Their Lordships were unanimous in deciding that the claimant could not be awarded damages for loss of the lucrative charter as this loss was too remote, although there were some differences in approach in the reasoning.

Baroness Hale had doubts and said that the case could be an examination question – one where there is no obviously right answer!

Lord Hoffman took the view that the court should decide objectively what the intentions of the parties were at the time of entering the contract. Had the charterers assumed the risk of the claimant's losses in respect of the re-charter of the ship? He thought they had not, taking into account the type of contract and its commercial background. Lord Hope gave a similar judgment.

Lord Rodger of Earlsferry took a more orthodox approach and said that neither party would reasonably have contemplated that the delay would 'in the ordinary course of things' cause the owners the kind of loss for which they claimed damages. That was not 'an ordinary consequence' of a breach of that kind. It occurred because of the extremely volatile market conditions and was too remote to give rise to damages.

The differences in the reasoning in this case make it difficult to find the *ratio decidendi*. Lord Hoffman considered assumption of responsibility and was clearly departing from the orthodox approach to remoteness as established in *Hadley v Baxendale*. Lord Hoffman wrote a comment on the case in the *Edinburgh Law Review* (2010) in which he said:

> The orthodox approach produces a high degree of indeterminacy because it relies on only two concepts: kind of loss and degree of probability. But the cases show that these are open to very considerable manipulation to achieve what the court considers to be a fair result. ...
>
> It seems to me that the time has come to look for a broader principle which can explain not only the, so to speak, run of the mill cases like *Hadley v Baxendale* but also the more puzzling cases like *The Achilleas*.

Lord Hoffman went on to say that the cases are explicable 'if one examines the nature of the obligation assumed by the contracting party and asks: for what kind of loss would he reasonably be taken to have accepted liability?'

In *The Achilleas* Lord Hoffman felt that the commercial background to the agreement made it clear that the charterer could not reasonably be regarded as having assumed the risk of the owner's loss of profit on the re-charter of the ship.

So, the question is how will the courts treat remoteness issues in future cases?

In *John Grimes Partnership Ltd v Gubbins* [2013] EWCA Civ 37, the Court of Appeal said that the test for remoteness (ie whether the loss claimed was of a kind which would have been within the reasonable contemplation of the parties at the time that the contract was made as being not unlikely to result) was 'the standard rule'. However, there might be unusual cases, such as *The Achilleas*, in which the particular commercial context and surrounding circumstances make it necessary to consider whether or not a party had assumed responsibility for losses of that particular kind.

The remoteness rule is really a way in which the law limits the amount of damages which may be recovered for a breach of contract. We shall now go on to consider two more ways in which damages may be limited, namely the mitigation rule and contributory negligence.

4.1.5 Mitigation

As you have seen, the claimant can claim damages for loss suffered due to the defendant's breach, provided that loss is not too remote. However, there is also a requirement that the claimant should mitigate their loss. This was explained by Viscount Haldane LC in *British Westinghouse Electric & Manufacturing Co Ltd v Underground Electric Railway Company of*

London Ltd [1912] AC 673. It means that the claimant should take reasonable steps to ensure that losses are kept to a minimum.

The claimant cannot recover damages for losses which the claimant could have avoided by taking reasonable steps. If the claimant does take reasonable steps to mitigate, the claimant can claim any expenses incurred in trying to mitigate even if the attempt is unsuccessful.

The onus of proof is on the party in breach to show that the claimant could have mitigated, but they did not do so. If the defaulting party can do this then the court will not award damages for that part of the loss which was caused by the claimant's failure to mitigate: that loss was not caused by the breach.

So let us now have a look at what a claimant might reasonably be expected to do to mitigate their loss in certain situations.

★ Examples

Situation	Mitigation
1. Sheila is dismissed from her job as a dental assistant in breach of contract.	Sheila should look for suitable alternative employment as a dental assistant.
2. In breach of contract, Ellery refuses to deliver goods to Nasser.	Nasser should go into the marketplace straight away and try to buy similar goods elsewhere.
3. Arjuna tries to deliver goods to Pauline, but in breach of contract she refuses to accept delivery.	Arjuna should go into the marketplace straight away and try to sell the goods elsewhere.
4. Hugh agrees to paint all the rooms in Elnora's house. He paints the kitchen, but then abandons the job because he can earn more money elsewhere.	Elnora should look for someone else to finish the painting at a reasonable price. (She should obtain two or three comparable quotations and accept the cheapest.)

4.1.6 Contributory negligence

In tort, it is well established that a claimant's damages may be reduced due to contributory negligence under the Law Reform (Contributory Negligence) Act 1945.

If the only cause of action for breach of contract is a negligent breach (eg breach of the term implied by s 13 of the Supply of Goods and Services Act 1982 that services performed in the course of a business will be carried out with reasonable care and skill) and this would also give rise to a claim in the tort of negligence, then the Law Reform (Contributory Negligence) Act 1945 would apply. In this case, the claimant's damages may be reduced on the basis of contributory negligence.

4.1.7 Time for assessment of damages

The basic rule is that damages are assessed by reference to the time of the breach. For example, assume that the claimant had agreed to buy goods from the defendant for £5,000. The goods were to be delivered on 31 January. The defendant refused to deliver the goods. On 31 January the claimant could have purchased similar goods for £7,000. At the time of the hearing, the goods cost £10,000. The claimant would be awarded £2,000 damages based on the cost of the goods at the date of the breach. This relates to the principle of mitigation which we considered earlier. The claimant should take reasonable steps to mitigate their loss, and if a seller refuses to deliver goods this usually means that the buyer should act quickly and buy replacement goods rather than delaying and risking a rise in prices.

There are exceptions to the basic rule, but a discussion of these is beyond the scope of this textbook.

Also, in the case of *Golden Strait Corporation v Nippon Yusen Kubishiki Kaisha* (*The Golden Victory*) [2007] 1 CLC 352 HL, the majority of the House of Lords said that the most important principle is that damages should reflect the loss suffered, and, although the assessment at the date of breach rule would normally achieve this, it should not be applied where it did not.

We have now considered all issues which may be relevant in the assessment of damages, ie aim or purpose in assessing damages and quantification, types of loss, remoteness rules, mitigation, contributory negligence and time of assessment.

Bringing a claim for damages can be costly and time-consuming, and so the parties may put a clause in their contract stating the amount of compensation to be paid if there is a breach. This is so particularly in commercial contracts. We now go on to consider the validity of such clauses.

4.1.8 Specified damages and penalty clauses

The parties may include a provision in the contract which states the amount of compensation which will be paid if the contract is broken.

Stating in the contract the amount of compensation to be paid helps to provide certainty. A party can see by looking at the contract the amount that will be paid or received in the event of a particular breach. If the contract is broken and both parties are willing to abide by the clause, the cost of going to court will be avoided. Also, depending on how the clause is drafted, the innocent party may not have to prove the extent of its loss, only that the breach has occurred.

4.1.8.1 The distinction between a specified (liquidated/agreed) damages clause and a penalty clause

A specified damages clause may be defined as a genuine attempt to pre-estimate the loss which is likely to be caused by the breach. Such a clause is binding, and the sum specified is the amount that will be paid regardless of the actual loss which the claimant has suffered. The usual rules of measure of damages, remoteness and mitigation do not apply, and the claimant may receive more or less than the loss suffered. The crucial figure is the amount of compensation stated in the clause. (Note that a specified damages clause is often referred to as a 'liquidated damages' or 'agreed damages' clause.)

A penalty may be defined as an attempt to put pressure on a party to perform the contract. A penalty is unenforceable. Where the clause is a penalty, the court is free to assess damages in the usual way and the usual principles of measure of damages, remoteness and mitigation will apply.

If both parties are happy to abide by the clause, the issue will not come before the court. However, one party might want to avoid the operation of the clause, and if this happens the court will then have to decide whether the clause is a specified damages clause or a penalty clause. From what we have just seen of the distinction between a specified damages clause and a penalty clause, when might the innocent party want to argue that the clause is a penalty clause and not binding? When might the party in breach want to argue that the clause is a penalty?

The innocent party might want to argue that the clause is a penalty and not binding if the claimant's actual loss is greater than the amount stated in the clause. The intended aim of the clause (ie to compensate for genuine loss or to put pressure on a party to perform) is judged by reference to circumstances at the time of the contract. At that time, the sum stated may well have been meant to have a punitive effect, but in the end turns out to be less than the actual loss suffered. If the clause is a penalty, it will be invalid, and the court is free to award damages for the full amount of the innocent party's loss.

The party in breach might want to argue that the clause is a penalty and not binding where the amount stated in the clause is greater than the actual loss of the innocent party. If the court is free to assess damages in the usual way, the innocent party would receive less than the sum stated in the clause.

4.1.8.2 How does the court decide whether the clause is a specified damages clause or a penalty clause?

As we have seen, if one of the parties wants to avoid the operation of the clause, the court will have to decide whether the clause is binding. The distinction between specified damages and penalty clauses was traditionally a question of construction, depending on the parties' intentions, judged in the light of all the circumstances at the time of the contract. In *Dunlop Pneumatic Tyre Co Ltd v New Garage & Motor Co Ltd* [1915] AC 79, Lord Dunedin set out the following guidelines for the courts to consider when deciding whether a clause is a specified damages clause or a penalty:

(a) If the sum stated in the clause is extravagant and unconscionable in amount in comparison with the greatest loss that could conceivably be proved to have followed from the breach then it will be a penalty.

Notice that whether, or not, the amount is extravagant and unconscionable is not judged by comparing it with the actual loss suffered. The amount specified in the clause must be compared with the loss that might have followed from the breach, which of course could be much greater than the loss which was actually incurred.

(b) If the breach consists only in not paying a sum of money then if the sum stated in the clause is greater than the amount which ought to have been paid it will be a penalty.

(c) If a single lump sum is payable on the happening of one or more of several events, some of which may cause serious and some minor damage, it is presumed to be a penalty.

Note that if (a) or (b) apply the clause will certainly be a penalty and so be unenforceable. Guideline (c) only raises a presumption that the clause is a penalty and this can be rebutted. This is illustrated by the *Dunlop* case itself, which is considered in more detail after the next guideline.

(d) The clause can be a specified damages clause even if it is difficult or impossible to pre-estimate precisely the loss which might be caused by the breach.

In fact, in the *Dunlop* case, it was difficult to pre-estimate the loss. The claimant agreed to supply tyres to the defendant dealers. The defendant agreed not to tamper with the marks on the tyres, not to sell the tyres below the claimant's list price and to certain other restrictions. The defendant agreed to pay the sum of £5 for each tyre sold in breach of the agreement. The defendant sold a tyre below the list price. The House of Lords found that the clause was a specified damages clause and not a penalty. Although a single lump sum was payable on the happening of several events, the presumption that this was a penalty was rebutted because the damage or loss that might be caused on the happening of each of these events could not easily be ascertained and the amount (£5) was relatively small.

In the *Dunlop* case the House of Lords also said that although the parties may use the words penalty or specified/liquidated damages, this wording is not conclusive. Therefore, a clause may be described as a penalty in the contract, but the court may decide that really it is a specified damages clause, and vice versa.

In the case of *Philips Hong Kong Ltd v Attorney-General of Hong Kong* (1993) 61 BLR 41, the Privy Council stressed that certainty is important in commercial contracts. The Privy Council thought that specified damages clauses could be valuable because they enabled the parties to know, with a reasonable degree of certainty, the extent of their liability and the risks they would run as a result of entering the contract.

The Privy Council also said that although the clause must be judged by considering the terms and circumstances of the contract at the time of formation, looking at subsequent events and what had actually happened could be valuable evidence as to what could reasonably be expected to be the loss at the time the contract was made.

Commercial considerations were also found to be important in the case of *Azimut-Benetti SpA (Benetti Division) v Healey* [2010] EWHC 2234 (Comm). The claimant entered into a contract to build a luxury yacht for the defendant. The price was €38 million, payable in instalments.

The buyer breached the contract, and the claimant lawfully terminated the contract. A clause in the contract provided that, in these circumstances, the yacht builder could retain out of payments made by the buyer and/or recover from the buyer an amount equal to 20% of the contract price by way of liquidated (specified) damages as compensation for its estimated losses. The clause also provided that, subject to this, the yacht builder would return any balance of instalments paid by the buyer. The buyer argued that this clause was a penalty.

The court decided that the clause was a liquidated (specified) damages clause. The evidence made it clear that the purpose of the clause was not deterrent, and that it was commercially justifiable as providing a balance between the parties upon lawful termination by the builder of the yacht. The court took into account that both parties had the benefit of expert representation at the conclusion of the contract.

The judge emphasised that the clause sought to balance the rights of the parties, ie it meant the buyer would be entitled to the immediate return of instalments paid over the 20% of the contract price figure. As the judge said, the alternative would have been that if the buyer defaulted, the claimant might continue to build the yacht and then sell it, with any remaining sums being returned only after the sale when the extent of the loss had been ascertained.

The leading case on penalty clauses is now *Cavendish Square Holding BV v Makdessi; ParkingEye Ltd v Beavis* [2015] 3 WLR 1373, in which the Supreme Court recognised the broader contractual issues and reformulated the test for a penalty.

The Supreme Court said that the penalty rule was concerned with two questions. The first was the circumstances in which the rule was engaged. The Supreme Court said a provision could not be a penalty unless it provided an exorbitant alternative to ordinary damages. The second question was concerned with whether the clause was penal and not whether it was a pre-estimate of loss (which had traditionally been one of the main guidelines). The fact that the clause was not a genuine pre-estimate of loss did not necessarily mean it was penal. The Supreme Court said that the real test of a penalty clause turned on whether the means by which the contracting party's conduct was to be influenced were unconscionable or extravagant. This was formulated as a test of whether the clause imposed a detriment on the contract-breaker out of all proportion to any legitimate interest of the innocent party in the enforcement of the contract.

In *ParkingEye Ltd v Beavis*, Mr Beavis had parked in a car park operated for the landowner by ParkingEye. There were prominent notices in the car park which said parking was limited to two hours and that a fee of £85 would be imposed for overstaying. Mr Beavis parked for three hours and ParkingEye demanded payment of the £85 fee. Mr Beavis argued it was unenforceable as a penalty. The Supreme Court dismissed his appeal. Although ParkingEye was not liable to suffer loss as a result of overstaying motorists, it had a legitimate interest which involved receiving income to meet the legitimate costs of running the car parking scheme. This in itself was a legitimate way for the landowner to regulate the efficient use of the car park.

Where compensation for breach, however, is the only legitimate interest, the Supreme Court said that the guidelines in *Dunlop v New Garage* would usually suffice to decide whether the clause was penal. But in a commercial context where compensation might not be the only legitimate interest of the innocent party and the contract was negotiated between properly advised parties of comparable negotiating power, the Supreme Court said the presumption had to be that the parties themselves were the best judges of their interests.

Damages is the most common remedy for a breach of contract. We are now going to consider other remedies which may be available, starting with an action for an agreed sum.

4.2 Action for an agreed sum

4.2.1 Introduction

If the contract provides that one party shall pay a definite sum of money to the other, then if the duty to pay has arisen but the payer refuses to pay, the payee can bring a claim for the agreed sum. This is not a damages claim so the remoteness and mitigation rules do not apply. It is a very straightforward claim for the amount due, ie a debt action.

4.2.2 The duty to pay must have arisen

To bring a claim for an agreed sum, the duty to pay must have arisen.

Please read clauses 6.1 and 6.2 in the Specimen Conditions of Sale (**Reading 1** in the **Appendix**).

Suppose the seller sent the buyer an invoice a week ago. The buyer has not yet paid and the seller has a cash flow problem. Could the seller bring an immediate action for the agreed sum?

The seller could not bring an immediate action for the agreed sum as the buyer's duty to pay has not yet arisen. The terms of the contract provide that the buyer has 21 days from issue of the invoice to make payment.

4.3 Termination of the contract

4.3.1 When can a party terminate the contract?

We saw in **Chapter 3** that a breach of contract by one party sometimes gives the other party the right to terminate the future performance of the contract, ie end the contract. In order to decide whether this right exists, it is necessary to consider the kind of term in the contract which has been broken. The right arises in two main circumstances: where there is a breach of condition (a particularly important term of the contract), and where there is a very serious breach of a term classed as an innominate term (see **Figure 4.1**). These are called repudiatory breaches – breaches that allow the non-defaulting party to treat the breach as having brought the contract to an end. Generally, the innocent party will have a choice:

- affirm the contract (ie treat the contract as ongoing); or
- discharge the contract.

So, the breach itself does not terminate the contract automatically. It is up to the innocent party whether, or not, to treat the contract as at an end. But if they affirm the contract, they cannot then change their mind. Affirmation is a bar to terminating a contract. (See **4.3.2** below for more detail.)

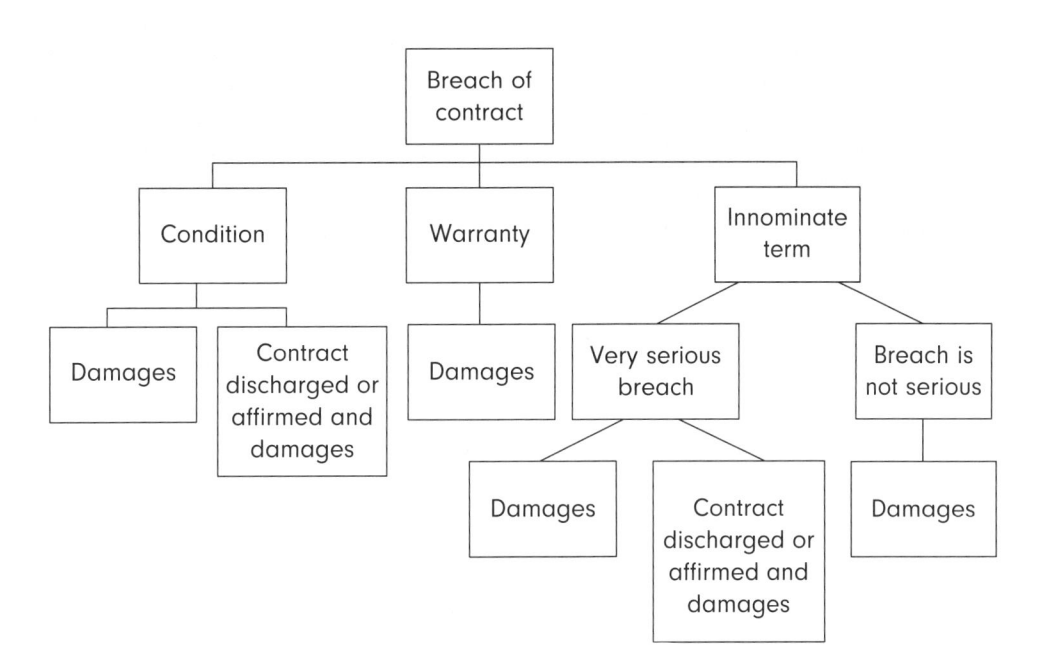

Figure 4.1 Consequences of breach of contract – summary

```
                        Breach of
                        contract
        ┌──────────────────┼──────────────────┐
    Condition           Warranty         Innominate
                                            term
    ┌───┴───┐               │          ┌──────┴──────┐
 Damages  Contract       Damages   Very serious   Breach is
          discharged or            breach         not serious
          affirmed and         ┌──────┴──────┐        │
          damages           Damages      Contract   Damages
                                         discharged or
                                         affirmed and
                                         damages
```

⭐ *Example*

Barot has engaged Attwal to build a house for her. Attwal has to carry out four stages of building, and Barot has agreed to pay for each stage in advance.

Barot pays the price for Stage 1 and Attwal completes Stage 1. Barot pays for Stage 2 and Attwal completes it. Barot pays for Stage 3, but then something goes badly wrong and Attwal breaches a condition of Stage 3.

Barot has the choice whether to treat the contract as terminated. She does not have to. She could affirm the contract and limit herself to a claim for damages for the breach. But if she does treat the contract as at an end then both parties are discharged from future performance of the contract. Barot does not have to pay any more but, equally, Attwal does not have to do any more building work.

Furthermore, if the breach of contract causes Barot any loss, she can sue for damages. For example, if it will cost her more than the outstanding payment for Stage 4 (the money she has saved to get the work completed) she is entitled to the excess as damages – though, as we have seen, she has to mitigate (take reasonable steps to reduce) her loss. For example, she would be expected to get a few quotes to complete the work from reputable builders and then accept the cheapest.

It is important to note that termination only operates to discharge parties from future contractual obligations: if there are none (eg because the contract has been performed), termination will be impossible. (Note: the rights and remedies for breach of contracts for the sale of goods are governed by the SGA 1979 and the CRA 2015 – see **Chapter 3**.)

It is important to note too that if there has been a breach of contract, it is only necessary to decide on the kind of term broken if the innocent party wants to terminate the contract. If the innocent party wants some other remedy, or if termination of the contract is not possible, then it is immaterial whether the term broken is a condition, a warranty or an innominate term.

When drafting a commercial contract, it is always useful to consider when a party might want to be able to terminate the contract if there is a breach and make this clear in the contract. If you look at clause 6.3 of the Specimen Conditions of Sale (**Reading 1** in the **Appendix**) you will see that the seller has stipulated that time for payment shall be of the essence. This means that the time for payment is a condition of the contract. If the buyer fails to pay on time, the seller may terminate the contract.

4.3.2 Right of election of the innocent party

If a contract has been fully performed by both parties, it will not usually be possible to terminate, although there are special rules which apply to sale of goods contracts (see **4.3.5** below).

If the innocent party has the right to terminate the future performance of the contract, the innocent party does not have to do so. The innocent party has a choice. It can either terminate the contract or affirm it, although in reality there may be no choice if the other party is refusing to perform its obligations. We shall now consider the effects of termination and affirmation.

4.3.3 Effect of termination

If the innocent party terminates, the contract is at an end and future obligations will be discharged. This means that neither party need perform any future obligations under the contract. The innocent party can also sue for damages for any loss suffered.

The decision to terminate must normally be communicated to the other party.

4.3.4 Effect of affirmation

If the innocent party affirms the contract then the contract is not over and both parties should continue to perform their obligations. If the innocent party does decide to affirm the contract, the innocent party should make it clear that they are treating the contract as continuing. The innocent party can still claim damages for loss suffered.

In some situations, affirmation may not be a realistic option. For example, if the continuation of the contract depends on the co-operation of the other party who is refusing to perform, eg the party is refusing to deliver goods or do work under the contract.

4.3.5 Special rules for sale of goods contracts

Usually, if a contract has been fully performed, it will not be possible to terminate; however, special rules apply to sale of goods contracts.

We saw in **Chapter 3** that if the seller breaches ss 9–11 of the Consumer Rights Act 2015 or s 13 or s 14 of the Sale of Goods Act 1979, the buyer may be entitled to reject the goods. So even though the contract has been fully performed (ie the buyer has received the goods and paid for them) the buyer may give them back and get a refund.

Remember though that a buyer may lose the right to reject – eg under the Sale of Goods Act 1979 – if the buyer has 'accepted' the goods (within the meaning of s 35 of the Act) or otherwise if the breach is so slight it would be unreasonable for the buyer to reject the goods.

4.3.6 Anticipatory breach

The breach which gives the innocent party the right to terminate the contract may be an anticipatory breach. What do you think is meant by an anticipatory breach of contract? A breach will be anticipatory if a party gives advance warning that they are not going to perform their contractual obligations when they fall due.

For example, suppose Raminder, a painter and decorator, agreed to decorate Martha's restaurant. Two weeks before he is due to start work, he telephones to say that he will not be doing the decorating for Martha. The breach is an anticipatory breach. Raminder has indicated *in advance* that he does not intend to perform his contractual obligations.

If one party does indicate they are not going to perform the contract when the time for performance falls due, then the other party can:

- terminate the contract and sue for damages immediately; or
- treat the contract as continuing and wait until the time fixed for performance in the hope that the party in breach will change their mind and perform the contract.

So far, we have looked at common law remedies, ie damages, an action for the agreed sum and termination of the future performance of the contract. We are now going to look at two equitable remedies – specific performance and injunction.

4.4 Specific performance

4.4.1 Introduction

Specific performance is an order of the court which requires a party to perform its contractual obligations. Failure to comply with the order will be contempt of court.

Specific performance is an equitable remedy and therefore discretionary. By contrast, common law remedies are available as of right provided any relevant conditions are fulfilled. For example, a claimant is entitled to the agreed sum where the duty to pay has arisen.

Specific performance can be combined with a claim for damages. For example, the claimant could ask for specific performance to compel the defendant to perform its contractual obligations and damages to compensate the claimant for the loss it has suffered already.

4.4.2 Restrictions on the availability of specific performance

Although specific performance is a discretionary remedy, the discretion is not supposed to be exercised in an arbitrary fashion. There are certain principles which govern the award of specific performance. We are going to look at some situations where specific performance will not usually be granted.

4.4.2.1 Damages is an adequate remedy

Traditionally, specific performance has not been granted where an award of damages is an adequate remedy. For example, if a seller refuses to deliver the goods, the buyer is unlikely to get specific performance where substitute goods can be purchased. Damages would be adequate compensation for any loss the buyer suffers. However, if substitute goods are not available, eg the contract is for the sale of a unique item such as a valuable painting, then specific performance may be granted.

4.4.2.2 Contracts requiring continuous supervision by the court

Specific performance may not be granted where the court would have to supervise the parties over a period of time because of the difficulty of continuous supervision.

4.4.2.3 Specific performance will not usually be granted for contracts involving services

An example of a contract involving services is an employment contract. Also, if you think back to the case of *Ruxley Electronics v Forsyth*, which we considered when looking at the remedy of damages earlier in the chapter, the contract there was a contract for services. The reason for the restriction on the grant of specific performance in relation to contracts for services is because such contracts usually depend on a certain amount of trust and confidence. If the relationship between the parties has broken down, it would not be advisable to force them to work together.

4.4.2.4 Specific performance will be granted only if it is just and equitable to do so

As specific performance is an equitable remedy, it follows that it will be awarded only when it is just and equitable to do so. The court will consider whether the claimant has acted equitably and will also look at whether the order would cause disproportionate hardship to the defendant. For example, if the claimant is seeking to take advantage of a mistake made by the defendant, specific performance may be refused.

4.5 Injunctions

An injunction may be prohibitory (which forbids a person doing a particular act) or mandatory. A mandatory injunction requires a person to put right a breach of contract. A mandatory injunction is rare in practice.

An injunction, like specific performance, is an equitable remedy and therefore available at the discretion of the court. An injunction will not be granted if the effect would be to compel the defendant to do acts which the defendant could not have been ordered to do by specific performance. We saw at **4.4.2.3** above that the court will not grant specific performance of a contract involving services such as an employment contract. The same restrictions apply in relation to injunctions, in that the court will not grant an injunction to force an employee to work for a particular employer.

However, a contract may contain a negative promise which can be enforced without directly compelling the employee to work for the employer. This occurred in the case of *Warner Brothers Pictures Incorporated v Nelson* [1937] 1 KB 209. In 1934 Nelson (known professionally as Bette Davis) entered into a contract with Warner Brothers, and one clause of the contract stipulated that 'she will not, *during the term of the contract render any services for or in any motion picture production or productions of any other person* ... or engage in any other occupation without the written consent of the producer being first had and obtained'. The contract could run until 1942.

In 1936 the defendant agreed to appear in a film for another film company. The claimants asked the court to grant an injunction to enforce that part of the negative stipulation printed in italics. They did not ask for an injunction preventing the defendant engaging in any other occupation.

Branson J granted the injunction, saying:

> ... The case before me is one in which it would be proper to grant an injunction unless to do so would in the circumstances be tantamount to ordering the defendant to perform her contract or remain idle or unless damages would be the more appropriate remedy.
>
> With regard to the first of these considerations, it would, of course, be impossible to grant an injunction covering all the negative covenants in the contract. That would, indeed, force the defendant to perform her contract or remain idle; but this objection is removed by the restricted form in which the injunction is sought. It is confined to forbidding the defendant, without the consent of the plaintiffs, to render any services for or in any motion picture or stage production for anyone other than the plaintiffs.
>
> It was also urged that the difference between what the defendant can earn as a film artiste and what she might expect to earn by any other form of activity is so great that she will in effect be driven to perform her contract. That is not the criterion adopted in any of the decided cases. The defendant is stated to be a person of intelligence,

capacity and means, and no evidence was adduced to show that, if enjoined from doing the specified acts otherwise than for the plaintiffs, she will not be able to employ herself both usefully and remuneratively in other spheres of activity, though not as remuneratively as in her special line. She will not be driven, although she may be tempted, to perform the contract and the fact that she may be so tempted is no objection to the grant of an injunction.

The result of this case then was that Nelson could not act in any film or stage production for any other film company for a number of years. The court was prepared to grant an injunction in this case because it felt that, although the defendant would probably earn more money as a film actress than working in some other capacity and might therefore be tempted to act for the claimants, she was not being forced to do so. There were other ways she could earn money. This does not seem to be very realistic, as a person who has a particular talent is unlikely to take up a new area of work.

This is illustrated by the case *Page One Records v Britton* [1968] WLR 157. The claimant was the manager of a pop group, 'The Troggs'. The group had appointed the claimant as their manager for a period of five years and in their contract they had agreed not to engage any other person, firm or corporation to act as managers or agents or to act themselves in such capacity. The group dismissed the claimant as their manager. The claimant applied for an injunction to prevent the group employing another person to act as manager.

The court refused to grant the injunction because if the group could not employ someone else, in practice this meant it would have to employ the claimant. Pop groups need managers. The court said it would be wrong to put pressure on the defendants in this way as the manager had duties of a personal and fiduciary nature to perform and the defendants had lost confidence in him.

In *Page One Records v Britton*, the court seemed to be taking a more realistic approach to the likely effect of an injunction than in *Warner Brothers v Nelson*, although the cases can be distinguished as trust and confidence was less of an issue in *Warner Brothers v Nelson*.

In summary, when deciding whether to grant an injunction enforcing a term of a contract whereby a party agrees not to work for someone else or in a particular capacity for a period of time, the court will consider such matters as:

- length of time – if the injunction will last for only a relatively short time (eg a few weeks), it is more likely to be awarded;

- whether granting the injunction will have the effect of seriously affecting the party's career – if so, it is unlikely to be granted.

An injunction will not be granted if the court feels that the inevitable result would be to compel the party to work for the original employer.

We have considered the remedies of damages, action for an agreed sum, specific performance and injunction. In the next section, we consider one final remedy which may be available – restitution.

4.6 Restitution

4.6.1 Introduction

A claim in restitution may arise in a number of different situations. The general idea behind a restitution remedy is to prevent one party being unjustly enriched at the expense of the other. However, it is important to note that a claim in restitution is not available in every case where there has been an element of unjust enrichment.

Contract

A claim may arise as a result of a breach of contract, or where no contract has come into existence. We are going to consider the following situations where a claim may arise:

- where money has been paid by one party to another under a contract and there has been a complete failure of the consideration; and
- where one party has done work for the other, or supplied goods to the other, and wants to be compensated for the work done or goods delivered.

4.6.2 Recovery of money which has been paid where there has been a total failure of consideration

If one party (the payer) has paid money to the other (the payee) under a contract, the payer can bring an action in restitution to recover the money if the payee is in breach and there has been a total failure of the consideration. A total failure of consideration is where the payee has not done any part of what the payee was supposed to do under the contract or what has been done is completely useless.

⭐ *Examples*

Situation	Total failure of consideration?
1. Shakira has paid £500 in advance for goods. The seller has agreed to deliver them.	A total failure of consideration would arise if the seller refuses to deliver the goods – for example if the seller knows they can sell the goods for more money to someone else.
2. Bill has paid £800 in advance to get his house painted. The painter is supposed to start work next week.	There will be a total failure of consideration if the painter does not turn up to paint Bill's house.

In both of the above situations, the payer will have received nothing at all for their money and so could bring a claim in restitution to recover the money. So, in situation 1, Shakira could bring a claim in restitution and recover the £500. If she can buy similar goods for £500 or less, she will not need any other remedy. If she has to pay more, though, then she will need to bring a damages action either as well as, or instead of, restitution.

Similarly, in situation 2, Bill could bring a claim in restitution and recover the £800. If Bill could then get his house painted by someone else for £800, or less, he will not need any other remedy. But if Bill has to pay more than £800 then he will need to bring a damages action.

Note that, in situation 2, if the painter had started the job and then abandoned it, this would not amount to total failure of consideration. So, Bill's only remedy would be damages for the amount he has to pay a new painter to finish off the work.

4.6.3 Compensation for work done or goods supplied

It is important to note that a party who has done work for another or supplied goods to another will not always be able to bring a claim in restitution for compensation.

We shall look at two examples where this claim might be relevant: first where the contract has been broken, and then where a contract was never formed.

4.6.3.1 The contract has been broken

If one party has supplied goods or done work for the other and the *other* party is in breach of contract, the party supplying the goods/doing the work may be able to bring a claim in restitution for a reasonable sum for work done or goods supplied as an alternative to a claim for damages.

Consider the following situation: Gavin agrees to build a garage for Ray. Gavin does some work and then Ray tells him to stop as he has changed his mind. Ray no longer wants the garage. Ray is in breach of contract. Gavin can sue for damages or he can bring a claim in restitution. If a claim is made in restitution then Gavin will receive what is called a *'quantum meruit'*, ie a reasonable sum for work done. We shall consider this again in **Chapter 5**.

4.6.3.2 A contract was never formed

In some cases, a party may do work for another before a contract has been formed, but expecting that a contract will come into existence. This sometimes happens for building work, where the negotiations between the parties may be complex and time-consuming but there is a desire to start the work as soon as possible. If a contract is not formed, can the party who has done the work recover payment for what has been done?

To answer this question, we will consider the facts and decision in *British Steel Corp v Cleveland Bridge and Engineering Co Ltd* [1984] 1 All ER 504.

The claimants were iron and steel manufacturers. The defendants asked the claimants to produce a variety of steel nodes for a construction project they were engaged in. The parties had not finalised the contract, but the defendants asked the claimants to start manufacturing the nodes straight away. The claimants prepared the nodes and delivered them to the defendants. The parties were unable to agree on some key terms of the contract. The claimants asked for a *quantum meruit* payment for the nodes.

Robert Goff J held as follows:

> ... In my judgment, the true analysis of the situation is simply this. Both parties confidently expected a formal contract to eventuate. In these circumstances, to expedite performance under that anticipated contract, one requested the other to commence the contract work, and the other complied with that request. If thereafter, as anticipated, a contract was entered into, the work done as requested will be treated as having been performed under that contract; if, contrary to their expectation, no contract was entered into, then the performance of the work is not referable to any contract the terms of which can be ascertained, and the law simply imposes an obligation on the party who made the request to pay a reasonable sum for such work as has been done pursuant to that request, such an obligation sounding in quasi contract or, as we now say, in restitution.

Both parties had expected a contract to be formed, and to expedite performance under that anticipated contract the defendants had asked the claimants to begin work, which the claimants had done. Goff J said that 'the law simply imposes an obligation on the party who made the request to pay a reasonable sum for such work as has been done pursuant to that request ...'.

If the parties had entered into a contract, the work done would be treated as having been performed under that contract and would be governed by the terms of the contract.

In summary, we have looked at three examples where a claim in restitution may be brought:

- If one party to a contract has paid money to the other, the payer can bring a claim in restitution to recover the money if the payee is in breach and there has been a complete failure of the consideration.
- If one party has agreed to do work for (or supply goods to) the other and the other is in breach, the party doing the work (or supplying the goods) may be able to bring a claim in restitution for a reasonable sum for work done (or goods supplied) as an alternative to a claim for damages.
- If goods have been supplied or work has been done but a contract has not been formed, the supplier may be able to bring a claim in restitution for a reasonable sum for work done or goods supplied (*British Steel Corp v Cleveland Bridge*).

4.6.4 Restitutionary damages

As you may recall from earlier in this chapter, the traditional purpose of an award of damages in contract is to compensate the claimant for the loss they have suffered as a result of the defendant's breach. Sometimes this is the expectation measure; sometimes it is the reliance loss measure – but, either way, its purpose is compensatory.

However, a line of cases has considered an award of remedies based, not on loss to the claimant, but on the gains made by the defendant. This feature also takes such awards outside the strict principles of restitution which, as we have just seen, come to the aid of a claimant when the defendant has made gains at the expense of the claimant. Here we are looking at gains made which do not, or at least do not necessarily, reflect the loss to the claimant.

The first example of this approach we will look at is the exceptional case of *Attorney-General v Blake* [2001] 1 AC 268. Blake was a notorious traitor. He was employed as a member of the secret service for 17 years from 1944. In 1951 he became an agent for the Soviet Union and disclosed valuable secret information. In 1961 he pleaded guilty to five charges of unlawfully communicating information and was sentenced to 42 years' imprisonment. In 1966 he escaped and fled to Moscow and then in 1989 wrote his autobiography. Blake entered into a publishing contract under which he would be paid £150,000 in advances against royalties. Plainly, had Blake not been an infamous spy who had also dramatically escaped from prison, his autobiography would not have commanded payments of this order. Certain parts of the book related to his activities as a secret intelligence officer; however, the information was no longer confidential, nor was its disclosure damaging to the public interest. So the money owed to Blake did not represent any loss to the Crown; it simply represented the benefit to Blake of the breach of his undertaking.

The case was decided on the basis that, even though the Crown had suffered no financial loss as a result of the publication of the book, it should receive the benefit of the profits from its publication.

Now an account of profits for misuse of confidential information would be a perfectly normal remedy for breach of fiduciary duty. The problem was that Blake had long since ceased to be employed by the Crown, quite apart from the fact that the material in his book was no longer confidential. So the argument that Blake still owed fiduciary duties was rejected.

Nevertheless, it was held that an account of the wrongdoer's profits was appropriate in these exceptional circumstances where it was a just response to the breach of contract.

But does that leave us with a stark choice between compensation for financial loss, in the vast majority of cases, and an account of profits only in truly exceptional cases? Or does the claimant have another recourse somewhere in the middle? Something which is an award of damages, rather than an account of profits, but which is not simply based on loss suffered by the claimant?

The answer appears to be a cautious yes; and the term for it is restitutionary damages. It may also arise, as in the case below, where the claimant may suffer no discernible financial loss other than the opportunity to negotiate a release fee and where it would be unfair to allow the defendant to take the full benefit of their breach of contract.

A case which illustrates this is *Wrotham Park Estate Co Ltd v Parkside Homes Ltd* [1974] 1 WLR 798. Parkside Homes had acquired a plot of land. The land was subject to a restrictive covenant, which purported to restrict further building without the consent of Wrotham Park Estate, the owner of the land which had the benefit of the covenant.

Parkside Homes nevertheless built on the land, and it made a handsome profit in the process. When Wrotham Park Estate discovered the breach, it sought a mandatory injunction ordering Parkside Homes to effectively demolish the development. A mandatory injunction is an extreme remedy and necessarily only awarded in exceptional circumstances. The development had caused no diminution in the value of the land owned by Wrotham Park Estate and to that extent no discernible financial loss. But Wrotham Park Estate had nevertheless lost the chance to negotiate a fee for relaxing the restrictive covenant.

The judge awarded damages to Wrotham Park Estate in substitution for the mandatory injunction which the judge was being asked to grant. The judge awarded a sum of 5% of the developer's profit, being:

> ... such a sum of money as might reasonably have been demanded by the claimants from Parkside as a quid pro quo for relaxing the covenants.

So, the damages in Wrotham Park were to compensate the claimant for the notional loss of the opportunity to bargain where that was the only loss.

Subsequently in *Morris-Garner & Another v One Step (Support) Ltd* [2018] UKSC 20, the Supreme Court referred to such damages as 'negotiating damages' and made it clear that they should not be awarded where the claimant has suffered clear financial loss as a result of the breach, even if that loss would be difficult to calculate. In the *Morris-Garner* case, the claimant had suffered a pecuniary loss as a result of the breach: it had lost profit when its business had been exposed to competition that it would otherwise have avoided. The fact that loss might be difficult to assess did not mean the claimant was entitled to negotiating damages instead. In other words, negotiating damages should only be awarded where the only loss is the opportunity to negotiate a release fee.

Now we are going to look at ways in which a non-defaulting party may be able to claim against a third party in the event of breach by either suing on a guarantee or claiming an indemnity.

4.7 Guarantees and indemnities

4.7.1 Guarantees

A contract of guarantee is a contract under which one person (the guarantor) guarantees that if another person (the debtor) does not pay back money owed then the guarantor will pay the money instead. For example, a parent might guarantee a child's overdraft so that the bank will agree to lend money to the child under the overdraft facility.

So, the essence of a contract of guarantee is that the guarantor agrees not to discharge the debt in any event, but only to do so if the debtor defaults. In other words, it is a secondary obligation to pay if, and only if, the debtor does not pay the money owed.

Contracts of guarantee must be 'evidenced in writing'. If not, they will be void and completely ineffective. 'Evidenced in writing' essentially means that although the contract itself need not be a written one, there must be some written evidence of the transaction. The evidence must have existed before the creditor seeks to enforce the contract and it must be signed by the guarantor. The note need not have been created for the specific purpose of enforcing the contract and may comprise a series of documents linked by reference.

4.7.2 Indemnities

An indemnity, on the other hand, creates a primary obligation. It is effectively where one party promises to reimburse pound-for-pound the other party in respect of a particular loss arising under the contract. As indemnities are primary obligations they do not have to be evidenced in writing.

Indemnities are often required by commercial buyers in relation to business acquisitions and purchases of land where there is a known specific liability/loss that the buyer will be taking on board. For example, a potential buyer of land discovers it is contaminated and that cleaning it up will cost £100,000. The buyer could negotiate an appropriate price reduction or alternatively seek an indemnity for £100,000. A price reduction would effectively solve the problem. An indemnity solves the problem provided the seller reimburses £100,000 as and when required to do so.

The practical difference between guarantees (as secondary obligations) and indemnities (as primary obligations) is illustrated below (**Figure 4.2**).

Figure 4.2 Guarantee and indemnity

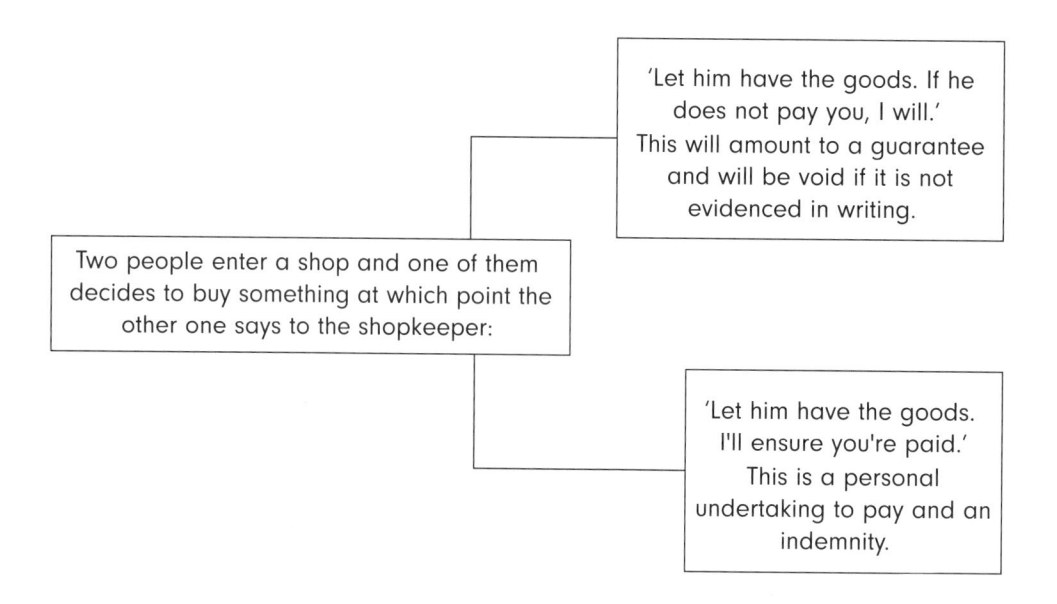

Two people enter a shop and one of them decides to buy something at which point the other one says to the shopkeeper:

- 'Let him have the goods. If he does not pay you, I will.' This will amount to a guarantee and will be void if it is not evidenced in writing.

- 'Let him have the goods. I'll ensure you're paid.' This is a personal undertaking to pay and an indemnity.

We have now considered the remedies which may be available if a term of a contract is broken, ie:

- damages;
- an action for an agreed sum;
- termination of the contract;
- the equitable remedies of specific performance and injunction;
- restitution (including restitutionary damages); and
- guarantees and indemnities.

Remedies for Breach of Contract

ACTIVITY 1 What is the most appropriate remedy?

Look at the following situations and select the most appropriate remedy.

1. J Paine, Painter & Decorator, contracted to paint Alison's house for £2,000 which Alison paid in advance. Paine does half the work, then abandons the job. Alison finds someone to finish the work for £500. What is the most appropriate remedy for Alison?

    - Restitution – total failure of consideration
    - Restitution – *quantum meruit*
    - Damages
    - Specific performance
    - Injunction
    - Action for agreed sum

2. Cave Builders contracted to repair Sumi's roof for £1,000. Sumi paid in advance. Cave Builders refused to do the work and Sumi got another contractor to do the job for £600. What is the most appropriate remedy for Sumi?

3. Shell Ltd contracted to sell goods to Bean & Co for £5,000, payment within seven days of delivery. Shell delivered the goods a month ago. Bean & Co is refusing to pay. What is the most appropriate remedy for Shell?

    - Damages
    - Restitution – *quantum meruit*
    - Action for agreed sum
    - Restitution – total failure of consideration
    - Injunction or specific performance

4. Barrett & Co asked Arcos Ltd to manufacture engine parts for it. Arcos manufactured the engine parts and Barrett accepted and used them, but the parties did not agree on a price or some other major terms. Consequently, there is no contract. What is the most appropriate remedy for Arcos Ltd?

    - Damages
    - Specific performance
    - Restitution – total failure of consideration
    - Restitution – *quantum meruit*
    - Injunction
    - Action for agreed sum

COMMENT

1. The most appropriate remedy for Alison is damages. She should receive £500 in order to put her in the position she would have been in had the contract been properly performed. She cannot recover the £2,000 she paid in advance in a restitution action as there has not been a complete failure of the consideration. The decorator did do some work.

2. The most appropriate remedy is an action in restitution to recover the £1,000 paid in advance as here there has been a complete failure of the consideration – Cave Builders did not even start the work.

117

3. The most appropriate remedy is an action for the agreed sum as payment should have been made within seven days of delivery.

4. The most appropriate remedy is an action in restitution for a *quantum meruit* payment – a reasonable sum for the work done.

SUMMARY

- If you are advising a client in respect of a breach of contract, you need to be aware of the range of remedies available and have a detailed knowledge of the main remedy, namely damages.

- Therefore, in this chapter, you have studied the key common law and equitable remedies, with the main focus being on damages. You have seen that the aim in awarding damages is to compensate a party for loss caused by the other party's breach and that the loss must not be too remote. We have examined how this aim can be achieved, ie generally by trying to put the innocent party in the position it would have been in if the contract had been properly performed. However, you should also appreciate that this is not always straightforward, as the *Ruxley v Forsyth* case illustrates.

- If you are drafting a contract, you need to consider whether to insert a clause specifying the amount of compensation payable in the event of a breach. You have looked at the difference between a specified damages clause and a penalty and the rules that you should bear in mind in order to draft an effective clause.

5 Performance and Discharge of a Contract

LEARNING OUTCOMES

When you have completed this chapter, you should be able to:

- explain and apply the rule relating to complete performance and the exceptions;
- identify and explain situations when a contract may be discharged;
- demonstrate a thorough knowledge and understanding of the nature and effects of frustration and apply the law to factual situations;
- understand the nature of a *force majeure* clause and explain why parties may wish to insert such a clause into their contract.

5.1 Order of performance

The parties may state in their contract when each party must perform their contractual obligations. Taking a commercial sale of goods contract as an example, what might the parties agree in relation to the order of performance?

The parties might agree that:

- the buyer will pay after delivery of the goods, eg payment within 21 days of delivery of the goods or issue of an invoice (have a look again at clause 6 of the Specimen Conditions of Sale which we dealt with in **Chapter 4**; the clause makes it clear that payment will be made only after the goods have been delivered);
- the buyer will pay on delivery;
- the buyer will pay before the goods are delivered.

If the parties do not make the order of performance clear in their contract, then there may be some statutory provision which can assist. For example, the Sale of Goods Act 1979 provides that unless otherwise agreed, in a contract for sale of goods, payment and delivery are concurrent provisions.

The order of performance is important when considering the doctrine of complete performance which we examine next.

5.2 The doctrine of complete performance

The contract may make it clear that one party only has to perform their obligations when the other party has performed their part of the contract. For example, suppose you enter

119

into a contract to have your house decorated. You may agree that the decorator will do the work first and you will pay when the decorating has been completed. Your obligation to pay arises only when the decorator has completed the work. If the decorator does a little work but then abandons the job, the general rule is that the decorator will not be entitled to any payment. Your obligation to pay was dependent on the decorator completing the work in its entirety and the decorator has not done so. The decorator's obligations are said to be 'entire'. The doctrine of complete performance would apply in this situation to prevent the decorator getting any payment.

The case of *Cutter v Powell* (1795) 6 TR 320 illustrates how the doctrine works.

Cutter was employed as second mate on a two-month voyage from Jamaica to Liverpool. The contract provided that Cutter would be paid 30 guineas 10 days after the ship reached Liverpool provided 'he proceeds, continues and does his duty' from Jamaica to Liverpool.

Cutter died about two weeks before the ship reached Liverpool, and his widow brought an action claiming payment for the work he had done on a *quantum meruit* basis (ie a reasonable sum in restitution for what he had done). We looked at restitution in **Chapter 4.**

The court decided that, as Cutter had not performed his obligations completely, the widow could not receive any money. The wording of the contract indicated that her husband would be paid a lump sum at the end of the voyage provided he completed it, but he had not done so. The court also took into account the fact that the sum he would receive if he completed the voyage was far more than a seaman would receive if he was paid at a monthly rate. Cutter had accepted the risk of only being paid if he completed the voyage.

To sum up, the doctrine of complete performance provides that performance of contractual obligations must be precise and exact. If one party has to pay only after the other has performed their obligations under the contract, then if performance is not precise and exact, the payer does not have to pay any part of the price (although the payer will not be able get back any money already paid unless there has been a complete failure of the consideration).

5.2.1 Exceptions to the doctrine of complete performance

5.2.1.1 Introduction

This doctrine could produce unfair results if applied in all circumstances and so there are exceptions. If an exception applies then some payment (albeit not the price) can be recovered, even though the contractual obligations have not been performed precisely and exactly.

The exceptions are:

(a) divisible obligations;

(b) substantial performance;

(c) wrongful prevention;

(d) voluntary acceptance of part performance.

Examples

Situation	Entitled to some payment – reason
1. Vince agrees to cut down the five trees in Elnora's garden for £900, payment on completion. He cuts down two trees but then Elnora says that she has changed her mind and she tells him to stop work.	Elnora has wrongfully prevented Vince from completing the work. She has broken the contract by telling him to stop.
2. AD Removals contract to transport two computers for Parke Co from Newcastle to Birmingham for £300, payment on completion. At Wolverhampton, AD Removals' van starts to overheat. Parke Co tell AD Removals that they will meet the driver at Wolverhampton and take delivery there.	It seems that Parke Co agreed to accept delivery in Wolverhampton, ie the company agreed to accept partial performance of the contract by AD Removals, so AD Removals should be entitled to some payment, ie a reasonable sum for taking the goods to Wolverhampton.
3. Benjamin has built a small extension to Michael's restaurant. The contract price is £10,000, payment on completion. Michael has discovered some minor defects, caused by faulty workmanship which will cost £100 to put right, and is refusing to pay Benjamin any money.	Although Benjamin has not performed his contractual obligations precisely and exactly, he has substantially performed his obligations as the defects are only minor. It will cost only £100 to put them right compared to a contract price of £10,000.

We shall now consider the four exceptions in more detail.

5.2.1.2 Wrongful prevention of performance by the other party

We saw in situation 1 above that Vince was entitled to some payment because Elnora changed her mind about having the trees cut down and wrongfully prevented him from completing his contractual obligations. It was not Vince's fault that he did not perform his obligations precisely and exactly, and it would be unfair if he was prejudiced because Elnora had changed her mind.

Elnora is in breach of contract and Vince could bring a claim to recover damages. As you have seen in the previous chapter, the aim of the court in awarding damages would be to put Vince in the position he would have been in if the contract had been properly performed, ie if Elnora had allowed him to complete the work (*Robinson v Harman* (1848) 1 Ex 850). Therefore, Vince would be able to recover his lost profit (ie the contract price less any expenses saved) subject to a duty to mitigate his loss by taking reasonable steps to look for alternative work.

Alternatively, Vince could claim a *quantum meruit*, which is a reasonable amount for the work he has done (*Planché v Colburn* (1831) 8 Bing 14). This is a claim in restitution, which we considered in **Chapter 4**.

It is often better to claim damages rather than a *quantum meruit*, as this usually enables a larger sum to be recovered. This is because the damages claim is for all losses arising from the breach which are not too remote (such as lost profits), whereas a *quantum meruit* represents a reasonable amount for the work actually done.

Also remember from **Chapters 3** and **4** that it is only in very limited circumstances that a non-defaulting party may be justified in terminating the future performance of a contract, ie where there has been a repudiatory breach (ie breach of a condition or otherwise a very serious breach of an innominate term).

Contract

The term implied by s 13 of the SGSA 1982 into business-to-business contracts that service/work will be carried out with reasonable care and skill is an innominate term (see **Chapter 3**), and it is in relation to breach of this term that problems may arise. How bad does the work have to be before the other party is justified in terminating the contract? If the other party terminates in circumstances falling short of a serious enough breach, then that will be wrongful prevention and a repudiatory breach. The other party has to make a judgement call.

> ⭐ *Example*
>
> *Wessex Builders Ltd agreed to build an extension to Sonia's cafe for £10,000, payment on completion. Halfway through the project, Sonia dismissed the builders because the work was very seriously defective. As the builders have committed a very serious breach of the term implied by s 13 of the SGSA 1982 to exercise reasonable care and skill, Sonia was justified in dismissing them. Sonia will have got the work done for nothing.*
>
> *However, if circumstances had been different and the work had not effectively deprived Sonia of the whole benefit she expected to receive under the contract then it would have been wrongful prevention by Sonia and she would be liable to the builders for breach of contract.*

5.2.1.3 Voluntary acceptance of partial performance by the other party

We saw in situation 2 above that AD Removals would be entitled to some payment as Parke Co had voluntarily accepted partial performance of the firm's contractual obligations. Note, however, that the non-defaulting party must have a genuine choice whether, or not, to accept the part performance. If they have no choice (eg because the supplier built something on the non-defaulting party's land and then abandoned the job), the non-defaulting party will not have to pay anything for what was done.

This is illustrated by *Sumpter v Hedges* [1898] 1 QB 673. In that case a builder agreed to construct two houses and a stable on the defendant's land for £565. However, he abandoned the project after completing £333 worth of work. The defendant had to complete the work himself and he used materials left behind by the builder. The builder claimed a reasonable sum for work done and materials supplied. The claim for the work failed as the defendant had no choice but to accept what had been done. However, the defendant did have a choice whether, or not, to use the materials that had been left behind and so was ordered to pay a reasonable sum for those. This is a claim in restitution, which we considered in **Chapter 4**.

Voluntary acceptance of part performance is reflected in the Consumer Rights Act (CRA) 2015 and the Sale of Goods Act (SGA) 1979. Section 25(1) of the CRA 2015 provides that where a trader delivers to a consumer a quantity of goods less than the trader contracted to supply, if the consumer decides to accept them then the consumer must pay for them at the contract rate. Similarly, s 30(1) of the SGA 1979 says, 'Where the seller delivers to a buyer a quantity of goods less than he contracted to sell, the buyer may reject the goods, but if the buyer accepts the goods so delivered he must pay for them at the contract rate.'

5.2.1.4 Substantial performance

A party who substantially performs their obligations may be able to claim some money for the work. For substantial performance to apply, the work must be 'finished' but slightly defective.

For example, suppose Tom agrees to build a garden wall for John at a price of £500, payment on completion. He builds 75% of the wall but then abandons the job. Tom could not argue that he has substantially performed his obligations as he has not finished the wall.

We shall now look at two cases where this topic was considered.

In *Hoenig v Isaacs* [1952] 2 All ER 176, CA, the defendant employed the claimant to decorate and furnish the defendant's flat for the sum of £750. The defendant paid £400 but refused to pay the balance on the ground that some of the work was defective. The contract provided that the balance was payable on completion. At first instance the official referee found that, although some of the work was defective (a wardrobe door needed replacing and alterations had to be made to a bookcase), there had been substantial performance.

He ordered that the defendant should pay the claimant the balance less the sum needed to remedy the defects (about £55). The official referee had relied on an earlier case of *H Dakin & Co Ltd v Lee* [1916] 1 KB 578. The defendant appealed. The Court of Appeal (per Somervell LJ) held as follows:

> The learned official referee regarded *H Dakin & Co Ltd v Lee* as laying down that the price must be paid subject to set-off or counterclaim if there was a substantial compliance with the contract. I think on the facts of this case where the work was finished in the ordinary sense, though in part defective, this is right.
>
> The learned official referee found that there was substantial compliance. Bearing in mind that there is no appeal on fact, was there evidence on which he could so find? The learned official referee having, as I hold, properly directed himself, this becomes, I think, a question of fact. The case on this point was, I think, near the border line, and if the finding had been the other way I do not think we could have interfered.
>
> I now come to the final question; the measure of damages ... The measure he (the official referee) applied was the cost of putting the work in accordance with the contract. The defendant is bound, he held, to pay for the furniture supplied less the cost of putting right the defects. This I think is, as the learned official referee thought, in accordance with *H Dakin & Co Ltd v Lee*.
>
> I therefore think the appeal must be dismissed. [The other two Court of Appeal judges also dismissed the appeal.]

So, in *Hoenig v Isaacs*, the decorator was entitled to the balance of the contract price less the cost of remedying the defects. It was not a clear case of substantial performance. The cost of remedying the defects was £55 compared to a contract price of £750, and this was regarded as borderline. So, if the cost of remedying the problem is more than 1/14 of the contract price (which was the case in *Hoenig v Isaacs*), it probably would not be deemed to be a case of substantial performance.

Having looked at a case where the court decided there had been substantial performance, we will now consider *Bolton v Mahadeva* [1972] 1 WLR 1009, CA, a case where the Court reached the opposite conclusion.

Here, the claimant agreed to install central heating in the defendant's house for the sum of £560. The claimant completed the work, but it was defective. The system did not heat the house adequately and fumes were given out which made the rooms uncomfortable. The Court held that the contractor had not substantially performed their contractual obligations. The heating system did not perform effectively its primary function. The defects were extensive and could not be remedied by some slight amendment of the system. The contract price was £560 and it would cost £174 to remedy the defects, ie about one-third of the contract price (unlike in *Hoenig v Isaacs* where the defects could be put right at a cost of about one-fourteenth of the total price).

Before resorting to litigation to try to recover the money, the contractor would have been well advised to offer to remedy the defects. If he had remedied the defects, he could then have justified claiming the full contract price.

5.2.1.5 Divisible obligations

The final situation where a party may be able to recover some money for work they have done, even though they have not performed their contractual obligations exactly, is if the obligations are divisible, eg if the parties have agreed payments for a distinct part or stage of the work. Each part or stage is treated like a separate contract.

⭐ *Example*

Situation	Entitled to some money – reason
Brooks agrees to decorate some rooms in Sarah's house. It is agreed that he will be paid £200 for painting the kitchen, £400 for the dining room and £300 for a bedroom, payment to be made as each room is completed. He paints the kitchen and dining room and starts work on the bedroom. Brooks then abandons the job for a more lucrative project.	It was agreed that Brooks would get £200 for painting the kitchen and £400 for painting the dining room, so he should be able to recover payment for the rooms he has finished; but nothing for the bedroom.

The decorator was entitled to be paid for the rooms completed, even though the decorator did not finish the job but abandoned the work for a more lucrative project. The obligations were not entire as in *Cutter v Powell*, where a lump sum was payable only if the voyage was completed. The work had been divided, with completion of each stage giving rise to the right to some payment. This often happens in building contracts.

⭐ *Example*

Nasser agrees to build a house for Keith for £160,000. Payment is to be made in three stages as each stage is completed:

Stage 1: £60,000

Stage 2: £60,000

Stage 3: £40,000

Nasser completes the first stage, does a little work on Stage 2, but then abandons the project as he has been offered more lucrative work elsewhere. Keith has not yet paid any money to Nasser. Keith gets another builder to finish the work for £80,000.

(a) *Nasser is entitled to £60,000 for Stage 1, which he has completed. The obligations in the contract were divisible and the completion of each stage gives rise to the right to payment. He is not entitled to any money for Stage 2 as he did not complete this part of the contract.*

Keith is also in breach of contract as he has not paid for Stage 1 after completion. It is possible to have situations where both parties have broken the contract.

(b) *It is not worth suing Nasser as Keith has not suffered any loss. Keith would have paid Nasser £100,000 for Stages 2 and 3, and he has arranged for someone else to finish the job for only £80,000.*

However, suppose that Keith had only been able to get another builder to finish the work for £120,000. If Keith pays Nasser £60,000 for Stage 1, he would end up paying £180,000 altogether. In that case he could sue Nasser for damages. The aim would be to put Keith in the position he would have been had his contract with Nasser been properly performed. If Nasser had performed the contract, Keith would have paid £160,000 for the house; therefore he should be awarded £20,000 in damages.

Figure 5.1 Exceptions to the doctrine of complete performance – summary

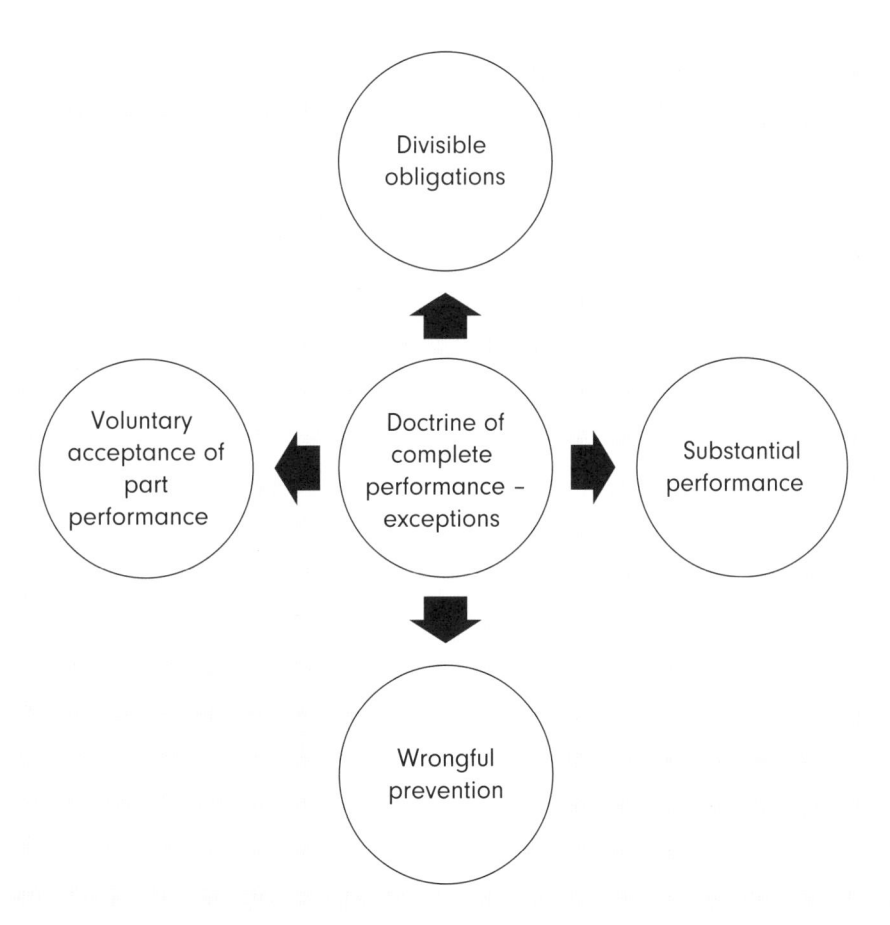

We have now covered the four exceptions to the doctrine of complete performance. But what if both parties perform all of their contractual obligations? Then the contract will be discharged. The contract is said to be discharged by performance, and this is the way most contracts come to an end.

However, there are other ways in which a contract may be discharged. We looked at one of these in **Chapter 4**, when considering remedies. You saw then that if there is a breach of a condition or a breach of an innominate term and the effects are major, the innocent party may terminate the future performance of the contract. If the innocent party does terminate then the contract is discharged and neither party need perform any future obligations, although the innocent party may still sue for damages for loss suffered.

As you worked through the material on the doctrine of complete performance and the exceptions, you may have noticed that there is a link with breach of contract.

Let's revisit a couple of situations we looked at earlier.

Situation	Entitled to some money – reason
Benjamin has built a small extension to Michael's restaurant. The contract price is £10,000, payment on completion. Michael has discovered some minor defects, caused by faulty workmanship which will cost £100 to put right, and is refusing to pay Benjamin any money.	Although Benjamin has not performed his contractual obligations precisely and exactly, he has substantially performed his obligations as the defects are only minor. It will cost only £100 to put them right, compared to a contract price of £10,000.

You can see that Benjamin is in breach of the term implied by s 13 of the Supply of Goods and Services Act 1982 as he was performing a service in the course of a business for a business customer (Michael) and did not use reasonable care and skill. Section 13 is an innominate term which means that Michael may only terminate the contract if the effects of the breach are major. Here the defects are only minor so Michael cannot terminate the contract. Therefore, technically, Michael should pay the contract price, although he can recover damages for loss suffered.

If Michael does not pay then Benjamin can bring an action for the contract price. There are two possible approaches.

First, Michael may try to rely on the doctrine of complete performance – ie argue that Benjamin has not performed the work precisely and so is not entitled to the money. In this case, Benjamin could rely on the substantial performance exception. This is what happened in *Hoenig v Isaacs* which we considered earlier.

However, there is another possible approach, ie Michael might argue that Benjamin is not entitled to be paid as he is in breach of the term implied by s 13 of the Supply of Goods and Services Act 1982. Benjamin would counter this by arguing that it is only a minor breach of an innominate term which does not justify Michael refusing the whole contract price.

Either way, Benjamin will be successful, and the court would order Michael to pay the contract price less an amount needed to remedy the defects.

Situation	Entitled to some money – reason
Wessex Builders Ltd agreed to build an extension to Sonia's cafe for £10,000, payment on completion. Halfway through the project, Sonia dismissed the builders because the work was very seriously defective.	No. The builders have committed a very serious breach of the term implied by s 13 of the SGSA 1982 to exercise reasonable care and skill. So Sonia was justified in dismissing them. Sonia will have got the work done for nothing.

If Wessex Builders sue Sonia for the contract price, Sonia could argue that Wessex had not performed its obligations exactly. Wessex could not rely on substantial performance (or any other exception to the complete performance doctrine). This was the line of argument adopted in *Bolton v Mahadeva*.

However, there is another approach. You can see that Wessex Builders has committed a major breach of the implied term that it will carry out the work with reasonable care and skill. Therefore, Sonia could terminate the contract which means that she is released from all future obligations. If Wessex Builders sue for the price, Sonia could argue that she has rightfully terminated the contract and does not have to pay the contract price.

Either way, Sonia will be successful and would not have to pay any part of the contract price.

These points bring together several areas of law. You have seen then that a contract may be discharged by performance and (in some cases) by breach. A contract may also be discharged by agreement and by frustration. We shall now examine each of these in more detail.

5.3 Discharge by agreement

The parties to a contract may agree to release one another from outstanding obligations, in which case the contract will come to an end.

The basic rule is that, in order to bind the parties, the agreement to end a contract (or to vary its terms) must itself contain all the elements of a contract, so there must be offer, acceptance, consideration and contractual intention.

Sometimes it can be difficult to establish all of these elements. For example, suppose that Marcus owes Ace & Co £2,000. Marcus says he can pay only £1,600, and Ace & Co agrees to accept this in full payment of the debt. Marcus pays £1,600, but Ace & Co then wants Marcus to pay the balance.

The agreement by Ace & Co to accept just £1,600 will be binding only if all the elements of a contract are present. Thinking back to **Chapter 2**, which essential element is missing here?

The missing element is consideration. Marcus has not given any consideration for Ace & Co's promise to release him from the balance of the debt. Consideration can be defined as the price one party pays for the other party's promise. Marcus has not paid the price for Ace & Co's promise. He has not done or promised to do anything in return. Marcus has only paid part of his debt and this is usually insufficient consideration for a promise to forgo the balance (*Pinnel's Case*, *Foakes v Beer*). To establish that Ace & Co's promise was binding, Marcus would have to show that an exception to this rule applied, either a common law exception or the doctrine of promissory estoppel. You covered these points in **Chapter 2**.

5.4 Discharge by frustration

5.4.1 What constitutes frustration

Frustration only operates in limited circumstances. The supervening event or change of circumstances must:

- make performance of the contract impossible, or radically different;
- be something beyond the ordinary risks that the parties can be treated as having taken on board when entering into their contract (ie something unexpected); and
- be something that was beyond the control of either party.

So where an unforeseen event occurs after the contract was formed, then generally if the parties are not at fault and such an event renders the performance of the contract very different, or even impossible to perform, a contract will be terminated by frustration as a matter of law. It is an exception to the general rule that requires complete performance of obligations to avoid being in breach of contract. We considered the doctrine of complete performance above.

Contract

5.4.1.1 'Radically different'

Most of the cases that have considered frustration have been placed into convenient categories of circumstances that render performance of the contract 'radically different'. These categories include:

(a) government intervention;

(b) unavailability of a specific person crucial to the contract;

(c) illegality;

(d) destruction of the subject matter;

(e) non-occurrence of a fundamental event.

But in all cases, it will be a question of degree.

⭐ Examples

Situation	Frustrated – reason
Shahid agrees to hire the local community centre for 1 June so his amateur dramatic group can perform a play. Before 1 June someone breaks into the centre and starts a fire. The centre is completely destroyed.	The subject matter of the contract (the centre) is accidentally destroyed so it is impossible to perform the contract.
Shirjel has agreed to write a book for Bharat. The book must be completed in six months' time. Shirjel writes a couple of chapters but then falls ill. He will not be able to work for at least a year.	Shirjel is not going to be able to complete the book in six months' time because of his illness. The contract is impossible to perform. Note: Shirjel was vital to performance of the contract.
Someone hires a room for two days (not the nights) for the sole purpose of viewing the coronation procession of Edward VII. The procession is cancelled due to the illness of the King.	The whole purpose for hiring the room had been to watch the procession and that is no longer possible.

Situation	Not frustrated – reason
A 10-year lease of a warehouse. For 18 months of the 10-year term the local authority closes the street giving the only access to the warehouse.	Whilst frustration may apply to leases of land, here the relative length of the interruption would not be sufficiently grave to amount to a frustrating event.
Sheila enters into a contract with Beautiful Interiors Ltd to have her house decorated. Mike, an employee of Beautiful Interiors, works on her house for a couple of days but then goes down with flu and is replaced by Phil, another employee. Sheila is looking for an excuse to end the contract as she would like to finish the decorating herself with the help of friends.	The contract has not become impossible to perform or radically different. Beautiful Interiors can still do the work by using Phil rather than Mike. Sheila makes her contract with Beautiful Interiors, and the identity of the employee who will do the work is not important so long as one of their employees can do it.
Someone agrees to hire a ship for two days to take people out to view the royal Naval Review and for a day's cruise round the fleet. The Naval Review is cancelled due to the King's illness.	The royal Naval Review had not been the sole purpose of the contract. A day's cruise round the fleet is still possible and so performance has not become radically different.

Figure 5.2 Consequences of non-performance

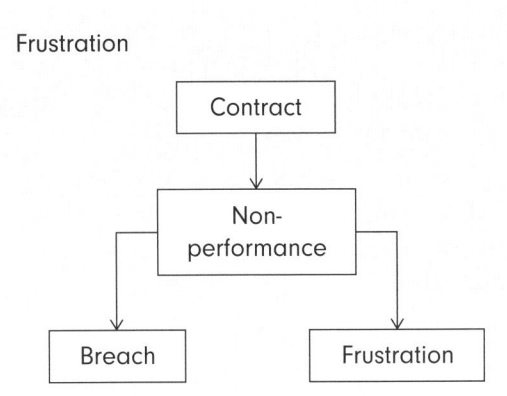

Frustration

```
        Contract
           │
           ▼
    Non-performance
       ╱      ╲
      ▼        ▼
   Breach   Frustration
```

If a contract is frustrated, there is no breach of contract in relation to the frustrating event. The contract comes to an end automatically at the time of the frustrating event and the parties do not have to perform their future obligations.

As there is no breach of contract when a contract is frustrated, the remedies associated with breach of contract (eg damages) will not be available.

It is for the above reasons that the party alleging frustration will almost invariably be the party who would otherwise have been in breach of contract for non-performance. They will be using it as a defence to an allegation of breach of contract (**Figure 5.2**).

You should now have a very general idea of when a contract will be frustrated, and we shall look in detail at when frustration will occur and the effects of frustration later. However, before we do that, we shall consider the original position at common law so you can see how this area of law has developed.

5.4.2 The original common law rule

The idea that a contract will be frustrated if it becomes impossible to perform has not always been the legal position.

Originally, at common law, if a party assumed an absolute obligation in a contract (ie the obligation was not qualified or modified in any way), then if circumstances made performance of the obligation impossible, the party would still be liable. The party concerned should have protected itself by making sure a suitable provision was included in the contract.

This approach was adopted in the case of *Paradine v Jane* (1647) Aleyn 26. In this case the claimant was claiming arrears of rent from the defendant. The defendant had been forced off the land by a hostile army and so argued it should not have to pay. The argument did not succeed. The court held that the defendant was still liable to pay the rent. This approach came to be seen as harsh and was modified in the mid-nineteenth century.

5.4.3 Modification of the original common law rule

5.4.3.1 Implied term theory

The modern law of frustration is often said to date from the decision in the case of *Taylor v Caldwell* (1863) 3 B & S 826. In this case the claimants hired a music hall from the defendants for a few days for the purpose of giving a series of concerts. Before the date of the first concert, the music hall was destroyed by fire and the concerts could not take place. Neither party to the contract was at fault. The contract was discharged by frustration.

Blackburn J justified the decision by saying that the existence of the music hall was essential for the fulfilment of the contract. He thought that there was an implied condition in the contract that the parties would be excused if performance became impossible because, without the fault of the parties, the music hall perished.

Note it was the party who would have been in breach by non-performance (ie the hirer of the music hall) who alleged the contract had been terminated by the supervening event. As you will see shortly (when we consider the effect of frustration), frustration of a contract yields a much more desirable result than liability for breach.

5.4.3.2 Construction theory

The idea of frustration resting on a term implied between the parties was dismissed as a fiction by the House of Lords in *Davis Contractors Ltd v Fareham Urban District Council* [1956] AC 696, as in most cases the parties could not have had such an intention.

Lord Radcliffe said:

> The legal effect of frustration 'does not depend on the [the parties'] intention or their opinions, or even knowledge as to the event.' On the contrary, it seems that when the event occurs 'the meaning of the contract must be taken to be, not what the parties did intend (for they had neither thought nor intention regarding it) but that which the parties, as fair, and reasonable men, would presumably have agreed upon if, having such possibility in view, they had made express provision as to their several rights and liabilities in the event of its occurrence.' ...
>
> By this time it might seem that the parties themselves have become so far disembodied spirits that their actual body should be allowed to rest in peace. In their place there rises the figure of the fair and reasonable man. And the spokesman of the fair and reasonable man ... is and must be the court itself.

5.4.4 Review

We have established that a contract is frustrated if an event occurs after the contract has been formed which makes the contract impossible to perform or radically different, and this event is outside the control of the parties to the contract.

We shall now look in detail at the situations which will cause a contract to become frustrated.

5.4.5 Events which will frustrate a contract

5.4.5.1 Unavailability of a specific thing or person vital to the contract

We saw at **5.4.1.1** that the unavailability of a specific thing or person vital to the contract can cause frustration. Three factors which determine whether a person not being available leads to frustration of the contract are:

(a) the length of the contract;

(b) the length of the period of absence; and

(c) whether the contract must be performed by that particular individual or whether a substitute can do the work.

⭐ Examples

Situation	Frustrated	Not frustrated
1. Elsie works as a computer programmer and has a five-year contract of employment. She has a bad cold and takes two days off work.		√ Short periods of illness in a long employment contract will not frustrate the contract. It is assumed that the employee may have some time off because of illness, and usually there will be express contractual provision covering it. Short periods of illness do not make a long-term employment contract radically different from what the parties envisaged.
2. Two weeks ago Dipa entered into a contract of employment for six months. She has now been taken seriously ill and will not be fit for work for at least nine months.	√ Looking at the length of the contract and the period of sickness, the contract will be regarded as impossible to perform. Dipa has only worked two weeks of her six-month contract. This is very different from a short period of illness in a long contract, which was illustrated in situation 1 above.	

Unavailability of a person vital to the performance of the contract caused frustration in *Morgan v Manser* [1948] 1 KB 184, where a music-hall artist, 'Cheerful Charlie Chester', was called up for military service. Also, the contract was frustrated in *Condor v Barron Knights* [1966] 1 WLR 87, when a drummer with a pop group was taken ill and was capable of working for only three or four nights a week, whereas the group had engagements for seven nights a week. The contract was frustrated as the drummer was not capable of performing the contract in the way intended.

We are now going to look at another situation which may frustrate a contract, and that is the non-occurrence of a fundamental event.

5.4.5.2 Non-occurrence of a fundamental event

If a particular event taking place is essential to the contract (ie the contract is dependent on it), and the event is cancelled, then this may frustrate the contract.

To give you a better idea of how this concept works, we shall look at two cases where an event was cancelled. Both cases involve the postponement of the coronation of Edward VII due to the King's illness. In the first case, the court decided that the contract had been frustrated, whereas in the second case the court came to the opposite conclusion.

In *Krell v Henry* [1903] 2 KB 740, CA, the defendant saw a notice in the window of the claimant's flat to the effect that windows to view the coronation procession of Edward VII were to be let. The defendant subsequently agreed to hire the flat for the two days (not the nights) when the coronation procession would take place. The contract contained no express reference to the procession or any other purpose for which the flat was taken. The defendant paid a deposit. When the procession was cancelled due to the King's illness, the defendant refused to pay the balance of the rent.

Vaughan Williams LJ said:

> In my judgment the use of the rooms was let and taken for the purpose of seeing the Royal procession. It was not a demise of the rooms, or even an agreement to let and take the rooms. It is a licence to use rooms for a particular purpose and none other. And in my judgment the taking place of those processions on the days proclaimed along the proclaimed route, which passed 56A, Pall Mall, was regarded by both contracting parties as the foundation of the contract ...
>
> ... in the case of the coronation, there is not merely the purpose of the hirer to see the coronation procession, but it is the coronation procession and the relative position of the rooms which is the basis of the contract as much for the lessor as the hirer; and I think that if the King, before the coronation day and after the contract, had died, the hirer could not have insisted on having the rooms on the days named ...

The rooms had clearly been hired for the sole purpose of seeing the Royal procession. Neither party in *Krell v Henry* was in breach of contract because the contract was frustrated. The postponement of the coronation procession frustrated the contract because the foundation of the contract was not just to hire rooms but to hire rooms in order to view the procession and this was not possible.

In the case of *Herne Bay Steamboat Co v Hutton* [1903] 2 KB 683, CA, the defendant agreed to hire a ship from the claimant for two days to take out a party 'for the purpose of viewing the Naval Review and for a day's cruise round the fleet'. The Naval Review was cancelled due to the King's illness. The Court of Appeal decided that the cancellation of the review did not discharge the defendant from his obligations under the contract, ie it did not frustrate the contract.

Vaughan Williams LJ said:

> The defendant when hiring this boat had the object in view of taking people to see the Naval Review, and on the next day of taking them round the fleet and also round the Isle of Wight. But it does not seem to me that, because those purposes of the defendant became impossible, it is a legitimate inference that the happening of the Naval Review was contemplated by both parties as the foundation of the contract, so as to bring the case within the doctrine of *Taylor v Caldwell*. On the contrary, when the contract is properly considered, I think that the purposes of the defendant, whether of going to the review or going round the fleet or the Isle of Wight with a party of paying guests, do not make those purposes the foundation of the contract within the meaning of *Taylor v Caldwell*.
>
> Having expressed this view, I do not know that there is any advantage to be gained by in any way defining what are the circumstances which might or might not constitute

the happening of a particular contingency the foundation of the contract. I will only say I see nothing to differentiate this contract from a contract by which some person engaged a cab to take him on each of three days to Epsom to see the races, and for some reason, such as the spread of an infectious disease or an anticipation of a riot, the races are prohibited. In such a case it could not be said that he would be relieved of his bargain. So in the present case it is sufficient to say that the happening of the Naval Review was not the foundation of this contract.

How can the decision in *Herne Bay Steamboat Co v Hutton* be distinguished from the decision in *Krell v Henry*, ie why was the contract in *Krell v Henry* frustrated whereas in *Herne Bay Steamboat Co v Hutton* the court came to the opposite decision?

One view is that *Krell v Henry* can be distinguished from *Herne Bay Steamboat Co v Hutton* on the basis that, in *Krell v Henry*, the cancellation of the procession meant that the foundation or basis of the contract could not be accomplished. The purpose was not just to hire rooms but to hire rooms in order to see the procession. (This was apparent from the terms of the contract. The room was hired out by the day; the night was not included in the hire.) By contrast, in *Herne Bay Steamboat Co v Hutton*, the defendant's motive in entering into the contract may well have been to see the review, but this was not the foundation of the contract. In addition, Stirling LJ emphasised that a cruise round the fleet was still possible.

Also, as Roger Brownsword says in his article, 'Henry's lost spectacle and Hutton's Lost Speculation. A Classic Riddle Solved?' (1985) 129 *Solicitors Journal* 860–62, Hutton was engaged in a business venture, Henry was not, and this may explain the different attitudes of the court.

Having looked at non-occurrence of a fundamental event, we shall now go on to consider other situations in which a contract may be frustrated.

5.4.5.3 Government intervention

It is not every form of government intervention which will frustrate a contract. It depends on the effect which the intervention has on the contract.

The case of *Metropolitan Water Board v Dick Kerr* [1918] AC 119 involved a contract to build a reservoir. Not long after the work had started, the government requisitioned the workforce and machinery because of World War I. Such a substantial interruption could not have been in the contemplation of the parties at the time the contract was made. The delay was such that the contract, if resumed, would be radically different from the contract the parties had originally made.

In *Metropolitan Water Board v Dick Kerr*, there had been a clause in the contract dealing with the possibility of an extension of time in the case of delay. However, the court decided that it was meant to cover temporary delays and not an interruption of such character and duration as World War I. As a matter of construction, therefore, the delay clause did not cover the situation which had arisen, and the court held that the contract had been frustrated.

We shall now look in more detail at when delay may cause a contract to be frustrated.

5.4.5.4 Delay: when will this cause frustration?

The case of *Metropolitan Water Board v Dick Kerr* is not just a case about government intervention; it is also a case about delay and when this will cause frustration.

It is not every case of delay which frustrates the contract. In fact, a delay is more likely to mean that a party is in breach of contract. For example, if it is a term of the contract that the seller delivers goods on 3 March but then does not do so, the seller is likely to be in breach of an express term of the contract and frustration would not apply.

Factors which are relevant when deciding if delay frustrates the contract include:

- whether the contract provides for what should be the consequences of the delay;
- the likely length of the delay;
- any time set in the contract for the obligations to be performed;
- if the contract is resumed after the delay, whether it is radically different from the contract the parties had originally made.

In the *Metropolitan Water Board* case, the delay was such that the contract, if resumed, would be radically different from the contract the parties had originally made.

It can sometimes be difficult to distinguish situations where delay frustrates the contract because the contract becomes impossible or radically different to perform from situations where the contract merely becomes more difficult to perform or less profitable. For example, the closure of the Suez Canal in 1956 led to many voyages being re-routed and the new voyage was longer and more expensive. The courts were reluctant to say that the contract was frustrated unless the route had been specified in the contract, or a precise delivery date had been agreed or the goods were perishable.

This is illustrated by the case of *Tsakiroglou & Co Ltd v Noblee Thorl* [1962] AC 93. Sellers agreed to ship groundnuts from Port Sudan to Hamburg. At the time of the contract, the parties assumed that the shipment would be via the Suez Canal, although the route was not specified in the contract. The closure of the Canal meant that the goods had to be shipped via the Cape of Good Hope. The sellers claimed that the contract was frustrated. The House of Lords found that the contract was not frustrated. The contract had become more difficult and expensive for the sellers, but the contract could still be performed (as no route had been specified) and had not become radically different.

Can you think of any policy reason why mere increased difficulty or expense does not frustrate a contract and bring it to an end?

Many contracts can become more difficult or more expensive to perform, eg if the cost of materials goes up. It would be very unsatisfactory if this could bring a contract to an end. It would open the floodgates to litigation with many claims that contracts had been frustrated. It would also lead to uncertainty if a party could say the contract was at an end just because performance had become more difficult or less profitable. It would be unfair to the other contracting party who would never know when this argument was going to be raised. Some contractors might underestimate the cost of their work, and it would be unreasonable if they could say that the contract was at an end.

Given that the cost of labour and materials often goes up, a party who wishes to protect itself against such increases should foresee the possibility and make express provision in the contract, eg by including a price escalation clause.

Having seen the reason behind the approach the court adopts, let us now look at the case of *Davis Contractors Ltd v Fareham Urban District Council* [1956] AC 696, HL.

Davis Contractors agreed to build 78 houses within a period of eight months for Fareham UDC. Davis Contractors experienced a number of difficulties, mainly caused by shortages of labour and materials. The contract took over 22 months to complete. Davis Contractors argued that the contract had been frustrated and that they should be entitled to be paid a reasonable sum for work done after the frustrating event. (If the contract was frustrated then the contractors would not be liable for breach of contract for taking longer than specified to finish the houses.) The House of Lords held that the contract was not frustrated.

Lord Radcliffe held:

> Frustration occurs whenever the law recognises that, without default of either party, a contractual obligation has become incapable of being performed because the circumstances in which performance is called for would render it a thing radically different from that which was undertaken by the contract.
>
> ... it is not hardship or inconvenience or material loss itself which calls the principle of frustration into play. There must be as well such a change in the significance of the obligation that the thing undertaken would, if performed, be a different thing from that contracted for.

The other reason given by Lord Radcliffe as to why the contract should not be frustrated was the fact that the parties could have foreseen the cause of the delay. He said that the possibility of enough labour and materials not being available was before their eyes and could have been the subject of special contractual stipulation.

We will consider this idea further when we look at the restrictions on the doctrine of frustration.

The final event we are going to consider which may cause frustration is illegality.

5.4.5.5 Illegality

The performance of a contract may become legally impossible, and this can frustrate the contract. This can occur as a result of a change in the law. Also, the outbreak of war will frustrate a contract where the other party is in enemy-occupied territory, as in time of war it is against the law to trade with the enemy.

This principle is illustrated by *Fibrosa Spolka Akcyjna v Fairbairn Lawson Combe Barbour Ltd* [1943] AC 32, HL. The respondent (an English company) had agreed to manufacture machinery for the appellant (a Polish company) and to deliver to Poland. Before the manufacture had been completed, the German army occupied Poland. The House of Lords held that the contract was frustrated.

Note that the effect of illegality is not something that can be expressly provided for in the contract. If performance of a contract subsequently becomes illegal, the contract will be frustrated.

Events which can cause frustration – summary

- Unavailability of a specific thing vital to the contract (*Taylor v Caldwell*).
- Unavailability of a specific person vital to the contract (*Morgan v Manser, Condor v Barron Knights*).
- Non-occurrence of a fundamental event (*Krell v Henry*, contrast *Herne Bay Steamboat Co v Hutton*).
- Government intervention (*Metropolitan Water Board v Dick Kerr*).
- Illegality (*Fibrosa*).

These are some of the events which could lead to a contract being frustrated. Other events, eg strikes, could also have this result. However, remember that the crucial thing is not the event itself, but the effect of the event on the contract. The contract will be frustrated only if a supervening event (ie one that happens after the contract has been formed) makes performance of the contract impossible or radically different from that originally envisaged. If the event simply makes the contract more difficult or more expensive to perform, as in *Davis Contractors v Fareham UDC*, the contract will not be frustrated.

We shall now consider some restrictions on frustration.

5.4.6 Restrictions on the doctrine of frustration

We have already considered the general conditions which must be fulfilled before a contract will be frustrated. You know that you are looking for a supervening event which makes performance of the contract impossible or radically different from that envisaged. If a restriction applies, then the contract will not be frustrated. We are going to consider two possible restrictions. The first is where the frustrating event was foreseen by the parties, and the second is where the frustrating event was 'self-induced'.

5.4.6.1 The event must not be foreseen by the parties

The parties may have made express provision in the contract covering the event which has occurred and explaining how any loss caused by the event will be borne by the parties. Alternatively, the court may feel that the parties foresaw or should have foreseen the event even though there is no express provision in the contract. We shall look at each possibility in turn.

Express provision in the contract covering the event which has occurred

A term known as a '*force majeure*' clause may be inserted to cover events outside the control of the parties. If the parties have made express provision in the contract covering the event which has occurred, then this may be binding on the parties. (Note, however, that a clause cannot prevent frustration applying in the event of the contract becoming illegal, eg because of outbreak of war as in the case of *Fibrosa* which we looked at earlier.)

Have a look at the Specimen Conditions of Sale (**Reading 1** in the **Appendix**) and see if you can spot the *force majeure* clause there.

The clause is clause 4.3 in the Specimen Conditions. You can see that the seller states that the seller will not be liable for any failure to deliver goods arising from circumstances outside the seller's control and then goes on to give a list of examples of such circumstances, including war, riots, strikes, fire, abnormal weather conditions and government action.

Why do you think it is advisable to insert such a clause?

- Inserting such provision in a contract brings greater flexibility than relying on the doctrine of frustration. For example, the parties can include events which would not normally amount to frustrating events. In clause 4.3 of the Specimen Conditions, the list of events includes shortage of labour and materials. You have seen in *Davis Contractors v Fareham UDC* that shortage of labour and materials did not cause the contract to be frustrated as the contract had not become radically different.

- The parties can specify what should happen if such an event occurs and how the loss should fall. See, for example, clauses 4.3.2–4.3.4 of the Specimen Conditions. As you will see later at **5.4.9**, the effect of the Law Reform (Frustrated Contracts) Act 1943 can be very uncertain.

- A *force majeure* clause can also provide a greater degree of certainty as it may often be difficult to decide whether a contract has been frustrated. The parties can list events which will be regarded as *force majeure* events and this will reduce the uncertainty. A well-worded clause will mean that disputes are avoided.

However, it is important to draft the clause carefully so that it does in fact cover all events which the parties intend. For example, you looked at the case of *Metropolitan Water Board v Dick Kerr* where the contract contained a clause covering delay. In this case the court decided that the delay clause in the contract did not actually cover the event which had occurred. The clause was meant to cover temporary delays and not an interruption of such a character and duration that it fundamentally changed the conditions of the contract.

Note also that a *force majeure* clause in a business-to-business contract limiting and/ or excluding liability may be subject to s 3 of UCTA 1977, in which case it will need to be reasonable in order to be upheld. We considered exemption clauses and UCTA 1977 in **Chapter 3**.

No express provision in the contract but the event is foreseen

If the parties have not made any express provision in the contract, there is a conflict of opinion as to whether there can still be frustration if the event is foreseen.

In the case of *Davis Contractors v Fareham UDC*, which we considered earlier, Lord Radcliffe took the view that if the event was foreseen, the contract would not be frustrated.

In the case of *The Eugenia* [1964] 2 QB 226, Lord Denning MR said, *obiter*, that the contract could still be frustrated even if the event was foreseen – the only essential thing was that the parties should not have made provision for the event in the contract.

We shall now consider the second restriction on the doctrine of frustration.

5.4.6.2 Event must be beyond the control of the parties

The event which makes the contract impossible or radically different must be beyond the control of the parties.

A party whose own act or election has given rise to the frustrating event cannot rely on the doctrine of frustration. The frustration is said to be 'self-induced' and the contract will not be at an end. The party will be in breach of contract if it cannot perform its contractual obligations. As you can see, therefore, 'self-induced frustration' is not frustration at all.

It would be unreasonable if a party could cause the event to occur and then plead frustration to end the contract and effectively defend an action for breach. In essence, the law takes the view that you should not be excused from what is your own fault.

This is illustrated by two cases: *Maritime Fish Ltd v Ocean Trawlers Ltd* [1935] AC 524 and *The Super Servant Two* [1990] 1 Lloyd's Rep 1.

In *Maritime Fish Ltd v Ocean Trawlers Ltd*, the claimants hired a trawler from the defendants. Both parties knew that the trawler could only be used with an otter trawl and that a licence was needed for this. The claimants had four other trawlers and applied for five licences. They were only granted three licences. They could have used one for the trawler they had hired from the defendants but decided not to do so. The court decided that the contract was not frustrated as it was the claimants' own election which had caused the problem.

In *The Super Servant Two*, the defendants agreed to transport the claimants' drilling rig from Japan to Rotterdam. The contract said the rig was to be carried using a 'transportation unit', defined as meaning Super Servant One or Super Servant Two. The defendants intended to use Super Servant Two, but it sank before the date due for delivery. The defendants had entered into other contracts that they could only perform using Super Servant One, and so two weeks after the sinking they informed the claimants that they would not be able to transport the rig. The Court of Appeal decided the contract had not been frustrated. What had happened was 'self-induced'. It was the defendants' decision to use Super Servant One for other contracts that had made performance of their contract with the claimant impossible. The impossibility of performance resulted from their own act and the choice they had made.

The decision that it was self-induced frustration can be criticised on the basis that the defendants did not have a genuine choice about the allocation of Super Servant One. The sinking of the other transporter left the defendants with only Super Servant One, and Super Servant One could not be allocated to all the contracts the defendants had made. Performance of some of these contracts had been made impossible by the sinking of Super Servant Two, regardless of how Super Servant One was allocated.

The contract would have been frustrated if the contract had provided for carriage by Super Servant Two with no alternative vessel and Super Servant Two had been lost without fault.

On the basis of the decision in *The Super Servant Two*, it seems that any act by a party which contributes to the event will prevent the contract from being frustrated. This shows the narrow limits within which the doctrine of frustration operates and the advantage of inserting a *force majeure* clause in the contract to avoid liability.

In fact, in *The Super Servant Two*, there was a *force majeure* clause in the contract. The defendants argued as an alternative defence that, if the contract was not frustrated, the loss of the ship was covered by the *force majeure* clause allowing them to cancel the contract. The clause referred to 'perils or danger and accidents of the sea'. The court held that the clause covered the sinking of Super Servant Two provided this was not caused by the negligence of the defendants.

Finally, on the topic of self-induced frustration, if one party alleges that the other party has caused the frustrating event then it seems that the burden of proving fault is on the party alleging it. This was stated in the case of *Joseph Constantine Steamship Line Ltd v Imperial Smelting Corporation Ltd* [1942] AC 154.

We have now looked at the two restrictions on the doctrine of frustration: self-induced frustration and events foreseen by the parties. We shall now go on to consider whether frustration can apply to leases of land.

5.4.7 Frustration and leases of land

For many years, it was thought that frustration could not apply to a lease of land because a lease actually created an interest in the land, and this interest endured even if you could not use the land for the intended purpose. An interest in land was not a perishable commodity like goods. You may be thinking that the idea that frustration cannot apply to a lease of land does not accord with the decision in *Taylor v Caldwell*. We looked at this case at **5.3**, and we saw that a contract for the hire of a music hall was frustrated. However, the problem of whether a lease could be frustrated did not arise in *Taylor v Caldwell* because the agreement was just a licence to occupy the premises. It was not a lease which created an interest in the land.

The House of Lords looked at whether frustration might apply to leases of land in the case of *National Carriers Ltd v Panalpina (Northern) Ltd* [1981] AC 675. Here, the appellants leased a warehouse from the respondents for a term of 10 years from 1 January 1974. In May 1979 the local authority closed the street giving the only access to the warehouse. This was because of the dangerous condition of a building opposite the warehouse. It was envisaged that the street would be reopened in January 1981. The closure of the street prevented the appellants from using the warehouse. The appellants argued that the lease was frustrated by the closure of the street giving access to the warehouse.

The House of Lords said that the doctrine of frustration was capable of applying to a lease of land so as to bring the lease to an end if a frustrating event occurred during the currency of the term. However, the circumstances in which the doctrine of frustration could apply to a lease of land were rare. On the facts of *Panalpina* the House of Lords decided that the lease was not frustrated.

Although by the time access to the warehouse was restored, the appellants would have lost two out of 10 years' use of the warehouse and their business would have been severely disrupted, the closure of access to the warehouse was not sufficiently grave to amount to a frustrating event since there would be a further three years of the lease remaining after the access was re-established.

Having considered when a contract may be frustrated, we shall now consider the effects of frustration at common law and the extent to which the common law rules have been altered by statute.

5.4.8 Effect of frustration at common law

5.4.8.1 Introduction

If a contract is frustrated, the future performance of the contract is terminated automatically as a matter of law. Therefore, both parties are released from all future obligations (ie obligations arising after the frustrating event) and neither party will be in breach of contract in respect of the frustrating event. It is for this reason that it will be the party who would otherwise be in breach by not performing, who will allege that the contract has been frustrated.

Note that discharge of the contract happens as a matter of law – the non-defaulting party does not have a choice whether, or not, to terminate the contract. If you recall, this is very different to the position where there has been a repudiatory breach of contract where the innocent party has a choice whether to affirm it or accept the breach as ending the contract. We looked at repudiatory breaches earlier in this chapter.

Having reviewed some of the effects of frustration, we shall now go on to consider some further points.

It may be that one party has already paid money to the other, or has incurred expenses in performing the contract, or has received a benefit under the contract. We shall consider whether money paid can be recovered and whether compensation can be claimed for expenses incurred, or a benefit conferred on the other party.

We shall look first at the original common law rules and then at the changes made by legislation.

5.4.8.2 The original position at common law when a contract was frustrated

Originally, at common law, if one party had paid money to the other before the frustrating event, it could not be recovered. Also, if any money was due and payable before the frustrating event, it still had to be paid. Therefore, it was necessary to examine the terms of the contract to decide when the money was due or payable.

Think back to the facts of *Krell v Henry* [1903] 2 KB 740, which we looked at in **5.4.5.2** when we were dealing with the non-occurrence of a fundamental event leading to frustration.

In *Krell v Henry*, the defendant agreed to pay £75 for the hire of rooms overlooking the route of the coronation procession. The defendant paid a deposit of £25. The coronation procession was then cancelled. This happened before the defendant was due to pay the balance of £50.

Applying the principles set out above:

- The defendant could not recover the £25 as this was money paid before the frustrating event.
- The defendant did not have to pay the outstanding £50 as the obligation to pay arose after the frustrating event, ie after cancellation of the coronation procession.

We are now going to compare the above outcome with another coronation case, *Chandler v Webster* [1904] 1 KB 493, where the claimant agreed to hire rooms for £141 to view the coronation procession. The contract stipulated that the entire sum was payable immediately, although the claimant had paid only £100 when the procession was cancelled. The court held:

- The claimant could not recover the £100 as this was money paid before the frustrating event.
- The claimant did have to pay the outstanding £41 as this was money due before the frustrating event occurred, ie before the coronation procession was cancelled.

The common law rules did not produce a fair outcome in cases like *Krell v Henry* and *Chandler v Webster*. In each case, the party who had hired the rooms paid money but received nothing in return when the coronation was cancelled. Clearly, the cancellation of the coronation was not their fault, so they were being severely prejudiced by an event outside their control. In both cases, money paid before the frustrating event could not be recovered. Also, in *Chandler v Webster*, the claimant was still liable to pay more money as this payment was due before the frustrating event occurred.

The injustice of this situation was addressed to a certain extent by the House of Lords in *Fibrosa Spolka Akcyjna v Fairbairn Lawson Combe Barbour Ltd* [1943] AC 32. In *Fibrosa*, the House of Lords stated that if there had been a total failure of consideration then money already paid could be recovered and money due and payable before the event need not be paid. This meant that if the payer had received absolutely no benefit under the contract, the payer could recover money paid and did not have to pay money that was due before the event. However, if any benefit had been received, the money could not be recovered or still had to be paid.

Viscount Simon LC thought that, even after the decision in *Fibrosa*, certain problems still remained. The decision did not address the problem of a party who had incurred expenses carrying out their contractual obligations before frustration occurred. Also, a party may have done almost all the work under the contract but would not be compensated for it.

Viscount Simon LC thought that it was up to the Parliament to deal with the problems which remained. We are now going to look at the legislation which was passed to deal with these issues.

5.4.9 The effect of frustration under the Law Reform (Frustrated Contracts) Act 1943

The Law Reform (Frustrated Contracts) Act 1943 tries to do justice between the parties when a frustrating event has occurred. The Act deals with the following:

- money paid and/or payable by a party before the frustrating event;
- expenses incurred by the payee; and
- valuable benefits obtained by either party.

Section 1(2) contains three key points:

- Money paid before the event can be recovered.
- Money that should have been paid before the event need not be paid.
- At the court's discretion, expenses incurred by the payee in performance of the contract can be recovered out of the total sums paid/payable before the event.

Section 1(2) deals with payments already made, or payments that should have been made but had not been made, before the frustrating event. Pre-payments can be returned. Also, money that should have been paid before the event need not be paid. But under the proviso to s1(2), there is a *very wide discretion* afforded to the courts to allow a payee to recover expenses out of the total money paid *and* payable before the frustrating event.

Note that there are effectively two maximum sums a court can award the payee under the proviso for expenses incurred. If the expenses incurred are less than the total pot of money available under the proviso, then the most the payee can recover is the amount of expenses incurred; otherwise the maximum that can be awarded is the total sum paid and payable before the frustrating event. However, the courts have a very wide discretion when it comes to awarding sums under the proviso to s 1(2) for expenses incurred by the payee, and this was made clear in *Gamerco SA v ICM/Fair Warning (Agency) Ltd* [1995] 1 WLR 1226.

In that case the defendant payee had incurred expenses of $50,000 in performing the contract before the frustrating event. Garland J said that there was no obligation on the court to award total retention or equal division. He said the court has a broad discretion and its task is to do justice in a situation which the parties had not provided for and to mitigate the possible harshness of allowing all loss to lie where it fell. In the event, Garland J did not make an award for expenses under s 1(2) as the payer's expenses were considerably higher than those of the payee.

The common law did not deal with the problem of expenses at all, so s 1(2) is an improvement on the position at common law. However, if no money was paid and/or payable before the frustrating event, s 1(2) does not help.

Section 1(3) of the Law Reform (Frustrated Contracts) Act 1943 applies where one party has conferred a valuable benefit on the other party before the frustrating event. Where this is the case, the court may order the party obtaining the benefit to pay such sum (if any) as the court considers just, but not exceeding the value of the benefit.

All of the circumstances must be taken into account, in particular any expenses that the party who receives the benefit may have incurred before the frustrating event. This includes any expenses which the court has ordered that party to pay to the other under s 1(2). Also, the court must consider whether the frustrating event itself affected the benefit.

The court considered s 1(3) of the Act in *BP Exploration Co (Libya) Ltd v Hunt* [1979] 1 WLR 783. Here, Goff J said that, in the case of an award under s 1(3), there are two distinct stages:

- First, the benefit has to be identified and valued and this then forms the upper limit of the award. Any expenses incurred by the party obtaining the benefit must be deducted from the value of the benefit (including any money ordered to be paid by that party to the other under s 1(2)).

- Secondly, the court has to assess the just sum (which must not exceed the value of the benefit). When assessing a just sum, the court may have regard to the consideration in the contract as evidence of the appropriate level of remuneration.

- Goff J also said that the benefit under s 1(3) is the end product of what the claimant has provided, taking into account the frustrating event, and not the value of work that has been done. To illustrate this argument, he uses the following example: 'Suppose that a contract for work on a building is frustrated by fire which destroys the building and which therefore destroys a substantial amount of the work already done by the [claimant] ... The effect of s 1(3)(b) will be to reduce the award to nil ...'

To sum up, s 1(3) provides that if one party has received a valuable benefit before the frustrating event because of something done by the other party in performance of the contract then the court may order the recipient to pay such sum as the court considers just, but not exceeding the amount of the benefit.

The common law did not deal with the provision of a valuable benefit at all, so s 1(3) is an improvement on the common law position.

Section 2 of the Act allows the parties to put a clause in the contract excluding the Act and making their own provision about the effects of frustration on their contract. We have considered *force majeure* clauses earlier in this chapter.

Section 2 also lists contracts to which the Act does not apply, eg certain charterparties and insurance contracts. In relation to insurance, s 1(5) of the Act specifically provides that the court shall not take into account insurance payments unless there was an express term of the contract imposing an obligation to insure. In the *Gamerco* case, both parties had taken out insurance cover against the particular risk, but as neither party had been bound to do so under the contract, the court ignored any sums paid out by the insurance companies when determining what to do about expenses under s 1(2).

Before we leave the Law Reform (Frustrated Contracts) Act 1943, we shall consider some of the weaknesses of the Act and some of the difficulties which may arise in applying it.

Section 1(2): expenses

The amount recoverable is limited to the total of the sums paid and payable before the frustrating event. Expenses incurred above this amount cannot be recovered. If no money was paid or payable before the frustrating event, s 1(2) does not help at all.

Section 1(2) does not make clear the basis on which an award for expenses is to be calculated. Garland J, in *Gamerco SA v ICM/Fair Warning (Agency) Ltd*, said that the court had a broad discretion. The absence of guidelines as to how this discretion is to be exercised could lead to inconsistencies.

Section 1(3): valuable benefit

It can be difficult to predict how much will be awarded under s 1(3). Also, is it reasonable for the valuable benefit to be the end product of what the claimant has provided rather than the value of the work done (*BP Exploration (Libya) Ltd v Hunt*)? Goff J's interpretation of s 1(3) can produce undesirable results, eg where fire destroys a building on which work had been done, the award under s 1(3) would be nil. (The person who had done the work could claim expenses under s 1(2), but this award would be limited to the amount of money paid and/or payable to that person before the frustrating event.)

It is because of the limitations and uncertainties identified above that parties to a commercial contract prefer to rely on a *force majeure* clause (such as clause 4.3 in the Specimen Standard Conditions of Sale (**Reading 1** in the **Appendix**)).

To appreciate how the common law and the 1943 Act operate in practice when a contract has been frustrated, we are now going to consider a particular set of facts.

Example

Moira agrees to hire a boat from Jane for six weeks beginning on 1 August. Moira pays a £200 deposit and agrees to pay a further £400 on 15 July and the balance of £2,400 on 1 August. They agree that Jane will install some extra bunks. Jane has spent £800 installing the bunks when a fire destroys the boat on 16 July. Moira has not yet paid the £400 due on 15 July.

Assume that the contract has been frustrated.

1. *Moira does not have to pay the balance of £2,400. Frustration of the contract discharges future obligations.*

2. *Section 1(2) says that money paid before the frustrating event can be recovered and money payable before the frustrating event need not be paid. So Moira could recover her £200 deposit and need not pay the £400 (but this is subject to any award that the court makes for Jane's expenses (see below)).*

3. *Under s 1(2) the maximum the court can award for expenses incurred by the payee is a sum equal to the total paid and payable before the frustrating event or the*

amount of the expenses incurred (whichever is the lower sum). In this situation, the total money paid and payable before the frustrating event was £600 (ie the £200 deposit and the £400 due on the 15 July); whereas £800 had been spent by Jane (the payee) in performance of the contract. Therefore, Jane could be awarded a maximum of £600 under s 1(2) and so would not be compensated in full.

The court has a broad discretion when it is contemplating an award for expenses under s 1(2). Its task is to do justice and it is not obliged to award the maximum amount.

4. *Jane has done some work installing extra bunks in the boat. This would constitute a valuable benefit under s 1(3) but, as the frustrating event completely wiped out the work Jane had done before Moira could benefit from it, a 'just sum' might be nil.*

If the fire had destroyed the boat on 8 August, Moira would have had use of the boat for one week and a court may decide that this amounts to a valuable benefit. The court would have to identify and value the benefit taking into account any expenses incurred by Moira, including any money that Moira has to pay Jane under s 1(2). Having done this, the court would then have to decide on a just sum (if any) that Moira should pay. The court could have regard to the consideration (ie the amount Moira agreed to pay for the hire).

The above example was focusing on the effect of frustration and so worked through on the basis that the contract had been frustrated. But where it is unclear on the facts, the first issue will be to determine whether the contract had been frustrated or indeed breached. Only if it has been frustrated will you need to consider the effects of frustration; otherwise you will be advising on the remedies for breach. Set out below is a suggested structure for tackling issues involving alleged frustration of a contract.

Structure for approaching problem questions on frustration

1. Identify which party which will wish to claim frustration, ie the party which would otherwise be in breach for non-performance.

2. General rule in *Paradine v Jane*. Contractual obligations are absolute, ie a party must perform its contractual obligations. If a party does not, it will generally be in breach of contract.

3. Frustration is an exception to this. Define frustration.

4. Go through the definition and apply each part to the facts. For example, has there been a supervening event which makes the contract impossible or radically different to perform? Is there a term in the contract covering the event? Is one of the parties at fault?

5. Effect if the contract is frustrated:
   - The contract comes to an end automatically at the moment of the frustrating event.
   - Neither party is in breach.
   - Each party is completely discharged from all future obligations. Apply to the facts.

Does the Law Reform (Frustrated Contracts) Act 1943 apply? Yes, unless excluded. Consider s 1(2) and (3) of the Law Reform (Frustrated Contracts) Act 1943. Look at each subsection in turn, explain what it says and apply to the facts.

6. If the contract is not frustrated then a party may be in breach of contract. If so, the innocent party can claim damages for breach of contract and may be able to terminate the contract. (We considered how damages are awarded and when a party can terminate in **Chapter 4**.)

So having looked at how to approach problem questions on frustration, let's now think about essay questions on the topic. Essays test your knowledge, but also your ability to critically evaluate a statement or quotation on a particular topic and to express a reasoned conclusion as to whether, or not, you agree with the statement/quotation. We looked at how to approach answering an essay question in **Chapter 2** in the context of downward contractual variations and in particular promissory estoppel.

Set out below is an essay question focussing on the effects of frustration and feedback on how you might approach answering it.

Sample essay question

While mitigating some of the harshness of the common law approach did not solve all the problems, the Law Reform (Frustrated Contracts) Act 1943 makes some attempt to solve these problems. (Wheeler and Shaw, *Contract Law: Cases, Materials and Commentary*)

Explain and comment on the law of frustration in the light of this statement.

In your answer you should demonstrate that you can:

- explain what is meant by frustration;
- refer to the rule of absolute obligations (*Paradine v Jane*). Frustration is an exception to this rule. Define frustration and give examples;
- explain the effect of frustration.

The contract comes to an end at the moment of the frustrating event, the parties are discharged from all future obligations, and damages cannot be recovered as no breach of contract.

Consider the common law rules and *Krell v Henry* and *Chandler v Webster*.

Originally, at common law, if one party had paid money to the other before the frustrating event, it could not be recovered, and if money was payable prior to the frustrating event, it still had to be paid. You should look critically at the decisions in *Krell v Henry* and *Chandler v Webster* and express an opinion on the fairness of the result.

Consider the modification of the common law position by the decision in *Fibrosa*. You should explain the decision in *Fibrosa v Fairbairn Lawson* and look at any problems which remained. The decision in *Fibrosa* only applied where there had been a total failure of consideration. If this condition was not satisfied then the money could not be recovered or still had to be paid.

The decision did not address the problem of a party who had incurred expenses before frustration. Also, a party may have done almost all the work under the contract but would not be compensated for it.

Set out the provisions of the Law Reform (Frustrated Contracts) Act 1943 and express an opinion on the extent to which the Act solves the problems which remained after *Fibrosa*. You should refer to relevant cases, eg Gam*erco SA v ICM Fair Warning (Agency) Ltd* and *BP Exploration (Libya) Ltd v Hunt*.

Section 1(2) is not dependent on a total failure of consideration.

The expenses provision in s 1(2) is an improvement on the common law which did not deal with the problem of expenditure. However, the amount recoverable is limited to the sum paid and payable to the payee before the frustrating event. Expenses above this amount cannot be recovered, and if no money was paid or payable to the payee before the frustrating event then s 1(2) does not help at all. It does not help the payer who may have incurred expenses.

Also, s 1(2) does not make clear the basis on which an award for expenditure will be calculated. Garland J in *Gamerco* said that the court had a broad discretion.

Section 1(3) – valuable benefit. The common law did not deal with the provision of a valuable benefit, so this section is an improvement. You should discuss the difficulty of valuing the benefit and the decision in *BP Exploration v Hunt*.

You might point out that the parties may make their own provision about the effects of frustration and discuss the advantages of doing so. You might also mention that the common law continues to apply to contracts excluded from the Law Reform (Frustrated Contracts) Act 1943.

Figure 5.3 Frustration – summary

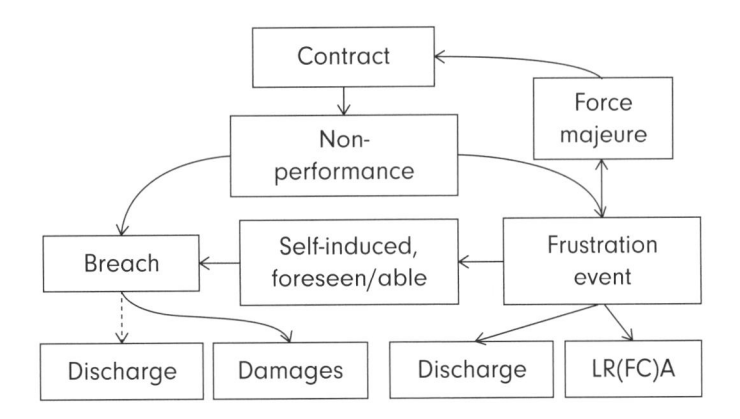

SUMMARY

- You started this chapter by examining the doctrine of complete performance and the exceptions. Therefore, you can see why it may be important to specify the order of performance in the contract and the consequences which may follow if a party has to perform its obligations first and does not do so precisely and exactly.

- You then looked at the ways in which a contract may be discharged. You saw that a party may be able to terminate the contract and the link here with the type of term broken. You also saw that a contract will normally be discharged by performance but could also be discharged by agreement between the parties and the link with consideration which you studied in **Chapter 2**.
- Lastly, you saw that sometimes a contract may come to an end automatically if a frustrating event occurs. Having examined the doctrine of frustration and its effects in some detail, you will appreciate that it is usually better to insert a *force majeure* clause into a contract in the interest of certainty.

6 False Preliminary Statements

LEARNING OUTCOMES

When you have completed this chapter, you should be able to:

- distinguish between different types of pre-contractual statements and explain and apply the guidelines used by the courts;
- explain and discuss in depth the law relating to misrepresentation;
- appreciate the relationship between the law of contract and the law of tort with reference to misrepresentation and breach of contract actions.

6.1 False preliminary statements made by a contracting party

Before we can look in detail at misrepresentation, it is necessary to appreciate when a false preliminary statement will be actionable and to distinguish between when it will amount to breach of an express term of the contract and/or a misrepresentation.

A statement made during contractual negotiations may be:

- A mere puff. This is usually a claim which is extravagant in an obvious way or an advertising gimmick. There is no right of action in respect of this type of statement.
- An express term. A term is part of the contract. If untrue, the innocent party will have a remedy for breach of contract. We dealt with terms in **Chapter 3** and with remedies for breach in **Chapter 4**.
- A representation. A representation is a statement made by one party to the contract which may have induced the other party to enter into the contract but does not form part of it. If untrue, the innocent party may have a remedy if the statement amounts to a misrepresentation.

The law relating to false preliminary statements is important in most areas of contract law. Where a lot of money is at stake, both individuals and business buyers will want assurances about what they are proposing to buy. The main difference is that in most commercial contracts there will be a clause purporting to exclude liability for false preliminary statements. This means that if, and when, a false preliminary statement is made, the initial focus is more likely to be on the validity of the exclusion rather than on the classification of the false statement.

For an example of how a company might seek to exclude liability in this respect, let us look at the Specimen Standard Conditions of Sale set out in **Reading 1** in the **Appendix**. Clause 2.2 provides, inter alia:

> The Seller's sales representatives are not authorised to do any of the following things on behalf of the Seller:
>
> 2.2.1 ... introduce any other terms, written or oral into the Contract and
>
> 2.2.2 ... make any representation ...

Thinking back to **Chapter 2** in which you studied agency, you will realise that this clause is to stop a sales representative binding the seller to any preliminary statement which they might make in trying to promote a sale. Where sales representatives are inexperienced and/or subject to ambitious sales targets, there will always be a risk that they might make exaggerated claims about the products they are selling.

A party may also put a clause in the contract limiting liability for misrepresentation. You can see an example in clause 8.4.1 of the Specimen Conditions of Sale.

Section 3 of the Misrepresentation Act 1967 provides that any clause in a non-consumer contract which purports to exclude or restrict liability for misrepresentation will only be upheld if it satisfies the reasonableness test set out in s 11 of the Unfair Contract Terms Act (UCTA) 1977. Similarly, if you remember back to **Chapter 3** in which you studied UCTA 1977, when one party deals on the other party's written standard terms, it is only possible to exclude liability for breach of an express term if it is reasonable to do so (UCTA 1977, s 3). So, in a commercial context where there is a clause purporting to exclude liability for a false preliminary statement, the main issue is often whether or not the clause is reasonable and as such valid. By contrast, where there is no such exclusion, the initial focus will be on the classification of the false preliminary statement(s) as that will determine the remedies available to the innocent party.

6.2 Distinguishing between terms and representations

It is because the remedies for breach of contract and misrepresentation differ that it is important to decide whether a false preliminary statement is a term or only a representation. In practice, the claimant might claim both breach of contract and misrepresentation in the alternative, but there will be no double recovery.

The primary test for determining whether a statement is a term or a representation is the common intention of the parties when they entered the contract. Did they intend the particular statement to be a contractual term, or did they intend it to be only a representation? If that intention is not clear, there are a number of guidelines the court will consider namely:

- Whether one party had greater skill or knowledge of the subject matter.
- Whether a statement made verbally was repeated in a written contract before it was agreed.
- Whether the recipient of the statement made clear it was of vital importance.
- Whether the statement maker invited the other party to verify it.
- Whether there was a lapse of time between the statement being made and the contract being formed.

We will now consider each of the above guidelines in more detail.

6.2.1 The relative skill and knowledge of the parties

If an expert makes a false preliminary statement to a non-expert, the statement may well be deemed to be a term of the contract; conversely, if a non-expert makes a false preliminary statement to an expert, the statement is more likely to be deemed a simple representation.

This guideline is well illustrated by *Oscar Chess Ltd v Williams* [1957] 1 WLR 370, CA and *Dick Bentley Productions Ltd v Harold Smith (Motors) Ltd* [1965] 1 WLR 623.

In *Oscar Chess Ltd v Williams* the defendant sold a second-hand car to the claimant, a motor dealer, for £290. The price had been calculated on the basis of information in the registration book (which was inspected by the claimant) which stated that the car was first registered in 1948, and the defendant had no reason to doubt that fact. The following year, the claimant discovered from the manufacturer that the car was a 1939 model. Had the claimant been aware of that fact, the claimant would only have paid the defendant £175 for the car. Thus, the claimant tried to recover the difference by bringing an action for breach of contract, but the action failed. The majority of the Court of Appeal held that as the claimant knew the defendant had no personal knowledge of when the car was manufactured, and as the claimant was in at least as good a position to know this, the defendant had simply made an innocent misrepresentation.

To quote Denning LJ:

> It is sometimes supposed that the tribunal must look into the minds of the parties to see what they themselves intended. That is a mistake ... The question whether a warranty was intended depends on the conduct of the parties, on their words and behaviour, rather than on their thoughts. If an intelligent bystander would reasonably infer that a warranty was intended, that will suffice ... When the seller states a fact which is or should be within his own knowledge and of which the buyer is ignorant, intending that the buyer should act on it and he does so, it is easy to infer a warranty ... So also if he makes a promise about something which is or should be within his own control ... But if the seller when he states a fact, makes it clear that he has no knowledge of his own but has got his information elsewhere, and is merely passing it on, it is not so easy to imply a warranty.

The case of *Dick Bentley v Harold Smith Motors* also involved the sale of a car, but in this case it was a car dealer selling to a private individual (the claimant). The defendant had told the claimant (relying on the odometer reading) that the car had only done 20,000 miles and this was one of the reasons that had prompted the claimant to buy the car. The claimant subsequently discovered that the car's stated mileage was false and sued for breach of contract. In this case, the claimant was successful.

6.2.2 Whether a statement made verbally was repeated in a written contract before it was agreed

If so, it is good evidence that the statement was intended to be a term but, if not, it could well be just a representation. As with all the factors though, this one is not conclusive. For example, in *Birch v Paramount Estates* the seller's oral promise was not repeated in the written contract but the court still decided it was a term of the contract. This meant that the contract in *Birch v Paramount Estates* was partly written and partly oral.

6.2.3 Whether the recipient of the statement made clear it was of vital importance

If so, it is likely the statement will be deemed a contract term. This guideline is illustrated by the case of *Bannerman v White* (1861) 10 CB NS 844 where the buyer of hops asked the seller if the plants had been treated with sulphur. The buyer added that, if they had, they would not even ask the price. The seller assured the buyer that sulphur had not been used. This assurance was held to be a term of the contract.

6.2.4 Whether the statement maker invited the other party to verify it

If so, the statement may well be just a representation. In *Ecay v Godfrey* (1947) 80 Ll L Rep 286, the seller of a boat asked the buyer if they were going to have it surveyed. The court decided that this question indicated that the seller did not intend their previous statement about the condition of the boat to be a term.

Conversely, if the seller tells the buyer not to bother with a survey, this points to a statement about the quality of goods being a term. The authority for this is *Schawel v Reade* [1913] 2 IR 81, HL.

6.2.5 Whether there was a lapse of time between the statement being made and the contract being formed

The longer the time lapse, the more likely the statement will be held to be a representation. Authority for this is *Routledge v McKay* [1954] 1 WLR 615. During pre-contractual negotiations for the sale and purchase of a motorcycle, the seller, taking information from the registration book, said on 23 October that the cycle was a 1942 model. On 30 October a written contract of sale was made which did not refer to the date of the model. The actual date was later found to be 1930. The buyer's claim for breach of contract failed. There had been a marked interval between the negotiations and the contract.

It is not a scoring system. Some of the above guidelines tend to carry greater weight than the others eg the relative skill and knowledge of the parties.

6.2.6 Summary – classification of actionable pre-contractual statements

We have seen that the test for determining whether a false preliminary statement is a term or a representation is the common intention of the parties. If that is not clear, the court will consider a number of guidelines and factors.

If, after having applied the guidelines, you conclude that a false preliminary statement may have been an express term of the contract, it is then necessary to consider remedies for breach (see **Chapter 4**). Furthermore, if the false preliminary statement is a misdescription of goods, it may amount to breach of the statutory implied condition that goods sold by description should match that description (Sale of Goods Act 1979, s 13, Supply of Goods and Services Act 1982, s 3 and Consumer Rights Act 2015, s 11), in which case you would need to consider damages, the possibility of rejecting the goods and, if appropriate, the additional remedies available to buyers dealing as consumers (see **Chapter 3**).

If you conclude that a false preliminary statement may have been a representation, the next step is to determine whether it amounts to a misrepresentation. If it does, you should consider the remedies available for misrepresentation. We shall now look at misrepresentation in detail.

6.3 Misrepresentation

6.3.1 What is a misrepresentation?

To have a remedy if a representation turns out to be untrue, the innocent party must establish that a misrepresentation has occurred. The definition of a misrepresentation is technical, but basically it is a false statement of fact made by one contracting party to the other before the contract was made and which was one of the factors which induced the other party to enter into the contract.

We shall now consider each part of the definition in turn.

6.3.1.1 False statement

There must be a false statement

The statement may be oral, in writing or by conduct.

In *Spice Girls v Aprilia World Service BV* [2000] EMLR 748, the court held that by participating in the filming of a TV commercial, the pop group Spice Girls represented that they did not know or have reasonable grounds to believe that any members intended to leave. This was untrue. Their participation in the filming amounted to a misrepresentation by conduct, and the sponsor who had relied on the misrepresentation when entering into the sponsorship contract was entitled to damages.

Conduct should be distinguished from silence

The general rule is that silence in itself will not amount to a misrepresentation (*Hamilton and Others v Allied Domecq plc* [2007] UKHL 33). There are four exceptions to this rule namely:

(a) where there is a fiduciary relationship between the parties, eg solicitor and client or trustee and beneficiary;

(b) where the contract is one of the utmost good faith, eg an insurance contract;

(c) where there has been a half-truth, ie where what was not said positively distorts what was actually said. For example, a car is advertised 'one lady owner'; this is true but ignores the other previous owners who happened to be men, giving the misleading impression that there has been just one owner and that the one owner was a lady – the moral is to tell the whole truth, or nothing at all. A case involving a half-truth is *Curtis v Chemical Cleaning and Dyeing* [1951] 1 KB 805. You considered the facts of this case in **Chapter 3** in the context of exemption clauses, and you will consider them again later in this chapter;

(d) where a statement of fact is true when made, but a change of circumstances occurs before the contract is formed which makes the statement untrue. Failure to disclose the change in circumstances may amount to a misrepresentation. This is illustrated by *With v O'Flanagan* [1936] Ch 575, where the vendor of a medical practice told the potential buyer in January that the practice was worth £2,000 a year. This was true at the time, but before the sale went through in May profits had dropped considerably due to the vendor having been ill. The change in circumstance was not disclosed to the buyer. This was held to be a misrepresentation and the contract was set aside.

6.3.1.2 The false statement must be fact not opinion or intention

To amount to a misrepresentation, the statement must be one of fact and not opinion. However, if the opinion is not genuine, or there are no reasonable grounds for the maker to believe it to be true, or if the statement is made by a person who is in the best position to know the true facts, then there may be an implied false statement of fact which may amount to a misrepresentation if the other elements of the definition are satisfied.

In *Smith v Land and House Property Corporation* (1884) 28 Ch D 7 the seller of a tenanted property described the tenant as 'most desirable'. The seller knew that the tenant was in arrears with the rent and so had no reasonable ground for describing the tenant as 'desirable'. Bowen LJ said: 'if the facts are not equally known to both sides, then a statement of opinion by one who knows the facts best involves very often a statement of fact for he impliedly states that he knows facts which justify his opinion.'

Contrast this with the case of *Bisset v Wilkinson* [1927] AC 177. In *Bisset v Wilkinson*, the seller of a farm was asked about the number of sheep the farm could sustain. The farm had never held sheep, but the seller said that in their personal judgement it would support 2,000 sheep. The statement was held to be opinion rather than fact, because both parties knew that the maker of the statement had not carried on sheep farming on the land and that the land had never been used for this purpose. By contrast, in *Smith*, the maker of the statement was in possession of facts (knowledge of the arrears of rent) which indicated that the tenant was not desirable.

A statement of intention will not amount to a misrepresentation unless it can be shown that the intention was never held. In *Edgington v Fitzmaurice* (1885) 24 Ch D 459, the directors of a company said the purpose of borrowing money was to expand the company's business. In fact, the loan was needed to pay the company's debts. The court held that the directors had made a misrepresentation. They never intended to use the money to expand the business; they had made a false statement about the state of their minds.

6.3.1.3 The statement must be made by one party to a contract to the other

If the maker of the statement is not the other contracting party, there cannot be a claim for misrepresentation. It may be possible to bring a claim in tort for negligent misstatement or deceit (both of which are dealt with later in this chapter) if the requisite conditions are satisfied.

6.3.1.4 The statement must have been one of the factors which induced the party to enter the contract

The statement does not have to be the only reason why a party enters into a contract provided it did encourage that party to do so. The authority for this is the case of *Edgington v Fitzmaurice*, which you considered earlier.

Where, however, a party does not rely on the other party's statement but instead has it checked out by their own experts, there will not have been a misrepresentation: the false statement did not act as an inducement to enter the contract. This principle was decided in the case of *Attwood v Small* (1938) 6 Cl&F 232.

A claimant may still claim that a false statement induced them to enter the contract if they were given the chance to verify the facts but did not take it up (*Redgrave v Hurd*). However, this principle may not be applied where the true position was set out in the contract signed by the claimant.

This is illustrated by *Peekay Intermark Ltd v Australia and New Zealand Banking Group Ltd* [2006] 2 Lloyd's Rep 511. The bank had described an investment to the claimant (an experienced businessperson) in general terms. The claimant was later sent a contract setting out the full terms and conditions. The claimant looked at the contract only briefly before signing it. The claimant assumed the terms were in line with what they had been told, but that was not the case. The claimant sued for misrepresentation, but the Court of Appeal held that the bank had not misrepresented the written contract itself. The claimant was an experienced businessperson and had looked at it and decided to sign it. It was not open to the claimant to argue they had been induced by an earlier representation.

The facts of this case need to be contrasted with those of *Curtis v Chemical Cleaning and Dyeing*, considered in **Chapter 3** in connection with incorporation of terms. In *Curtis* the claimant was a consumer who had been misled about the extent of an exclusion clause in a document which had been signed when handing over a wedding dress (for dry cleaning). The claimant in that case asked about the contents of the document before signing and was entitled to rely on what the claimant had been told by the dry cleaners about the exemption. In *Peekay Intermark Ltd*, however, the claimant was an experienced businessperson and should have known better than simply to rely on a rough and ready explanation of the investment.

6.3.1.5 Burden of proof

The party who alleges that a misrepresentation has occurred bears the burden of proving that the definition of a misrepresentation has been satisfied.

We have looked at what constitutes a misrepresentation. We shall now consider the remedies which may be available.

6.3.2 Remedies for misrepresentation

To some extent, the remedies available for misrepresentation depend on whether the misrepresentation is fraudulent or non-fraudulent.

We shall start by considering the remedy of rescission, which is available whether the misrepresentation is fraudulent or non-fraudulent.

6.3.2.1 Rescission

The effect of any misrepresentation is to make the contract voidable, ie the contract is valid unless and until the innocent party rescinds it. If a contract is rescinded, it is sometimes said that the contract is 'set aside' or 'avoided'.

The innocent party does not have to rescind the contract – they may affirm the contract, ie treat the contract as continuing.

(a) How to rescind a contract

In order to rescind the contract, the innocent party must notify the other party so that they are aware that this is what the innocent party has decided to do. But what if the other party has disappeared? What then can the claimant do to rescind?

Imagine for a moment that you sell your car through your local newspaper to a stranger. A couple of days later, you discover you have been conned (eg the cheque you were given as payment is dishonoured). What you would want to do is rescind the contract and get back your car, but the rogue buyer has disappeared. What would you do? Report the incident to the police?

In *Car and Universal Finance Co Ltd v Caldwell* [1964] 1 All ER 290, the innocent party, in similar circumstances, tried to recover the car by reporting the matter to the police and the Automobile Association. The court held that by doing this, the innocent party had made it clear that they sought to rescind the contract, and as such ownership of the car immediately reverted to them. Consequently, when the rogue buyer *later* purported to sell the car to an innocent third party, the rogue no longer owned it (as ownership had reverted to the original owner) and so the rogue could not pass ownership of the car on to the buyer. So, as regards the two innocent parties (ie the original seller and the ultimate buyer), it was the original seller who was held entitled to the car.

As well as giving notice to the defaulting party, a claimant can always apply to court for a formal order of rescission. In fact, in some cases the claimant may have to apply for an order of rescission if the other party will not cooperate.

One of the main things to remember about rescission is that it is potentially available for all forms of misrepresentation, whether fraudulent or non-fraudulent, provided it is not barred in either practical or legal terms. You will be looking at the bars to rescission shortly.

Having looked at how to rescind a contract, we shall now consider the effect of rescission.

(b) The effect of rescission

The aim of rescission is to restore both parties as far as possible to their pre-contract positions. So, if a contract is rescinded, each party should return to the other money or property transferred under the contract, and neither party need perform any future obligations. Think of it as hitting the rewind button – to go back to the start.

> ⭐ **Example**
>
> Zena has bought a car from Keith. Keith has delivered the car to her and she has paid him £7,000. She still has a further £500 to pay and she will pay this when he installs a Sat Nav in the car.
>
> Assume that Keith has made a misrepresentation to Zena, eg about the age or mileage of the car. If Zena rescinds:
>
> - Zena will return the car to Keith.
> - Keith will return the £7,000 Zena has already paid.
> - Keith will not have to install a Sat Nav.
> - Zena will not have to pay Keith the further £500.
>
> Notice that each party must return to the other money or property transferred.
>
> If Zena wishes to recover the money she has paid to Keith, she must be prepared to return the car. She cannot keep the car and get her money back. The principle behind this rule is to make sure that Zena is not unjustly enriched by rescinding the contract.

(c) Bars to rescission

Rescission is an equitable remedy and the right to rescind will be lost in certain situations. When this happens, there is said to be a bar to rescission. There are four bars to rescission namely:

- where a bona fide purchaser has acquired rights in the property;
- affirmation;
- undue delay;
- where restitution is impossible.

The first three listed above are equitable bars. The last one is a practical bar to rescission. Let us now consider each of these bars in turn.

Where an innocent purchaser acquires an interest in the property before the contract is rescinded

Think back to the case of *Car & Universal Finance v Caldwell* where a rogue bought a car as a result of a misrepresentation and then disappeared. Can you remember what the innocent party did as soon as they discovered that they had been conned?

The seller notified the police and the Automobile Association (AA), and that had the effect of immediately transferring ownership of the car back to them. This was important on the facts, as following notification to the police and the AA the rogue had sold the car to an innocent third party, and the main question before the court was which of the two innocent parties (ie the original seller or innocent buyer) should get the car, and which should be left having to sue the rogue for their loss. As the original seller was deemed to have rescinded the contract (and thus regained ownership of the car) before the sale to the innocent purchaser, the court found in favour of the original seller.

Had the facts been different and the rogue had resold the car to the innocent purchaser before the police and the AA had been notified, rescission would have been barred. An innocent purchaser who acquires an interest in the property before the contract is avoided is a bar to rescission.

Affirmation

A second bar to rescission is affirmation. On discovery of a misrepresentation, an innocent party has a choice: elect to affirm the contract, or rescind it. If the innocent party elects to affirm, they cannot then change their mind.

Affirmation may be express (ie the misled party may tell the other they are continuing with the contract) or implied. Affirmation will be implied if the misled party behaves in such a way as to lead the other to believe that they are continuing with the contract.

Going back to the Example above, if Zena knew about Keith's misrepresentation but did something that indicated she was treating the contract as continuing (eg, she got him to fit the Sat Nav and paid him the £500), she would probably be regarded as affirming the contract and would lose her right to rescind.

Undue delay

A third equitable bar to rescission is undue delay, which is illustrated by the case of *Leaf v International Galleries* [1950] 2 KB 86. The claimant had bought a painting which had been described as an original John Constable. Five years later, the claimant discovered it had not been painted by Constable. As a result, the claimant sought to rescind the contract for the purchase of the painting, but the action failed due to lapse of time.

Lord Denning thought that the claimant's claim to rescind was barred because the right to reject the goods for breach of a condition of the contract would have been barred (**Chapter 3**). The claimant had had the chance to examine the picture within a few days of purchase and discover the misrepresentation. A delay of five years meant the contract could not be rescinded.

The *Leaf* case illustrates that, in calculating delay, the court does not necessarily look at when the misrepresentation was actually discovered, but at when it should have been discovered. Lord Denning thought the misrepresentation should have been discovered very soon after purchase. It was not.

However, the principle that time runs from when the misrepresentation should have been discovered does not apply to a fraudulent misrepresentation. If there is a fraudulent misrepresentation then time runs from when the misrepresentation was actually discovered. We shall look at what constitutes fraudulent misrepresentation later in this chapter.

Where it is impossible for a party substantially to restore goods or property to the other

We saw in the Example above that if a contract is rescinded then each party should return to the other property and money which had been transferred under the contract. So Zena had to return the car to Keith, and Keith had to refund the price. But what if in the meantime the car had been involved in an accident and had been damaged, or even destroyed? Would rescission then have been possible?

If the car had simply been damaged then substantial restoration would be possible and a court would probably order Zena to return the car, but she would not get back the full price she had paid; instead, the price would be reduced to reflect the extent of the damage to the car. If the car had been destroyed, arguably restoration would be impossible and rescission would be barred.

A case which illustrates the fact that restoration does not have to be exact is *Erlanger v New Sombrero Phosphate Co* (1878) 3 App Cas 1218. There, a contract for the purchase of a mine was rescinded even though the mine had been worked and was therefore not in the same state as when it had been purchased. Lord Blackburn said that the court:

> can take account of profits and make allowance for deterioration and I think the practice has always been for a court of equity to give this relief whenever it can do what is practically just, though it cannot restore the parties precisely to the state they were in before the contract.

In the *Erlanger* case, the purchaser returned the mine, and the court ordered that the purchaser should give an allowance to the seller for the profit they had made using it, and for the deterioration in the state of the mine.

One case in which this bar did operate and where the contract was not rescinded is *Crystal Palace FC (2000) Ltd v Iain Dowie* [2007] EWHC 1392 (QB). The claimant had entered into a compromise agreement with Iain Dowie (its former manager) releasing him from his employment contract with the club. Under the employment contract, the defendant had been required to pay the club £1 million compensation if he left prematurely to work for a premiership club. The compromise agreement released the defendant from this obligation to pay the compensation. Very shortly after entering the compromise agreement, the defendant was appointed manager of a premiership club.

The court held that the defendant had deceived the claimant into entering the compromise agreement. He had lied about his reasons for wanting to leave, but the court refused an order for rescission. If the compromise agreement had been rescinded, it would have revived the defendant's employment contract with the claimant. The claimant had in the meantime appointed another manager, and the defendant was now employed as a manager of another club. The defendant could not perform two employment contracts at the same time. Practical justice meant the making of appropriate orders for damages, but not an order for rescission.

It is for this reason that a contract for the sale of a business is rarely rescinded. A business is likely to have changed its position (eg by entering into contracts with third parties), rendering rescission impossible.

Summary

To sum up, there are four bars to rescission, ie:

- where an innocent purchaser has acquired an interest in the subject matter of the contract before purported rescission of the contract;
- affirmation;
- undue delay;
- where it is impossible substantially to restore goods or property.

(d) Indemnity

If a contract is rescinded then the innocent party can claim an indemnity for expenses necessarily incurred as a result of entering into the contract. This means the indemnity is very restricted and is only available as part of rescission.

In *Whittington v Seale-Hayne* (1900) 82 LT 49 the claimant took a lease of premises belonging to the defendant. A clause in the lease provided that the tenant had to do certain repairs and pay rent and rates. The claimant planned to use the premises to breed chickens. Before the contract, the defendant told the claimant that the premises were in a good sanitary condition, but this was not the case. The water supply was polluted and the claimant and their manager became ill and many chickens died. The claimant wanted to rescind the contract (ie give up the lease) and also asked for an indemnity to cover the following:

- cost of the chickens;
- loss of profit on the sale of the chickens;

- rent paid to the defendants;
- vet's bill;
- medical expenses;
- repairs carried out under the provisions of the lease; and
- rates paid in accordance with the lease.

Which items do you think an indemnity would cover? Which losses had necessarily been incurred under the contract, ie the lease? Only the rent, repairs and rates, all of which had been obligations under the lease.

The lease did not say the farm had to be used to breed chickens, so the claimant could not get an indemnity for the loss of the chickens, loss of profit and vet's and medical bills.

The claimant in *Whittington v Seale-Hayne* wanted the indemnity because, when the case was decided in 1900, damages were only available for fraudulent misrepresentation and here the misrepresentation had not been made fraudulently. Asking for an indemnity was a way of getting financial compensation. Now, damages are usually available for non-fraudulent misrepresentation, and an indemnity is only likely to be claimed in a situation where the claimant has no right to damages. We will consider when damages are available for non-fraudulent misrepresentation later in the chapter.

(e) Damages in lieu of rescission

In certain cases where the claimant asks the court for an order of rescission, the court may award damages in lieu of rescission under s 2(2) of the Misrepresentation Act 1967:

> **2**(2) Where a person has entered into a contract after a misrepresentation has been made to him otherwise than fraudulently, and he would be entitled, by reason of the misrepresentation, to rescind the contract, then, if it is claimed, in any proceedings arising out of the contract, that the contract ought to be or has been rescinded, the court or arbitrator may declare the contract subsisting and award damages in lieu of rescission, if of opinion that it would be equitable to do so, having regard to the nature of the misrepresentation and the loss that would be caused by it if the contract were upheld, as well as to the loss that rescission would cause to the other party.

Note the following:

- The court can award damages in lieu of rescission only if the misrepresentation is non-fraudulent.
- The claimant does not have a right to damages under s 2(2). The court has a discretion to award damages in lieu of rescission.
- The court will not award damages in lieu of rescission under s 2(2) if the right to rescind has been lost, ie if one of the bars to rescission applies.
- A court is likely to exercise its discretion only where the false statement was about a minor matter and it would be unjust to allow the other party to rescind the contract.

6.3.2.2 Damages

Where a misrepresentation has occurred, the innocent party may be able to claim damages in addition to either rescinding the contract or affirming it. The nature of the claim depends to a certain extent on whether the misrepresentation was fraudulent or non-fraudulent.

(a) Damages for fraudulent misrepresentation

If the innocent party can prove that the misrepresentation was made fraudulently then they can sue for damages in the tort of deceit.

If a party wishes to allege fraudulent misrepresentation then the onus is on that party to prove fraud, ie they must show the false representation was made knowingly or without belief in its truth, or recklessly, careless whether it be true or false (per Lord Herschell in *Derry v Peek* (1889) 14 App Cas 337).

A statement made honestly will therefore not be fraudulent. Unless it is an obvious case of fraud, it may be difficult to prove. It will often be one person's word against another's.

Damages are assessed on tort principles, ie the court will aim to put the innocent party in the position they would have been in if the misrepresentation (and the contract) had not been made. So, basically, it calculates how much the claimant is 'out of pocket' as a result of the misrepresentation.

However, the damages for fraudulent misrepresentation may be more extensive than is usually the case in tort because the usual tortious remoteness rule of reasonable forseeability does not apply, and the claimant can recover for all loss directly resulting from the defendant's misrepresentation.

The case of *East v Maurer* [1991] 2 All ER 733 involved a fraudulent misrepresentation by the seller of a hair dressing salon. East had bought the business in reliance on the seller's deliberate false assertion that he (Maurer) intended to stop working at his other hair dressing salon in the same town. As a result of the unexpected competition from Maurer, East's business was unsuccessful and was eventually sold at a loss. One of the questions the Court of Appeal had to consider was what could be claimed in damages to represent the loss of profit suffered by East as a result of the false statement. The court concluded that tortious principles should be used to calculate the loss of profit suffered – meaning that the innocent party should be put into the position they would have been in, had the misrepresentation not been made. If the misrepresentation had not been made, East would not have bought that particular hair dressing salon; he would have bought a similar one instead. So East was awarded damages representing the difference between the profit he in fact made and the profit he would have made had he bought a similar business. This is a different calculation to that which is used when determining damages under ordinary breach of contract principles that you considered in **Chapter 4**. There the aim of damages is to put the innocent party, so far as money can do it, into the position they would have been in, had the contract been properly performed, ie loss of bargain damages (*Robinson v Harman*). So, if damages in *East v Maurer* had been awarded on this basis, East would have got a sum representing the difference between the profit he actually made and the profit he would have made had the statement been true.

Having looked at fraudulent misrepresentation, we shall now go on to consider liability for non-fraudulent misrepresentation.

(b) Damages for non-fraudulent misrepresentation

The claimant may ask for damages under s 2(1) of the Misrepresentation Act 1967. All the claimant has to show is that there was a misrepresentation that caused loss.

Damages under s 2(1) are awarded in accordance with tort principles. The aim of the court is to put the innocent party in the position they would have been if the misrepresentation (and the contract) had not been made.

Also, in the case of *Royscot Trust Ltd v Rogerson* [1991] 3 All ER 294, the Court of Appeal held that damages under s 2(1) should be awarded in the same way as damages for fraudulent misrepresentation in the tort of deceit. The effect of this decision is that when damages are awarded under s 2(1), the usual forseeability rule does not apply.

We shall now look in more detail at s 2(1):

> **2**(1) Where a person has entered into a contract after a misrepresentation has been made to him by another party thereto and as a result thereof he has suffered loss, then, if the person making the misrepresentation would be liable to

damages in respect thereof had the misrepresentation been made fraudulently, that person shall be so liable notwithstanding that the misrepresentation was not made fraudulently, unless he proves that he had reasonable ground to believe and did believe up to the time the contract was made that the facts represented were true.

Note the following:

- Section 2(1) can only be used by a party to a contract against the other contracting party. The section applies 'where a person has entered into a contract after a misrepresentation has been made to them by another party thereto'.

- If the false preliminary statement has not been made by the other contracting party then s 2(1) will not help the claimant. The only claims will be in the tort of deceit or for a negligent misstatement. (We shall look briefly at negligent misstatements later in this chapter.)

- Once the claimant establishes that a misrepresentation has been made then the defendant will be liable to pay damages under s 2(1) unless the defendant proves that they had reasonable grounds to believe and did honestly believe up to the time the contract was made that the facts represented were true. Notice, therefore, that the burden of proof is on the party making the misrepresentation.

- Part of s 2(1) says '... if the person making the misrepresentation would be liable to damages in respect thereof had the misrepresentation been made fraudulently, that person shall be so liable ...'.

In the case of *Royscot Trust Ltd v Rogerson* [1991] 2 QB 297, Balcombe LJ interpreted the words 'so liable' literally, ie to mean liable as if the misrepresentation had been made fraudulently; rather than to mean simply 'liable in damages'. Literal interpretation of the words 'so liable' ignores the policy behind the introduction of s 2(1), which was to allow damages to be recovered where the misrepresentation had been made negligently (rather than fraudulently).

The damages available under the tort of negligence are for reasonably foreseeable losses, whereas in the tort of deceit a claimant is entitled to recover all losses, even if not reasonably foreseeable. The policy behind the broader principle of damages for deceit was to punish a deliberate wrongdoing.

As the purpose behind s 2(1) was simply to introduce a right to damages for negligent misrepresentation, is it likely to have been Parliament's intention that more extensive damages should be available under the section than under the tort of negligence?

Balcombe LJ's interpretation has been criticised, and in the case of *Smith New Court Ltd v Scrimgeour Vickers Ltd* [1996] 4 All ER 769, Lord Steyn said:

> The question is whether the rather loose wording of the statute compels the court to treat a person who was morally innocent as if he was guilty of fraud when it comes to the measure of damages. There has been trenchant criticism of the *Royscot* case ... since this point does not directly arise in the present case, I express no concluded view of the correctness of the *Royscot* case.

The decision in *Royscot* has the effect of reducing the importance of the tort of deceit. There seems little point in trying to establish that the defendant was fraudulent when damages will be awarded in the same way under s 2(1) and the burden of proof is reversed (ie, the defendant will be liable to pay damages under s 2(1) unless they can show that they honestly and reasonably believed the statement to be true). For the time being, however, the *Royscot* case represents the legal position.

We have seen that once the claimant establishes that a misrepresentation has been made which has caused loss, the defendant will be liable to pay damages under s 2(1) unless the defendant proves that they had reasonable grounds to believe, and did believe, up to the time the contract was made, that the facts represented were true.

The difficulty faced by the misrepresentor in discharging the burden of proof under s 2(1) is illustrated by *Howard Marine & Dredging v Ogden* [1978] 2 All ER 1134, CA. In this case the owner of a barge (the defendant) told a potential charterer that its capacity was about 1,600 tonnes. The defendant based this figure on their recollection of the relevant entry in the *Lloyd's Register*, which stated that the capacity was 1,800 tonnes. The capacity was in fact much less, and the defendant would have discovered this if they had consulted the ship's documents. The charterers later sought to claim damages from the defendant under s 2(1) of the Misrepresentation Act 1967 and succeeded.

The defendant had failed to prove that it had had reasonable grounds to believe in the truth of the statement. The defendant had only consulted *Lloyd's Register*. This was not enough to give reasonable grounds for believing it to be true. The correct information could be found in the shipping documents, which had been seen, but then forgotten.

This case shows how difficult it is to establish reasonable grounds for belief. The maker of the statement had checked an authoritative source which most people would assume would be accurate, but the defendant was still liable under s 2(1).

If the defendant does establish reasonable grounds to believe the statement was true then the claimant will have no right to damages under s 2(1). However, as we have seen, the claimant may be able to rescind the contract (if rescission is not barred and the court does not exercise its discretion to order damages in lieu of rescission under s 2(2) of the Misrepresentation Act 1967).

So, if the defendant establishes the defence to the claimant's s 2(1) damages claim and rescission is barred, the claimant will have no remedy.

Misrepresentation Act 1967, s 2(1) – summary of key points

- Section 2(1) provides that once the claimant has established that a misrepresentation has been made and that they have suffered loss as a result, then the defendant will be liable to pay damages unless the defendant can prove that they had reasonable grounds to believe, and did believe up to the time the contract was made, that the statement was true.

- The burden of proving reasonable grounds for belief is on the party making the statement and this may be difficult to do – *Howard Marine & Dredging v Ogden*.

- Damages under s 2(1) are awarded in accordance with tort principles. The aim of the court is to put the claimant in the position they would have been if the misrepresentation (and the contract) had not been made.

- Damages under s 2(1) are awarded in exactly the same way as damages for fraudulent misrepresentation in the tort of deceit, which means that the usual foreseeability rule does not apply – *Royscot Trust Ltd v Rogerson*.

6.4 Negligent misstatements

It may be possible for a person to sue for damages in the tort of negligence if there has been a negligent misstatement. Generally, pure economic loss is not recoverable in tort. However, in the case of *Hedley Byrne & Co v Heller* [1964] AC 465, the House of Lords recognised an exception to this rule in the case of a negligent misstatement which caused economic loss.

A negligent misstatement is not limited to a statement of fact, eg it can be a statement of opinion. Also, it is not limited to a false statement made by the other contracting party.

In *Hedley Byrne*, the House of Lords said, *obiter*, that a duty of care can extend to careless statements where a 'special relationship' exists between the parties. Briefly, it means the statement was relied on, the maker knew it was being relied on, and it was reasonable to rely on it.

One advantage of suing for negligent misstatement is that the statement need not amount to a misrepresentation as such, eg there need not be a contractual relationship between the parties and the statement need not be one of fact. If, however, misrepresentation can be proved, it is usually better to bring an action under s 2(1) of the Misrepresentation Act 1967, as the burden of proof is reversed and the damages are better (eg as a result of *Royscot* there is no longer a problem with remoteness of damage under s 2(1)).

The claimant in a negligent misstatement claim must prove that the maker of the statement owed them a duty of care and had breached this duty causing loss, and the normal negligence remoteness rules will apply – ie the loss must be forseeable.

6.5 Conclusion

You have now completed the topic of false preliminary statements. Set out below is a suggested structure for tackling problem questions on this topic.

Suggested structure

1. Is there a contract? Usually there is no difficulty establishing that all the essential elements are present.
2. Is the statement a term and/or a representation? The test is the intention of the parties. Consider the guidelines.
3. If the statement is a term of the contract, the maker of the statement will be in breach of contract. Briefly consider remedies available.
4. If the statement is a representation, can the injured party prove misrepresentation? Define misrepresentation. Is each part of the definition satisfied?
5. If there has been a misrepresentation, consider the remedies available:
   (a) Rescission.
      - Do any of the bars to rescission apply?
      - Damages under s 2(2) in lieu of rescission?
   (b) Damages. What kind of misrepresentation is it? Even if fraudulent, it may be easier to sue for damages under s 2(1) of the Misrepresentation Act 1967. Deal with the burden of proof and how damages are assessed.
6. If a false statement has been made by a person who is not a party to a contract, consider negligent misstatement.

ACTIVITY 1 False preliminary statements

Using the suggested structure above attempt to answer the problem question set out below. Then compare your answer with the Feedback to see how well you have remembered and understood the rules relating to the classification of pre-contractual statements and the remedies available if they are actionable. The question also creates links with some of the statutory implied terms you looked at in **Chapter 3**.

Contract

Facts

On 1 December, Michael, a private collector of antiques, saw a carved ivory elephant in an antiques shop on the local high street. Andrea, the owner of the shop, told him that in her opinion it was from the Mogul period in the sixteenth century. She added that she was sure that the elephant's eyes were made out of precious stones.

Michael did not buy the elephant but said he would think about it. The next day he went to see his friend Carol in her office. She specialises in sixteenth-century history. Michael asked her to look at the elephant for him. Carol did so and assured Michael that it was genuinely from the Mogul period in the sixteenth century. Carol did not know, however, if Andrea's statement about the eyes was true. On 8 December, Michael bought the elephant for £300.

Six months later he took the elephant to be valued by an auctioneer. The auctioneer told him, correctly, that it was a nineteenth-century reproduction, the eyes were not made from precious stones, and that it was worth only £100.

Explain Michael's legal position as regards Andrea.

FEEDBACK

Is there a contract?

Michael clearly has a contract with Andrea.

Are the statements made by Andrea terms or only representations?

A term is part of the contract, whereas a mere representation does not form part of the contract.

Whether a statement is a term or a representation depends on the intention of the parties. If the intention is not clear, then the court will apply an objective test. The court decides whether a reasonable person would consider the statement to be a term or a representation. There are various guidelines to help the court. The statements were not made immediately before the sale as Michael only bought the elephant a week later. This timing suggests the statements are just representations (*Routledge v McKay*). Consider which party has special skill and knowledge. If the maker of the statement has special skill and knowledge, this suggests the statement is a term of the contract (*Dick Bentley v Harold Smith Motors*), whereas if the other party has special skill and knowledge, it is more likely to be a representation (*Oscar Chess v Williams*). Here Andrea only has a local high street antique shop, and Michael is a collector and may have greater skill and knowledge. Also, Andrea said that in her opinion the elephant was sixteenth century and, although she said she was sure the eyes were made out of precious stones, 'precious' is rather vague. She did not seemingly encourage Michael to check, which would have suggested that the statements were representations (*Ecay v Godfrey*), nor did Michael indicate that these matters were of vital importance to him, as in *Bannerman v White*, which would have suggested that the statements were terms.

However, looking at the guidelines overall, it seems likely that the statements are just representations.

(If this is a sale by description, then a term will be implied by s 11 of the Consumer Rights Act 2015 that the goods shall match the description (**Chapter 3**).)

Consider remedies for breach of contract.

If either statement is a term, then Andrea will have committed a breach of contract. If a condition of the contract is broken, the buyer can prima facie reject the goods; if the term implied by s 11 of the Consumer Rights Act 2015 has been breached, Michael will have lost the short-term right to reject (as he has had the goods for six months), but he could still ask for a price reduction or exercise the final right to reject.

However, as we have already seen, it is more likely that the statements are representations.

Consider misrepresentation.

Michael may be able to establish that there have been misrepresentations made by Andrea.

Define misrepresentation.

A misrepresentation is a false statement of fact made by one party to the other which induces the other party to enter into the contract. The burden of establishing misrepresentation will be on Michael.

Go through the definition to see whether it is satisfied.

To be a misrepresentation, the statements must be statements of fact and not opinion (*Bisset v Wilkinson, Smith v Land and House Property Corporation*). Andrea's statement about the elephant being sixteenth-century appears to be an opinion (provided it was an honestly and reasonably held one) and so will not be a misrepresentation. She said she was sure the eyes were made from precious stones. This may be a statement of fact.

If either statement is a statement of fact, for it to be a misrepresentation it must also have induced Michael to enter into the contract. If he relied on the advice of his friend Carol, and has not relied on what Andrea said at all, then he will have no action in misrepresentation (*Attwood v Small*). Carol assured Michael the elephant was from the Mogul period, but did not know whether Andrea's statement about the eyes was true. He may well have relied on what Carol said about the age of the elephant and on what Andrea said about the eyes. In any case, it is not necessary for Andrea's statement to be the sole inducement for him to have a claim in misrepresentation (*Edgington v Fitzmaurice*).

Consider remedies for misrepresentation

Misrepresentation makes the contract voidable so Michael can rescind the contract by notifying Andrea. The aim of rescission is to restore the parties to their pre-contractual position so Michael will return the elephant and Andrea will return the money. However, the fact that Michael has delayed for six months may constitute a bar to rescission (*Leaf v International Galleries*). If so, he will not be able to return the elephant and get his money back.

However, he can still claim damages, which can be awarded regardless of whether the contract is rescinded. There is no suggestion on the facts that Andrea made a fraudulent misrepresentation. Michael would have the burden of proving fraud and this is often difficult to do. It is easier for Michael to claim under s 2(1) of the Misrepresentation Act 1967. Andrea will be liable under s 2(1) unless she can show she had reasonable grounds to believe that the statements were true. This is very difficult to do (*Howard Marine & Dredging v Ogden*). Damages will be awarded in the same way as for fraudulent misrepresentation (*Royscot Trust Ltd v Rogerson*). The aim of the court will be to put Michael in the position he would have been in if the misrepresentation had not been made (the usual aim in tort), and he can recover for all direct loss. The usual remoteness rules will not apply. He will recover the amount he paid less the value of the elephant.

If Andrea can show reasonable grounds for believing what she said was true, then Michael will not obtain damages under s 2(1). The court would not be in a position to award damages in lieu of rescission under s 2(2) of the Misrepresentation Act 1967 if rescission is indeed barred by undue delay (as mentioned above).

SUMMARY

- When advising a client about a false preliminary statement (whether as a potential claimant or defendant), you must be able to classify the false statement to see if it is actionable and, if so, what will be the likely outcome of a case in terms of success and remedies. Only with that information to hand will the client be able to make a risk/cost assessment of the claim and decide whether it is worth pursuing/defending.
- So, in this chapter, you have analysed what constitutes a misrepresentation (in the technical sense) and compared it with breach of an express term. You have studied the remedies available for misrepresentation, considered rules of statutory interpretation in the context of s 2(1) of the Misrepresentation Act 1967 and compared and contrasted the different methods of assessing damages in contract and tort.

7 Duress and Undue Influence

LEARNING OUTCOMES

When you have completed this chapter, you should be able to:

- explain and discuss the law relating to duress and undue influence;
- advise businesses of the main legal issues involved in contractual variations (eg in terms of consideration and economic duress);
- assess the legal and practical implications for financial institutions, where security is being offered in a situation where there is a risk of undue influence.

As the essence of agreement (upon which contract law is based) is that the parties freely consent to the agreed terms, it follows that a party who has been forced into a contract by threats or undue pressure should not necessarily be bound by it. Note we are only talking about some sort of improper pressure. A party cannot generally complain about ordinary commercial pressure or mere inequality of bargaining power. It is only where there has been duress or undue influence that a contract will be voidable, thus giving the innocent party the option to rescind it.

7.1 Duress

7.1.1 What constitutes duress in contract law?

Traditionally, duress was confined to violence or illegitimate threats of violence or damage to property which effectively coerced the other party into entering a contract or varying a contract.

A case which involved threats of physical violence is *Barton v Armstrong* [1975] AC 104. Armstrong had threatened to kill Barton, if Barton did not buy his shares in the company. Barton agreed to do so, but not only because of the threats to his life. There was evidence to suggest that he thought it to be a satisfactory business arrangement in any event (he believed it would prompt the company's principal lender to advance further money to it). Nevertheless, it was held that Barton should not be bound by the agreement.

Lord Cross of Chelsea made it clear that duress need not be the only reason why the innocent party entered the contract. He said:

> ... if Armstrong's threats were 'a' reason for Barton [entering the contract] he is entitled to relief even though he might well have entered into the contract if Armstrong had uttered no threats to induce him to do so .... It was for Armstrong to establish, if he could, that the threats he was making ... in fact contributed nothing to Barton's decision to sign.

So traditionally duress was some sort of violence, illegitimate threat or pressure, and the burden of proof was on the party alleging it.

In practice, threats of physical violence to encourage a person to enter into a contract are quite rare. In the commercial world, illegitimate threats to a person's economic or business interests are far more common. But illegitimate threats need to be distinguished from straightforward hard bargaining, such as threats to take business elsewhere, sell to a competitor, or not to give a discount in future, which may amount to acceptable commercial pressure.

To amount to economic duress, the threat must be an improper threat (ie a threat to breach a contract or commit a tort). It can sometimes be difficult to draw a distinction between legitimate commercial pressure and illegitimate threats.

One case in which economic duress was established is *Atlas Express v Kafco* [1989] 1 All ER 641. The claimants were a road haulage company. The defendants were a small firm of manufacturers. The defendants had managed to secure a contract with Woolworths stores around the country. The defendants entered into a contract with the claimants whereby the claimants agreed to transport the defendants' goods to the various Woolworth stores. The goods were to be transported in cartons, and the defendants agreed to pay £1.10 per carton. The contract did not specify how many cartons the defendants would supply per load.

For the first load the defendants supplied 200 cartons. The claimants had expected more. They thought there would be 400–600 cartons. The claimants refused to make any more deliveries unless the defendants agreed to pay a minimum of £400 per load. The defendants were a small business. It would have been difficult for them to find another haulage company to deliver to Woolworths on time. If the goods were not delivered on time, their business relationship with Woolworths would have been ruined. They therefore agreed to pay the extra amount, but in the event did not do so.

When sued for the extra money, Kafco successfully defended the claim on the basis that the agreement to pay more money had been obtained by economic duress.

Kafco's agreement had been obtained by illegitimate pressure and Kafco had had no practical alternative but to agree. It would have been very difficult for Kafco to find someone else to deliver the goods, and if the goods had not been delivered, Kafco's customer, Woolworths, would have sued Kafco and would not have dealt with them again. In other words, Kafco had no practical choice but to concede.

An alternative argument raised by Kafco was that Atlas had given no consideration for its promise to pay more money on the basis that Atlas was simply performing an existing contractual duty (*Stilk v Myrick* (1809) 2 Camp 317 – **Chapter 2**). The argument succeeded.

It is important to note that *Atlas Express v Kafco* was decided before *Williams v Roffey* [1991] 1 QB 1, CA, where the Court decided that performing an existing contractual obligation owed to the other contracting party can be good consideration for a promise of more money, provided the person promising the money obtains a practical benefit in return. However, the principle in *Williams v Roffey* could not in any event have been used to allow Atlas Express to recover the extra money. Why not? The principle in *Williams v Roffey* can only apply where the promise is not obtained as a result of fraud or duress. (In *Williams v Roffey* the defendant did not argue that there had been duress.) The fact that Atlas Express had used duress to obtain the promise from Kafco meant that the principle in *Williams v Roffey* could not be used to allow Atlas Express to recover the extra money. The duress made the renegotiation voidable.

The early cases on economic duress emphasised that there must be coercion of the will so as to vitiate consent (*Pao On v Lau Yiu Long* [1980] AC 614). However, it may be misleading to say that duress is based on consent being vitiated so that the resulting act is not voluntary. The person alleging duress does consent. The problem with the contract is not the lack of consent, but the fact that the consent was obtained by improper pressure.

Given that the courts are no longer emphasising consent being vitiated as the key aspect of duress, more attention may have to be paid to the nature of the pressure in order to decide whether this pressure is illegitimate. Illegitimate pressure includes unlawful threats, such as a threat to commit a crime or a tort, or a threat to break a contract. (In *Atlas Express v Kafco*, Atlas Express were threatening to break their contract when they said they would not deliver the goods unless they were paid more money.)

In the case of *Carillion Construction Ltd v Felix (UK) Ltd* [2001] BLR 1, Dyson J summed up the ingredients needed to establish economic duress as follows. The ingredients of actionable duress are that there must be pressure:

(a) whose practical effect is that there is compulsion on, or a lack of practical choice for, the victim;

(b) which is illegitimate; and

(c) which is a significant cause inducing the claimant to enter into the contract.

Dyson J also said that, in determining whether there has been illegitimate pressure, the court will take into account a range of factors. These include:

- whether there has been an actual or a threatened breach of contract;
- whether the person allegedly exerting the pressure has acted in good or bad faith;
- whether the victim had any realistic practical alternative but to submit to the pressure;
- whether the victim protested at the time; and
- whether they affirmed and sought to rely on the contract.

Dyson J emphasised that illegitimate pressure must be distinguished from the rough and tumble of the pressures of normal commercial bargaining.

A case in which the court considered and applied the *Carillion* guidelines (and also the principle laid down in *Williams v Roffey*) is *Adam Opel GmbH and Renault SA v Mitras Automobile (UK) Ltd* [2007] EWHC 3205 (QB), in which the renegotiation was held to be voidable due to duress. More recently, the Supreme Court in *Pakistan International Airline Corporation v Times Travel (UK) Ltd* [2021] UKSC 40 considered economic duress in depth. It effectively confirmed the *Carillion* guidelines by endorsing that there are three elements to economic duress: (i) an illegitimate threat/pressure by the defendant; (ii) the illegitimate threat/pressure caused the claimant to enter the contract/contractual variation; and (iii) the claimant must have had no reasonable alternative but to concede to the threat/pressure. Note that the Supreme Court in this case also discussed at length lawful act duress (ie whether lawful (albeit unreasonable) demands can amount to illegitimate pressure for the purpose of economic duress). However, lawful act duress is beyond the scope of this textbook.

7.1.2 Effect of duress and remedy

Duress, like misrepresentation (which you considered in the previous chapter), makes an original or renegotiated contract voidable. However, unlike for misrepresentation, there is no remedy of damages. Rescission is the only available remedy for duress.

Remember that the easiest way to rescind a contract, or variation to a contract, is for the innocent party to notify the other party that it wants to rescind. But what if it is impossible to find the other party, or the other party refuses to return money or property? Well, if the other party cannot be traced then one option open to the innocent party is to notify the police. In any event, an innocent party may apply to court for an order of rescission.

But there are bars to rescission, and in cases involving duress if one, or other of them, applies, it means that the innocent party will have no recourse for having been improperly coerced into the contract or contractual variation: rescission is the only remedy for duress. The bars to rescission (which you looked at in **Chapter 6**) are:

(a) affirmation;

(b) undue delay;

(c) where an innocent purchaser has already acquired an interest in the property;

(d) where it is impossible to substantially restore goods or property, eg property has been consumed or destroyed.

One case in which rescission was barred is *North Ocean Shipping v Hyundai Construction Co (The Atlantic Baron)* [1979] QB 705. The case involved the construction of a ship. Building started, but the shipbuilders demanded more money and threatened to stop work unless the claimants agreed to pay the extra money. The claimants agreed to pay the extra money as they had no practical choice but to concede to the demand. They desperately needed the ship to be finished on time as they had made a contract to hire out the ship on completion. The ship was delivered on time and the shipbuilders were paid in full. Eight months later the claimants asked for repayment of the extra money on the grounds of duress. (The shipbuilders had provided consideration for the extra money and so consideration was not an issue.)

The court held that there was economic duress, but it refused to rescind the variation on the bases of both affirmation and undue delay. The court found that when the payment was made, there was no longer any pressure on the claimants, as market conditions had changed and there was no likelihood that the shipbuilders would refuse delivery. Payment therefore amounted to affirmation. Also, the claimants had left it too long (eight months) before asking for the return of their money.

Thinking back to *Atlas Express v Kafco*, what would have been the most sensible thing for the ship owners to have done once the ship had been delivered and the pressure taken away? Simply not to have paid the extra money. Then, if and when the ship owners were sued, they could have raised duress as a defence.

Note, in both *Atlas Express v Kafco* and *The Atlantic Baron*, that it was only the later variation which was affected by the duress, and therefore only the variation (ie the promise to pay the extra money) which was capable of being rescinded, not the original contract.

Duress – summary

- To establish duress, the innocent party must establish that there has been an illegitimate threat which left them with no practical choice and which was a significant factor in inducing them to enter the contract or variation (*Carillion Construction Ltd v Felix (UK) Ltd*).
- The effect of duress is to make the contract (or variation) voidable.
- Rescission is the remedy available to a victim of duress, provided it is not barred (eg by undue delay or affirmation (*The Atlantic Baron*)). Rather than rescind as such, we have also seen that duress can be used as a defence if the other party tries to enforce the renegotiated terms or otherwise claim damages for breach (*Atlas Express v Kafco*).

7.2 Undue influence

Undue influence, like duress, makes a contract voidable. The remedy is rescission, and the same bars apply as for duress. There is, like duress, no remedy of damages, and so if rescission is barred, a victim of undue influence has no remedy.

Undue influence consists not of threats or violence, but of influence which goes beyond what is regarded as acceptable. Just as it can be difficult to decide where legitimate commercial pressure ends and economic duress begins, it can be difficult to say at what point acceptable influence becomes 'undue' influence. The approach adopted by the law is to identify relationships which are unequal and then to consider whether the transaction resulted from the dominant person abusing that relationship.

Thinking back to duress, you may recall that the onus is on the innocent party to prove duress. That is not necessarily the case with undue influence, because as well as actual undue influence (ie proved on the facts), there is presumed undue influence. Basically, undue influence will be presumed where there is a fiduciary relationship (ie a relationship of trust and confidence) between the parties and a transaction which calls for explanation. As undue influence tends to be something which goes on 'behind closed doors', it will often be very difficult to prove, so most innocent parties will try to raise a presumption of undue influence. We shall now consider both types of undue influence in the context of established case law.

7.2.1 Actual undue influence

Here the claimant must prove that the defendant used undue influence. This might be difficult to do as it is often one person's word against another's, ie the evidence of the innocent party against that of the influencing party. One case in which the evidence of the innocent party (supported by a witness) was preferred to that of the influencing party (who was found to be 'not completely credible') is *Daniel v Drew* [2005] EWCA Civ 507. Mrs Drew was an elderly lady who intensely disliked confrontation and was afraid of her nephew and the prospect of going to court. So, when he told her to sign the contract under the threat of taking court action, she had felt unable to refuse.

Unlike duress, the threat may be entirely legal, such as, in this case, taking court action.

7.2.2 Presumed undue influence

For undue influence to be presumed, there must be a relationship of trust and confidence *and* the transaction must be one that calls for an explanation. The need for these two things to be established in order to raise a presumption of undue influence was laid down by the House of Lords in *Royal Bank of Scotland v Etridge (No 2)* [2001] 4 All ER 449. This is now the leading case on undue influence.

We shall now consider each element in turn.

7.2.2.1 Relationship of trust and confidence

In certain categories of relationship (eg solicitor and client, doctor and patient), it is irrebuttably presumed that one party places trust and confidence in the other. This is also the case with parents and children (under 18) and religious advisers and followers, but not, however, with the relationship of husband and wife.

In any case, such as husband and wife, where the relationship is not presumed to be one of trust and confidence, the innocent party will have to prove it was in fact a relationship of trust and confidence. For example, a wife may be able to prove that she actually did place trust and confidence in her husband in relation to financial matters.

One case where a relationship of trust and confidence was established is *Tate v Williamson* (1866) 2 Ch App 55. In this case, the defendant became financial adviser to an extravagant Oxford undergraduate who was being pressed by creditors. Having recommended the sale of the undergraduate's estate, the defendant offered to buy it for £7,000 without disclosing that it was in fact worth double that amount. The offer was accepted and the conveyance executed. The sale was later set aside as the defendant had wrongfully exploited, to their own advantage and knowledge, the commanding position in which the defendant stood. The undergraduate had taken the advice without questioning it.

Another, more recent case in which a relationship of trust and confidence was established on the facts is *O'Sullivan v Management Agency Ltd* [1985] QB 428. Here the relationship of trust and confidence was between Gilbert O'Sullivan, a young, unknown singer/songwriter and his manager.

Contract

7.2.2.2 The transaction must call for an explanation, ie the transaction is not readily explicable by the relationship between the parties

To raise any presumption of undue influence, however, it is not enough for there simply to be a relationship of trust and confidence between the parties. In addition, the transaction which the parties enter into must be such that it is not readily explicable by the relationship between them, ie the transaction must call for explanation (*Royal Bank of Scotland v Etridge (No 2)*).

7.2.2.3 Rebuttable presumption

Lastly, note that as with most presumptions, the presumption of undue influence is rebuttable. For example, it could be rebutted if there was evidence to show that the innocent party had taken independent advice.

Figure 7.1 sets out the steps for establishing undue influence.

Figure 7.1 Is there undue influence?

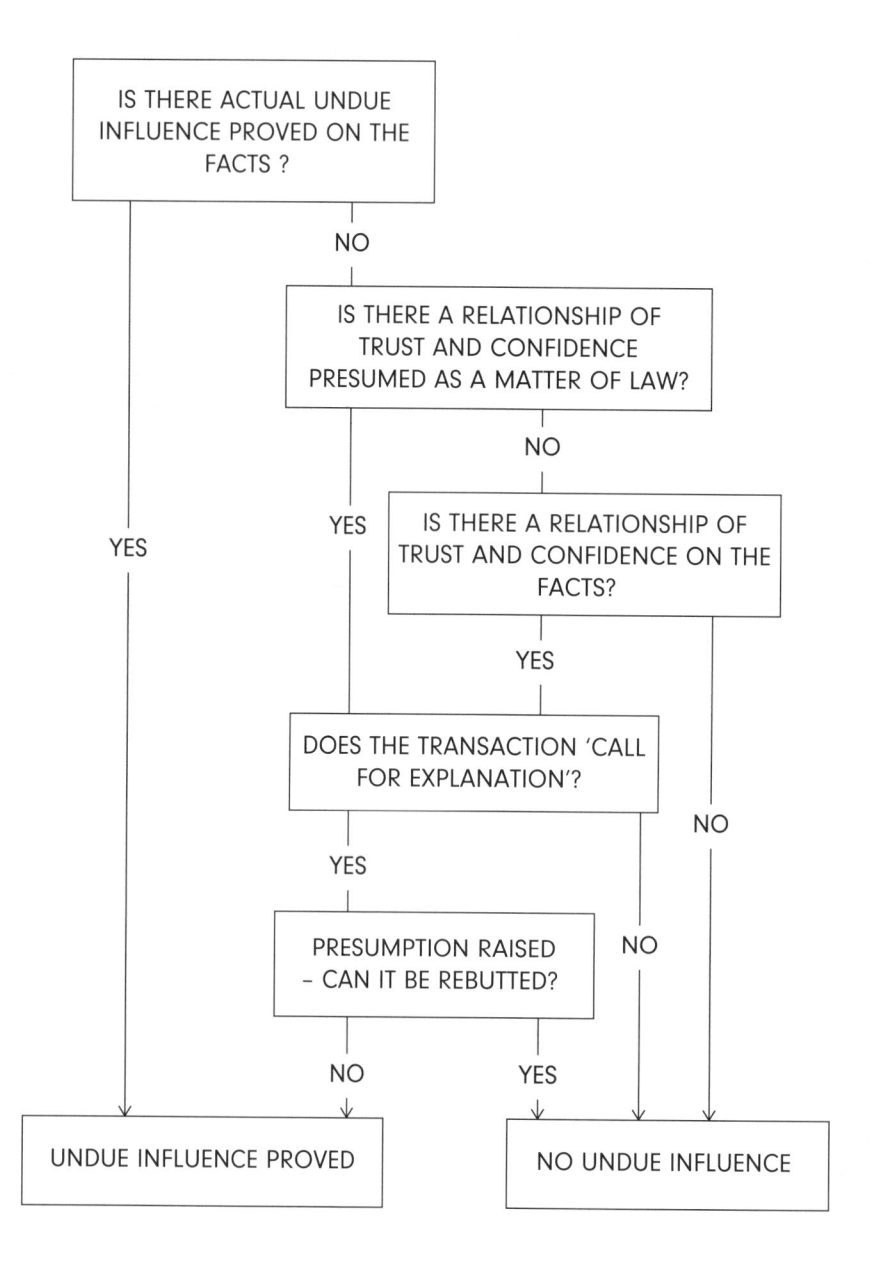

```
        ┌─────────────────────────┐
        │  IS THERE ACTUAL UNDUE  │
        │ INFLUENCE PROVED ON THE │
        │         FACTS ?         │
        └─────────────────────────┘
             │              │
             │             NO
             │              │
             │     ┌─────────────────────────┐
             │     │ IS THERE A RELATIONSHIP OF │
             │     │   TRUST AND CONFIDENCE     │
             │     │ PRESUMED AS A MATTER OF LAW?│
             │     └─────────────────────────┘
             │              │
             │             NO
             │              │
             │     ┌─────────────────────────┐
             │ YES │ IS THERE A RELATIONSHIP OF │
            YES    │ TRUST AND CONFIDENCE ON THE│
             │     │          FACTS?            │
             │     └─────────────────────────┘
             │              │
             │             YES
             │              │
             │     ┌─────────────────────────┐
             │     │  DOES THE TRANSACTION 'CALL│
             │     │      FOR EXPLANATION'?     │
             │     └─────────────────────────┘
             │              │                NO
             │             YES               │
             │     ┌─────────────────────────┐│
             │     │    PRESUMPTION RAISED   ││
             │     │   – CAN IT BE REBUTTED? ││
             │     └─────────────────────────┘│
             │         │         │            │
             │        NO        YES           │
             ▼         ▼         ▼            ▼
        ┌──────────────────┐    ┌──────────────────┐
        │ UNDUE INFLUENCE  │    │ NO UNDUE INFLUENCE│
        │      PROVED      │    │                  │
        └──────────────────┘    └──────────────────┘
```

7.2.3 Undue influence and the position of third parties

7.2.3.1 Establishing the basic principles

The law on undue influence has become important over recent years in relation to the notion of tainting a contracting party (typically a commercial lender) with the undue influence of a third party.

⭐ Example

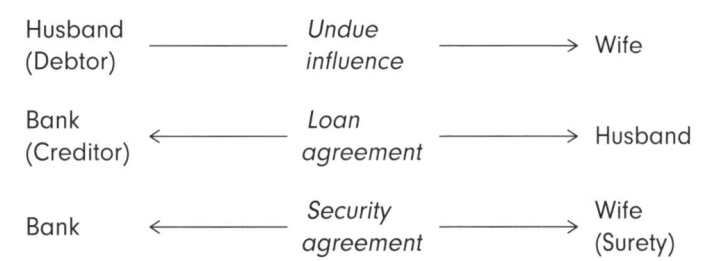

```
Husband        Undue
(Debtor)   ——influence——→  Wife

Bank                Loan
(Creditor) ←——agreement——→  Husband

Bank       ←——Security   ——→  Wife
              agreement         (Surety)
```

- *Husband defaults on the loan*
- *Bank seeks to enforce the security agreement for the loan against the wife*
- *Wife argues that the security agreement should be set aside (ie rescinded) on the basis of undue influence*
- *The bank argues that the undue influence was not exerted by it, ie the other contracting party to the security. It was exerted by the husband (third party debtor) and so should not affect the contract between the bank and the wife.*

Let us take a look at the typical situation (outlined above) in more detail and consider the legal, practical and commercial issues it raises.

A husband's business needs an injection of capital, and he approaches a commercial lender for a loan. The lender is prepared to advance the money, subject to taking security by way of a charge over the matrimonial home. As the matrimonial home is owned jointly by husband and wife, the wife will need to be a party to the security agreement and as such a surety, ie a person who gives security for the debts of another. As a result of the husband's undue influence, the wife signs the relevant documentation and the husband gets the money needed for the business.

The husband's business has problems: the loan is not repaid, and the lender seeks to enforce its security and repossess the matrimonial home. It is at this stage that the wife alleges undue influence by the husband and that the security agreement should be set aside (ie rescinded) as a result. If the security agreement is set aside, the lender will have lost its security and will be left suing the husband as an unsecured creditor. If the security agreement is not set aside, the lender will repossess the matrimonial home and the wife will effectively be left homeless.

The dilemma in this type of situation is that there are two innocent parties, the wife and the lender. To what extent, if any, should either, or both of them, be offered protection by the law? It would clearly be unfair to a lender if it was always affected by the undue influence of the husband. Also, as a matter of commercial reality, small businesses need loans, and lenders will often insist they are secured, and the main asset that can be offered as security is the matrimonial home. Consequently, lenders need to be able to take security with some reassurance that they will be able to enforce it if necessary. On the other hand, what about the wife? The wife trusted the husband and only signed the documentation because he told her to do so. The wife was unaware of the risks and practical implications involved.

Barclays Bank v O'Brien [1994] 1 AC 340

Until the case of *Barclays Bank v O'Brien*, the general view was that a commercial lender would not be affected by the undue influence of a third party debtor unless the debtor had been acting as agent for the lender in obtaining security for the loan (we looked at agency in **Chapter 2**).

There were flaws with the agency theory. For example, the aim of a potential debtor is to get the loan they require; whereas the aim of a creditor is to ensure repayment of the loan. On that basis, why would a creditor use the debtor as its agent to get security for the loan? Their interests are at odds.

Lord Browne-Wilkinson in *Barclays Bank v O'Brien* introduced the idea of notice, ie if the creditor had actual or constructive notice of the debtor's impropriety, it would be tainted with it, and any security contract obtained as a result would be voidable.

Constructive notice in this context is not the same as the constructive notice in land law. In this situation, the creditor will have constructive notice if it ought to have been put on inquiry of the risk of undue influence by the debtor *and* it did not take reasonable steps to ensure that the surety was aware of the implications of what they were signing.

We shall look in detail later at when a creditor will be put on inquiry, and what are the reasonable steps it should take to ensure the surety (in our example the wife) is aware of the risks, especially in the context of *Royal Bank of Scotland v Etridge (No 2)* [2001] 4 All ER 449 (the leading case in this area). For the moment, it is enough that you know that if the creditor had notice (actual or constructive) of the impropriety by the third party debtor, the creditor will be tainted with it and any security can be set aside.

CIBC Mortgages plc v Pitt [1993] 4 All ER 433

A case in which the lender did not have actual or constructive notice is *CIBC Mortgages plc v Pitt*. Here, the wife was able to prove actual undue influence by the husband. Mr Pitt had wanted to raise a second mortgage on the matrimonial home in order to finance share dealings. Mrs Pitt was not convinced, but eventually, worn down by her husband's persistence, she signed the mortgage application. Unfortunately for Mrs Pitt, the application did not state the true purpose of the loan. For all intents and purposes, it was a straightforward mortgage transaction to finance the purchase of a holiday home, and as a result there was nothing to alert the lender to any risk of impropriety. The House of Lords held that Mrs Pitt was not entitled to have the transaction set aside as against the lender as it had no notice (either actual or constructive) of the undue influence.

Lord Browne-Wilkinson thought it would go against practical common sense to say that lenders should be fixed with constructive notice of possible undue influence in every transaction involving husband and wife, as it would make such transactions impossible. On every purchase, if a home is in joint names, the bank or building society would have to meet the wife separately from the husband, advise the wife about the nature of the transaction and the need to take legal advice separate from the husband. This would not benefit the average married couple and would discourage institutions from lending.

Lord Browne-Wilkinson distinguished a joint advance (as in *CIBC Mortgages v Pitt*) from a situation where a wife stands as surety for the husband's debts, on the basis that in the latter case there is an increased risk of undue influence having been exercised. On the face of it, a guarantee by a wife of the husband's debts is not for the wife's benefit. This is relevant in deciding whether the bank has constructive notice of the undue influence.

Royal Bank of Scotland v Etridge (No 2) [2001] 4 All ER 449

The leading authority on this area is now the House of Lords decision in *Royal Bank of Scotland v Etridge (No 2)*. This is another case where the wife argued that the bank had constructive notice of the husband's undue influence and so should not get possession of the house. This argument failed because the solicitor acting for Mrs Etridge had confirmed to the bank, in the event falsely, that the solicitor had advised about the content and effect of the charge. The bank was entitled to rely on the solicitor's confirmation, and there were no further steps that the bank could reasonably have been required to take.

The House of Lords confirmed that if the creditor had actual or constructive notice of the debtor's undue influence then the security contract obtained as a result would be voidable. The House of Lords also stated that a creditor will have constructive notice if it ought to have been put 'on inquiry' and did not take reasonable steps to ensure that the surety was aware of the implications of what was being signed.

The House of Lords discussed the circumstances in which a creditor would be put 'on inquiry' and the sort of reasonable steps it should take to protect itself where it had been put on inquiry about the risk of undue influence.

Lord Nicholls said that if a wife acts as surety for the husband's debts then the bank is put on inquiry. On the other hand, if money is advanced to a husband and wife jointly (as in *CIBC Mortgages v Pitt*), the bank is not put on inquiry, unless the bank is aware the loan is being made for the husband's purposes alone.

Note: later in his judgment Lord Nicholls said that banks should be put on inquiry in every case where the relationship between the surety and the debtor is non-commercial, unless money is being advanced to a husband and wife jointly. So in the example at **7.2.3.1**, the bank would automatically be on inquiry as the relationship between the debtor (the husband) and the surety (the wife) is clearly non-commercial and the money is not being advanced to them jointly – it is being advanced to the husband for his business.

A bank can satisfy the requirement to take reasonable steps in two ways. First, if it insists that the wife attend a private meeting with a representative of the bank at which the wife is:

- told of the extent of liability as surety;
- warned of the risk the wife is running; and
- urged to take independent legal advice.

(In exceptional cases, the bank, to be safe, has to insist that the wife is separately advised (see *Credit Lyonnais v Burch* discussed at **7.2.3.2** below).)

Secondly, if the bank gets written confirmation from a solicitor that the wife (surety) has been independently advised and been made aware of the inherent risks. Not surprisingly, it is this second option which banks now tend to prefer: it transfers the risk of inadequate advice from the bank to a solicitor. Written confirmation from a solicitor that the wife has been independently advised guarantees that the security transaction will be upheld.

In the *Etridge* case, Lord Nicholls also made it clear that the same principles would apply if there had been some other wrongdoing on the part of the debtor, such as misrepresentation. In fact, this is what had happened in the *O'Brien* case, as Mr O'Brien had misrepresented the amount and duration of the loan.

7.2.3.2 Cases not involving husbands and wives

Although most of the cases have involved a husband taking advantage of his wife, the principles apply equally to other relationships. One case which did not involve a husband and wife is *Credit Lyonnais Bank Nederland NV v Burch* [1997] 1 All ER 144. The case involved a relationship between an employer (who owned the business) and a junior employee. The employee remortgaged their flat (valued at £100,000) to secure the unlimited liabilities of the employer's business in which the employee had no financial interest. The bank's solicitors wrote to Miss Burch on several occasions and told her that she should seek separate legal advice before entering the transaction, emphasising that the document she was being asked to sign was unlimited as regards amount and time. Miss Burch acknowledged receipt of the letters and confirmed that she was aware of the implications of the deal. When the business failed, and the bank tried to enforce the agreement against the employee, she pleaded undue influence. The court decided that there was a presumption of undue influence.

It was held that the bank was precluded from enforcing the security. In the circumstances, the bank had not done enough to satisfy itself that the employee's consent to the deal was freely given. The transaction was so disadvantageous to the employee that the bank should not have proceeded unless and until the bank had explained to her the full extent of the business's borrowing and its overdraft limit. Nor should it have done so until the employee had actually received independent legal advice. Thus, the security was unenforceable against her.

The decision in *Burch* demonstrates that in some circumstances it will not be enough for a creditor to urge a surety to take independent legal advice. It must insist that the surety does so, or otherwise not take the proposed security.

The position of lenders in relation to undue influence exerted by third-party debtors is summarised in **Figure 7.2**.

Figure 7.2 The effect of undue influence on the lender

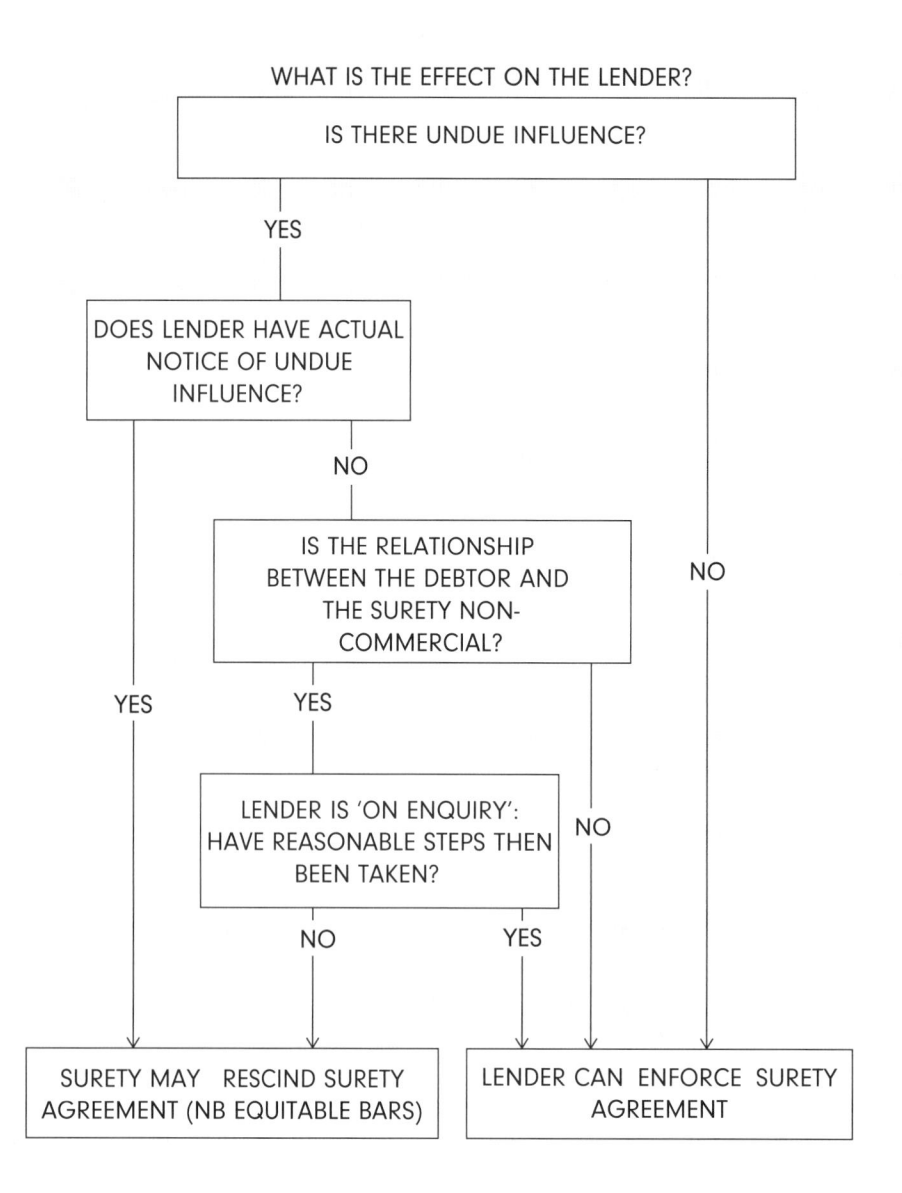

Put together **Figures 7.1** and **7.2** above and you have a suggested structure for tackling problem questions involving undue influence by a third-party debtor in the context of secured lending.

Suggested structure

1. Define undue influence.
2. Was there undue influence?
   (a) Actual undue influence? This may be difficult to prove.
   (b) Presumed undue influence? Is there a relationship of trust and confidence, either by its nature or otherwise on the facts?
   Does the transaction call for explanation?
   Can any presumption of undue influence be rebutted?
3. Position of the bank. If there has been undue influence, will this affect the bank?
   (a) Did the bank have actual or constructive notice? Explain what is meant by constructive notice.
   (b) Bank should be regarded as put on inquiry in every case where the relationship between a surety and debtor is non-commercial and not for their joint benefit (*Royal Bank of Scotland v Etridge (No 2)*). Apply to the facts.
   (c) Did the bank take reasonable steps to satisfy itself that the practical implications of the transaction had been brought home to the party alleging undue influence? Apply to the facts.
   (d) What if the bank did/did not take reasonable steps? Is rescission barred?

Undue influence – summary

- Like duress, the effect of undue influence is to make a contract voidable, and the only remedy is rescission.
- Unlike duress, there is no established definition, and undue influence may be presumed. It will be presumed where there is a relationship of trust and confidence, a transaction which calls for explanation and nothing to rebut the presumption.
- Where the undue influence has not been exerted by the other contracting party (eg the lender in relation to a second mortgage) but by a third party, the contract will nevertheless be voidable if the contracting party had notice (actual or constructive) of the undue influence.
- A contracting party (such as a lender) will have constructive notice if it should have been put on inquiry as to the risk of undue influence and did not take reasonable steps to ensure that the other party was aware of the implications of what they were signing (*Royal Bank of Scotland v Etridge (No 2)*).
- The House of Lords in *Royal Bank of Scotland v Etridge (No 2)* said that a creditor will be put on inquiry in every case where the relationship between the debtor and surety is non-commercial (except where money is being advanced to a husband and wife jointly). This case also set out what the creditor had to do in order to take reasonable steps to ensure that the other party was aware of the implications of what they were signing. Typically, the reasonable steps will be to ensure that the surety is independently advised by a solicitor, and that the solicitor sends a written confirmation of this.

We have looked at duress and undue influence. There now follows an Activity on these topics.

ACTIVITY 1 Problem question on economic duress and undue influence

This activity is in two parts. In Part 1 you will consider a question on economic duress, and in Part 2 you will consider a question on undue influence. In your answer, please include references to relevant cases.

PART 1

Facts

George is in the business of importing Persian carpets from the Middle East into the UK. He sold a consignment of the carpets to Threadworths Department Store, his main customer, and agreed to arrange delivery of the carpets to six Threadworths stores in different parts of England on Monday, 6 June. He rang up Mercator Carriers (a haulage firm which he regularly uses) and they agreed to pick up the carpets from George's warehouse and deliver them to the six stores on Monday 6 June at a total price of £300.

On Friday 3 June, Mercator telephoned George and told him that they had made a mistake in calculating the mileage involved. As a result, the agreed price of £300 was incorrect and they were substituting a new price of £500. When George protested, they replied that if he refused to pay the extra they would cancel the agreement. However, if he agreed to pay extra, they would make an extra delivery of carpets to other stores in those areas.

George spent the rest of Friday and the weekend ringing up other haulage firms, but none could do the job at such short notice. He also rang up Threadworths, who were very unsympathetic and told him they would never buy his carpets again if he delivered the consignment late.

Early on Monday morning, George telephoned Mercator and told them that they had left him with no choice but to agree to their terms. He asked them to make additional deliveries to two other shops near to one of the Threadworths stores. Mercator made all the deliveries and George paid them £500. Now, two weeks later, George is having second thoughts and wants to reclaim the extra £200.

Explain George's legal position.

COMMENT

Variation. The parties have purported to vary their contract. The same elements are needed for variation as for the formation of a contract, ie agreement, intention and consideration. As the parties have basically agreed and are in business (so contractual intention is presumed), the main issue is consideration.

Consideration. Mercator must have provided consideration for George's promise of more money.

Define. Consideration can be defined as the price the claimant pays for the defendant's promise. The basic rule is that consideration must be sufficient, but it need not be adequate (*Chappell v Nestlé*).

Just performing an existing contractual obligation has been held to be insufficient consideration for a promise of more money (*Stilk v Myrick*). However, in this case, Mercator are doing more than they had originally agreed to do (they are making extra deliveries), so there will be consideration for George's promise of more money (*Hartley v Ponsonby*). (Note: it is not necessary to consider *Williams v Roffey* because Mercator have obviously done more than they had agreed to do. It is not a case where Mercator have just performed their contractual obligations.)

Duress. Even though Mercator have given consideration for George's promise, George may avoid paying if the promise was obtained by economic duress.

What is meant by economic duress? Economic duress must be distinguished from legitimate commercial pressure. Economic duress usually involves an improper (unlawful) threat, and the innocent party has no practical alternative but to agree.

Burden of proof. George must establish there has been economic duress.

The facts here are very similar to those in the case of *Atlas Express v Kafco* (except that in *Atlas Express* the court also held there was no consideration for the promise of more money as Altas Express was not doing anything extra in return for increased payment). In *Atlas Express* there had been an improper threat to break the contract unless more money was paid, and Kafco would have found it very difficult to find someone else to deliver the goods. If the goods had not been delivered, Kafco's customer would not have dealt with them again. This is very similar to the situation involving George and Mercator. Mercator have also made an improper threat to break the contract, and George found it impossible to find someone else to deliver the goods at such short notice. Also, George's main customer, Threadworths, said they would never buy his carpets again if they were delivered late.

It seems as if there has been economic duress, and this conclusion is supported by considering the guidelines in *Carillion Construction Ltd v Felix (UK) Ltd*. The ingredients of actionable economic duress are:

- an illegitimate threat/pressure;
- compulsion on, or a lack of practical choice for, the victim;
- the threat/pressure was a significant cause inducing the claimant to enter the contract.

After considering the facts of *Atlas Express v Kafco* and the above guidelines, it does seem as if there has been economic duress.

Effect of economic duress. Duress renders a contract voidable, ie it is a valid contract until the innocent party avoids (rescinds) it. Here, it was only the variation that was brought about by duress, so only the variation is voidable. The main contract still stands.

George wants to rescind the variation for the payment of the extra money and recover the extra £200. Rescission will be possible unless a bar to rescission applies, eg affirmation or delay. In *The Atlantic Baron*, both of these bars applied. However, here George has only waited two weeks. This is unlikely to be long enough to bar rescission. However, George has paid the extra £200, unlike in *Atlas Express v Kafco*. This might be a bar as in *The Atlantic Baron*, although unlike in that case George did protest and the subsequent delay was much shorter.

Conclusion. It looks as if the variation to pay the extra £200 may be voidable for economic duress. If so, George should be able to rescind the contract and recover the extra money.

PART 2

This part of the activity deals with undue influence.

Facts

Kate and Steve are an unmarried couple. Kate is a consultant at the local hospital, and Steve runs a small manufacturing business in which Kate has no interest. Steve arranged a large overdraft facility for the business with Quality Finance Company. He was to guarantee repayment, and his liability to the finance company was to be secured by a second mortgage on the house, which he owns jointly with Kate. A representative from Quality Finance visited them at home and left the papers, suggesting that Kate take some time to think the matter over. Kate said she would discuss the matter with Steve as she left financial arrangements up to him. A few days later, Steve reminded her about the papers. As usual, she signed the papers without reading them. She had not taken independent legal advice. Steve has fallen behind with the repayments, and last week they received notice that Quality Finance has started possession proceedings.

Explain Kate's legal position.

COMMENT

Undue influence consists of influence which goes beyond what is regarded as acceptable.

Was there undue influence?

Actual undue influence. The burden of proof would be on Kate to show actual undue influence by Steve. This can be difficult to do, and there is little evidence of actual undue influence on the facts, eg, there is no evidence of overbearing, improper pressure. We are just told that he reminded her about the papers. It would depend on how he reminded her.

Presumed undue influence. It is probably easier to establish presumed undue influence. Kate would have to prove that she placed trust and confidence in Steve and that the transaction called for an explanation, ie it was not readily explicable by the relationship between the parties (*Etridge*). Applying these principles to the facts, it seems that Kate could prove that she placed trust and confidence in Steve. We are told that she was used to leaving all financial matters to him, and it seems she usually signed business papers without reading them. Also, the second condition seems to be satisfied, as the transaction was to provide security for a large overdraft facility for a business in which she had no interest.

It seems very likely that there will be a presumption of undue influence. There is no suggestion that she obtained independent legal advice which could rebut this presumption.

It is now necessary to consider whether the finance company will be affected by the undue influence of Steve.

The position of the finance company. It does not look as if Quality Finance had actual notice. Following the approach adopted by Lord Nicholls in *Royal Bank of Scotland v Etridge (No 2)*, it seems that Quality Finance will have constructive notice of Steve's undue influence and Kate's right to set aside the transaction. This is because the relationship between Steve and Kate is non-commercial and the loan was not for their joint benefit.

There is no evidence that the finance company took reasonable steps to satisfy itself that the practical implications of the transaction had been brought home to Kate. The finance company should have had a private meeting with Kate. The finance company did not warn Kate of the risks involved. Also, there is no indication that the representative told Kate to get independent legal advice or that she did in fact consult a solicitor. He just told her to take a few days to think it over, and Kate said she would discuss it with Steve as she left financial arrangements to him.

Alternatively, the finance company could rely on confirmation from a solicitor, acting for Kate, that they had fully explained the financial risks and nature of documentation to her. There is no indication that this occurred.

Effect of undue influence. Undue influence makes a contract voidable. It seems that the contract can be set aside, and the finance company will be unable to enforce the mortgage against Kate. The finance company would still be able to sue Steve on the original loan as an unsecured creditor.

SUMMARY

- In a commercial context, you have seen how economic duress can impact on contract formation but more particularly on contractual variations. You have looked at the practical and legal options when there has been duress.
- In contrast to duress, you will appreciate that undue influence does not necessarily have to be proved by the innocent party. In some circumstances, a presumption of undue influence will be raised. You also looked at how a lending institution can be tainted with the undue influence exerted by a third-party debtor, and hopefully you will have formed a view as to whether the law in this respect is fair.

8 Mistake and Illegality

LEARNING OUTCOMES

When you have completed this chapter, you should be able to:

- recognise when a client may need to argue that a contract is void for mistake or illegality;
- advise on the different types of mistake;
- advise on when, and how, a contract may be illegal.

This chapter is intended to provide you with an introduction to some of the basic legal principles governing mistake and illegality. You will be introduced to the different types of fundamental mistakes that may result in a contract being declared void, eg where both parties have been mistaken as to the existence of the subject matter – there clearly cannot be a contract if there is nothing to contract about. You will also be made aware of the main ways in which contracts may be illegal, eg sometimes they will be illegal from the outset, but in other cases they may become illegal through the way in which they are performed. Covenants in restraint of trade commonly found in employment contracts and sale and purchase agreements of businesses are prima facie void, but they may be upheld if they protect a legitimate business interest and are reasonable.

8.1 Mistake

8.1.1 What is mistake?

The first thing to appreciate in this area of law is that the word 'mistake' has a much more restricted meaning than in common parlance. Many examples might be given of situations where a 'mistake' in the popular sense is denied legal significance (eg because when viewed objectively the parties appeared to be in agreement) or otherwise where a remedy might be granted on some other ground such as misrepresentation. The doctrine operates only in exceptional circumstances where one party, or indeed both parties, can establish that the contract was entered into under a mistake which was so fundamental as to effectively negate agreement and therefore the existence of a contract.

8.1.2 Types of mistake

There are basically three different types of mistake:

- common mistake, ie where both parties have made the same fundamental mistake;
- cross-purpose mistake – where the parties are literally at cross purposes about some crucial aspect of the contract;

- unilateral mistake – where only one party is mistaken, eg mistaken as to the very identity of the other contracting party.

In all cases, the mistake must precede the contract and have induced it.

8.1.2.1 Common mistake

This is sometimes known as 'identical mistake' or 'shared mistake' because both parties have made the same fundamental mistake.

As with frustration (which is a supervening rather than a preceding impossibility (see **Chapter 5**)), there are strict limitations on the operation of common mistake:

- It will not operate if one party is at fault.
- The contract must not make express provision on the matter.
- The mistake must be fundamental, ie render performance of the contract impossible or radically different from what the parties anticipated.

One instance where the courts will find a fundamental mistake is where both parties are mistaken as to the very existence of the subject matter of the contract.

For example, imagine I agree to sell you my car, but unbeknown to either of us my car has already been destroyed in a fire. Our contract will be rendered void as there is nothing to sell or buy.

On the other hand, a simple mistake as to the quality of the subject matter will not usually be deemed sufficiently fundamental to affect the validity of a contract.

This is illustrated by the case of *Bell v Lever Bros* [1932] AC 161. Bell and another (B and A) were made executive officers of a subsidiary of Lever Bros. The subsidiary was closed down, and Lever Bros entered into contracts with B and A terminating their service contracts in return for substantial compensation. It was then discovered that B and A had previously breached their service contracts and so could have been dismissed without compensation. It was accepted that both B and A had forgotten about the earlier breaches when they entered their settlement agreements with Lever Bros.

Lever Bros sued B and A for the return of the compensation payments on the basis that the settlement agreements were void for mistake. Both parties had wrongly thought that the service contracts had been valid; but the House of Lords said the mistake was not fundamental enough to render the settlement agreements void.

Because a mistake as to quality is unlikely to make performance radically different, it is generally viewed as a last resort argument, ie where there is no other cause of action open to the claimant, as was indeed the case in *Bell v Lever Bros*. A and B had not lied about the status of the settlement agreement – they had genuinely (albeit conveniently) forgotten about their earlier breaches. So there had been no prospect of Lever Bros suing them for misrepresentation and/or breach of an express term of the contract. Lever Bros' only option had been to argue mistake.

8.1.2.2 Cross-purpose mistake

In the case of cross-purpose mistakes, the problem is that although one or other party may assert that a contract exists, each on terms favourable to that party, objectively it is impossible to resolve the ambiguity over what was agreed. That being the case, the only possible conclusion is that there was no contract.

A classic example of a cross-purpose mistake is *Raffles v Wickelhaus* (1864) 2 Hurl & C 906. It concerned a contract to sell cotton *'ex Peerless* from Bombay' (ie cotton from the ship named

'Peerless' which had sailed from Bombay). In the event, there were two ships named 'Peerless' which had sailed from Bombay – one had sailed in October and the other in December. The seller brought an action against the buyer for failing to take delivery of the cotton from the ship that had sailed in December. The buyer argued that there was a latent ambiguity in the contract and that they believed the ship in the contract to be the one that had sailed in October. On an objective analysis, there was no way to resolve the ambiguity, so the court found for the buyer, ie the contract was void.

8.1.2.3 Unilateral mistake

Unilateral mistake (ie where only one party is mistaken) is often relied on where there has been a mistake as to the identity of the other contracting party. However, only a genuine mistake of this nature where the identity of the other party is of vital importance will render the contract void. If the mistake is as to anything less (eg a mistake simply as to the other party's attributes such as creditworthiness) then it will not generally affect the validity of the contract.

A case in which the identity of the other party was held to be crucial is *Cundy v Lindsay* (1878) 3 App Cas 459. It involved a contract concluded by written correspondence. A rogue set up business under the name 'Blenkarn' at 37 Wood Street. A reputable company, Blenkiron and Co, traded at 123 Wood Street. The rogue ordered goods from the plaintiff, making their signature look like 'Blenkiron'. The plaintiff sent the goods to 'Blenkiron and Co' at the rogue's address. Before the rogue paid for the goods though, the rogue resold them to innocent purchasers. The plaintiff's only hope to recover the goods was to argue mistaken identity on the basis that it intended to deal specifically with Blenkiron and Co and not with whatever firm happened to be operating from 37 Wood Street. The plaintiff's argument succeeded, and the contract was held to be void for mistake.

In the above case, the plaintiff could not rely on misrepresentation to recover the goods as rescission was barred. The goods had been resold to innocent purchasers.

Where a bona fide purchaser has already acquired the goods, there are two innocent parties – the mistaken party and the innocent purchaser. Only one of them will be entitled to the goods; the other will be left suing the rogue (if the rogue can be found) for damages. The mistaken party's damages claim would be for breach of an express term and/or misrepresentation. The innocent purchaser's claim would be for breach of the statutory implied condition in contracts for the sale of goods that the seller has title to the goods which they can pass on (Sale of Goods Act 1979, s 12, in relation to business-to-business contracts and Consumer Rights Act 2015, s 17, in relation to business-to-consumer contracts). Of the two innocent parties, the courts tend to have less sympathy for the mistaken party – hence why mistaken identity rarely succeeds where the deal was struck in a face-to-face situation.

As a general rule in face-to-face situations, it will be much more difficult for a person to argue they intended to deal with someone other than the person physically present in front of them.

In *Lewis v Averay* [1972] 1 QB 198, the plaintiff advertised their car for sale. The man who turned up claimed to be the well-known actor, Richard Greene (who had played Robin Hood in a long-running TV series). He signed a cheque 'R.A. Green' and produced photographic identification in the form of an official pass for Pinewood Studios. On that basis, the plaintiff let the man take the car and log book in return for the cheque. The man then sold the car to an innocent purchaser (the defendant). The man's cheque was dishonoured and he turned out to be a fraudster. The plaintiff's only hope of getting back their car from the defendant was to establish mistake (as rescission for misrepresentation would be barred – see **Chapter 6**). But the court said that the plaintiff had been more concerned about the creditworthiness of the man, rather than what he actually called himself. So, it was a mistake as to an attribute (rather than identity) and as such was not fundamental enough to invalidate the contract.

So, if faced with a particular set of facts, how do you work out whether the contract is voidable (for misrepresentation) or void (for mistake)? Looking at the case law, it is far from straightforward, but the following guidelines can be deduced from it:

(a) If the parties are dealing face-to-face, there is a strong presumption that the innocent party intends to deal with the person in front of them (ie the rogue) rather than the person being impersonated. In that case, the contract is unlikely to be declared void for mistake, although it might be rescinded for misrepresentation.

(b) Where dealings are conducted exclusively in writing, the above presumption does not apply. Instead, the written agreement must be construed to determine with whom the innocent party intended to contract. If it was with someone other than the rogue then the contract might be void for mistake.

(c) The nature of the transaction may indicate to the rogue that it is vital the rogue possess a particular attribute and, if they do not do so, the offer is not addressed to the rogue. For example, if someone orally commissions a portrait from an unknown artist passing themselves off as a famous painter, the rogue could not accept the offer. In other words, there would be no contract with the rogue.

(d) If the person/entity whom the rogue is pretending to be actually exists and is known to the mistaken party (eg a registered company), it suggests that the offer is not addressed to the rogue. So, again, there could be no contract with the rogue; it would be void.

8.2 Illegal contracts

8.2.1 Illegality

The other argument for saying that a contract is void is because it is illegal. Contracts may be illegal either at the time of formation (eg because they involve the commission of a crime) or because of the way they have been performed.

A contract is illegal where its formation, purpose or performance involves the commission of a legal wrong, eg breach of a statutory provision or violation of public policy. Consequently, as a general rule, illegal contracts are void, and courts will not allow recovery of benefits conferred in the performance of an illegal contract.

Examples of contracts that are illegal in themselves are not difficult to identify (eg a contract to commit a crime).

Some contracts, however, are formed legally but then carried out in a way that is illegal. If the illegal act is purely incidental to performance of the contract, it is unlikely to affect the validity of the contract; it is enough that the wrongdoer is punished for what they did. For example, a contract to deliver goods would not be voided if the driver delivering the goods was caught speeding.

A case which illustrates this is *St John Shipping Corp v Joseph Rank Ltd* [1957] 1 QB 267. A statute made it an offence to load a ship to such an extent that the load line was below water. The offence was punishable by payment of a fine. When the plaintiff charterers committed this offence, the defendant sought to withhold payment for the goods on the basis that there was an illegal contract. The court held that the statute did not prohibit contracts performed in breach of the load line rule. It was enough that the charterers should be fined for the breach.

Where a contract is performed illegally, it is possible for either both, or only one, of the parties to intend illegal performance. Where both parties were aware that performance was illegal then the courts tend to take the view that neither party should be entitled to enforce the contract; the contract is void.

This is illustrated by *Ashmore, Benson, Pease & Co Ltd v AV Dawson Ltd* [1973] 1 WLR 828. The defendant agreed to transport boilers owned by the plaintiff and did so by carrying them on lorries which could not lawfully carry them. The plaintiff knew this to be the case. The boilers were damaged in transit and the owner sued for damages. Needless to say, the claim was rejected on the basis that the owner had effectively participated in the illegality.

On the other hand, where one party did not know of the illegal performance of the contract by the other party, the innocent party may be able to enforce it. Clearly, the illegal performer should not be permitted to enforce the contract.

8.2.2 Contracts illegal under statute

Identifying contracts that are illegal under statute is not difficult. For example, the Competition Act 1998 renders unenforceable contracts that have the effect of restricting, preventing or distorting trade within the UK.

8.2.3 Contracts illegal at common law

The courts will refuse to enforce some contracts at common law on the basis that they are contrary to public policy or morality, eg contracts that challenge the sanctity of marriage, contracts which are sexually immoral and contracts that seek to challenge the jurisdiction of the court.

8.2.3.1 Covenants in restraint of trade

Common form clauses which are prima facie void as being contrary to public policy are covenants in restraint to trade, eg clauses in employment contracts restraining senior employees from working for a competitor when their employment ends, or clauses in a sale and purchase agreement of a business stopping the seller setting up a competing business nearby. As a matter of public policy, individuals and businesses should be able to work and operate to generate income for themselves.

However, restraints of trade may be enforceable if:

- there is a legitimate business interest to protect, eg customers, employees and trade secrets; *and*
- the restraint is reasonable in terms of geographical area, duration and scope of the prohibited activities.

> ⭐ *Example*
>
> *NW Coaches Ltd (NWC) is a coach operator based in the north west of England. It employs a wide range of people, including coach drivers, business development managers and senior executives.*
>
> *In relation to the coach drivers, it may be argued that NWC has no legitimate business interest to protect, eg it is unlikely the coach drivers will be privy to confidential information, and if they leave and work for a competitor it is unlikely to adversely affect business. So, any covenants in restraint of trade in the contracts of employment of the coach drivers may well be unenforceable.*
>
> *With the more senior employees, however, NWC may well have legitimate business interests to protect (eg trade secrets and goodwill), but any restraints of trade would have to be reasonable, eg limited to working for a coach operator in the north west of England for an appropriate length of time. It would be unreasonable to restrain them after termination of employment from working for a coach operator, say, based in Scotland, or otherwise from working for a 'tour operator' when the extent of NWC's business interest is coach operator. In terms of duration, the longer the duration of the restraint, the more likely it is to be unreasonable, but it depends on all the circumstances. For example, a reasonable period of restraint for a senior executive is going to be longer than that for a recently appointed business development manager.*

Contract

Where there are legitimate business interests to protect, it makes sense for contracts of employment to incorporate covenants in restraint of trade, but they must be drafted appropriately. They must be reasonable in scope in relation to individual employees and their status and seniority within the organisation. Provided the clauses are reasonable, they will be upheld and the former employer will be granted injunctive relief and/or otherwise awarded damages to compensate for loss suffered as a result of any breach (see **Chapter 4**).

Figure 8.1 Enforceability of covenants in restraint of trade

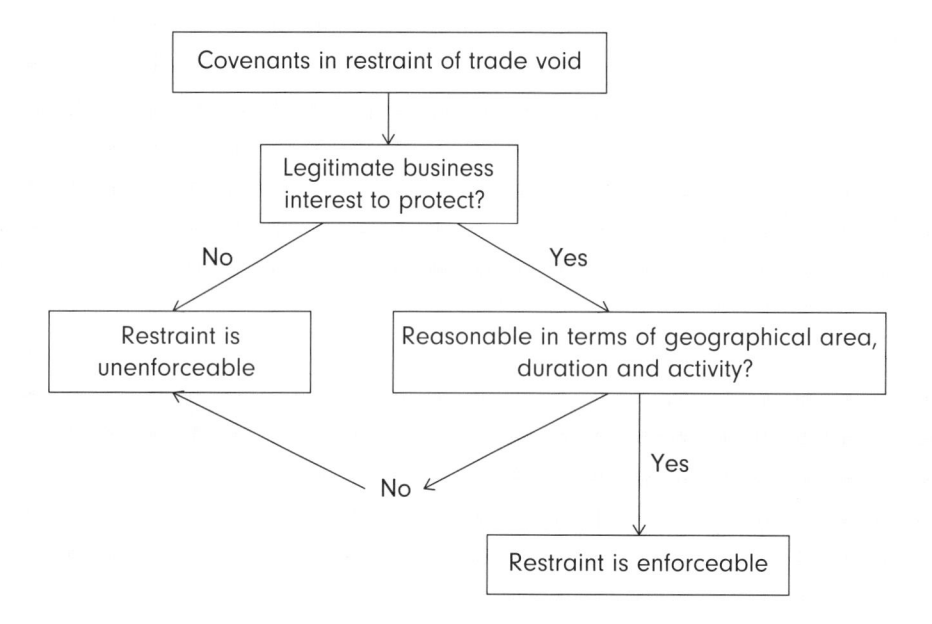

```
        Covenants in restraint of trade void
                        │
                        ▼
              Legitimate business
              interest to protect?
              ╱                ╲
           No                    Yes
           ╱                      ╲
    Restraint is         Reasonable in terms of geographical area,
    unenforceable               duration and activity?
           ▲                              │
           │                             Yes
           └──── No ──────                │
                                          ▼
                                 Restraint is enforceable
```

SUMMARY

- There are three kinds of mistake: common, cross-purpose and unilateral.
- The mistake must be fundamental and precede the contract.
- The effect of mistake is to render a contract void.
- Mistake tends to be pleaded as a last resort where there is no other effective cause of action (eg there was no breach of contract or misrepresentation).
- Contracts may be illegal from the start or otherwise illegal in the way in which they are performed.
- Contracts may be illegal because they violate a statutory provision, the common law or public policy.
- As a general rule, illegal contracts are unenforceable.
- Covenants in restraint of trade are prima facie void as being contrary to public policy. However, if there is a business interest to protect and the restraint is reasonable, the covenant will be enforceable.

Appendix
Resource Materials

Reading 1

NOTE: This document is for teaching purposes only. It is not to be used as a precedent.

SPECIMEN STANDARD CONDITIONS OF SALE (COMMERCIAL)

1. Definitions and Interpretations

In these Conditions of Sale

'the Seller' means   (Company Number)   whose registered office is at

'the Buyer' means

'the Contract' means any contract made between the Seller and the Buyer for the sale and purchase of the Goods incorporating these Conditions of Sale.

'the Goods' means the goods which the Seller is to supply in accordance with these Conditions of Sale. Any reference to the Goods shall, where appropriate, include a reference to part of them.

2. Application of Terms

2.1 These Conditions of Sale shall prevail over any inconsistent terms which the Buyer may seek to introduce. Such inconsistent terms shall have no effect.

2.2 The Seller's sales representatives are not authorised to do any of the following things on behalf of the Seller:

2.2.1 remove or vary any of these terms or introduce any other terms, written or oral, into the Contract; and

2.2.2 make any representation, or enter into any collateral contract.

3. Price

The price of the Goods is the price stated in the Seller's quotation or such other price as is expressly agreed in writing by the Buyer and Seller. Any quotation given by the Seller is valid for 21 days only.

4. Delivery

4.1 No order placed by the Buyer shall be deemed to be accepted until received by the Seller.

4.2 Unless otherwise agreed in writing by the Seller delivery of the Goods shall take place at the Seller's place of business.

4.3 The Seller shall not be liable for any failure to deliver the Goods arising from circumstances outside the Seller's control.

    4.3.1 Non-exhaustive illustrations of circumstance outside the Seller's control include act of God, war, riots, explosion, abnormal weather conditions, fire, flood, Government action, strikes, lockouts, delay by suppliers, accidents and shortage of materials, labour or manufacturing facilities.

    4.3.2 If the Seller is prevented from delivering in the above circumstances, it shall notify the Buyer of the fact in writing within 10 days commencing with the contractual delivery date.

    4.3.3 If the circumstances preventing delivery are still continuing 3 months from and including the date the Seller sends such notice, then the Seller may give written notice to the Buyer cancelling the contract.

    4.3.4 If the contract is cancelled in this way, the Seller shall be entitled to retain any payment which the Buyer has already made on account of the price.

4.4 The Buyer will take delivery of the Goods within [] days of the Seller giving it notice that the Goods are ready for delivery.

4.5 Any dates specified by the Seller for delivery of the Goods are intended to be an estimate and time for delivery shall not be made of the essence by notice. If no dates are so specified, delivery will be within a reasonable time.

4.6 Subject to the other provisions of these Conditions of Sale, the Seller will not be liable for any loss (including loss of profit), costs, damages, charges or expenses caused directly or indirectly by any delay in delivery of the Goods (even if caused by the Seller's negligence), nor will any delay entitle the Buyer to terminate or rescind the Contract unless such delay exceeds [] days.

4.7 If for any reason the Buyer will not accept delivery of any of the Goods when they are ready for delivery, or the Seller is unable to deliver the Goods on time because the Buyer has not provided appropriate instructions, documents, licences or authorisations:

    4.7.1 risk in the Goods will pass to the Buyer;

    4.7.2 the Goods will be deemed to have been delivered; and

    4.7.3 the Seller may store the Goods until delivery whereupon the Buyer will be liable for all related costs and expenses (including without limitation storage and insurance).

5. Quality

5.1 The Seller shall not be liable for any defects in the Goods unless the Buyer gives written notice of the defect to the Seller within 14 days of the time when the Buyer discovers, or ought to have discovered the defect.

5.2 The Seller shall not be liable for any defect if:

    5.2.1 the Buyer makes any further use of the Goods after giving such notice; or

Appendix

5.2.2 the defect arises because the Buyer failed to follow the Seller's instructions as to storage, installation or maintenance of the Goods or (if none) good trade practice; or

5.2.3 the Buyer alters or repairs the Goods without the written consent of the Seller.

5.3 Subject to conditions 5.1 and 5.2 if any of the Goods are defective, the Seller shall at its option repair or replace such Goods (or the defective part) or refund the price, provided that if the Seller so requests, the Buyer shall return the Goods, or the part of the Goods which is defective, at the Buyer's expense, to the Seller.

6. Payment

6.1 The Seller may invoice the Buyer for the price of the Goods on or at any time after delivery of the Goods.

6.2 The Buyer must pay the price of the Goods within the period of 21 days beginning with the date on which the Seller issues the invoice.

6.3 Time for payment shall be of the essence.

7. Risk/Title

7.1 The Goods are at the risk of the Buyer from the time of delivery.

7.2 Ownership of the Goods shall not pass to the Buyer until the Seller has received in full (in cash or cleared funds) all sums due to it in respect of:

7.2.1 the Goods; and

7.2.2 all other sums which are or which become due to the Seller from the Buyer on any account.

8. Limitation of Liability

8.1 Subject to conditions 4.3 and 5, the following provisions set out the entire financial liability of the Seller (including any liability for the acts or omissions of its employees) to the Buyer in respect of

8.1.1 any breach of these conditions; and

8.1.2 any representation, statement or tortious act or omission, including negligence arising under or in connection with the Contract.

8.2 All warranties, conditions and other terms implied by statute or common law are excluded.

8.3 Nothing in these Conditions of Sale excludes or limits the liability of the Seller for death or personal injury caused by the Seller's negligence.

8.4 Subject to conditions 8.2 and 8.3:

8.4.1 The Seller's total liability in contract, tort (including negligence) misrepresentation or otherwise shall be limited to £......; and

8.4.2 The Seller shall not be liable to the Buyer for any indirect or consequential loss or damage (whether for loss of profit, loss of business or otherwise) costs, expenses or

Contract

other claims for consequential compensation whatsoever (howsoever caused) which arise out of, or in connection with the Contract.

9. **Notices**

9.1 Any notice which must be given under the Contract may be either delivered personally or posted.

9.2 Notice given by post must be pre-paid and correctly addressed

9.2.1 in the case of a registered company, to its registered office; and

9.2.2 in any other case, to the recipient's address as set out in the Contract unless the recipient has notified another address to the other party to the Contract.

9.3 A posted notice which complies the sub-clause (b) above is deemed served:

9.3.1 when posted on a business day, on the second business day thereafter; and

9.3.2 in any other case, on the third business day thereafter.

10. **General**

10. The Court may strike out or override any part of the Contract which is considered unreasonable, invalid or unlawful (whether an entire clause or only part of one) and enforce the Contract as if the offending clause had never formed part of it.

11. The formation, existence, construction, performance, validity and all aspects of the Contract shall be governed by English law and the parties submit to the exclusive jurisdiction of the English courts.

Reading 2

CONSUMER RIGHTS ACT 2015

Part 1

Chapter 2

Goods

Section 5 – Sales contracts

(1) A contract is a sales contract if under it-

(a) the trader transfers or agrees to transfer ownership of goods to the consumer, and

(b) the consumer pays or agrees to pay the price.

...

Section 8 – Contracts for transfer of goods

A contract to supply goods is a contract for transfer of goods if under it the trader transfers or agrees to transfer ownership of the goods to the consumer and-

(a) the consumer provides or agrees to provide consideration otherwise than by paying a price, or

(b) the contract is, for any other reason, not a sales contract or a hire-purchase agreement.

Section 9 – Goods to be of satisfactory quality

(1) Every contract to supply goods is to be treated as including a term that the quality of goods is satisfactory.

(2) The quality of goods is satisfactory if they meet the standard that a reasonable person would consider satisfactory, taking account of-

    (a) any description of the goods,

    (b) the price or other consideration for the goods (if relevant), and

    (c) all other relevant circumstances …

(3) The quality of goods includes their state and condition; and the following aspects (among others) are in appropriate cases aspects of the quality of goods-

    (a) fitness for all the purposes for which goods of that kind are usually supplied;

    (b) appearance and finish;

    (c) freedom from minor defects;

    (d) safety;

    (e) durability.

(4) The term mentioned in subsection 1 does not cover anything which makes the quality of the goods unsatisfactory-

    (a) which is specifically drawn to the consumer's attention before the contract is made,

    (b) where the consumer examines the goods before the contract is made, which that examination ought to reveal, or

    (c) in the case of a contract to supply goods by sample, which would have been apparent on a reasonable examination of the sample.

…

Section 10 – Goods to be fit for particular purpose

(1) Subsection (3) applies to a contract to supply goods if before the contract is made the consumer makes known to the trader (expressly or by implication) any particular purpose for which the consumer is contracting for the goods.

…

(3) The contract is to be treated as including a term that the goods are reasonably fit for that purpose, whether or not it is a purpose for which goods of that kind are usually supplied.

…

Section 11 – Goods to be as described

(1) Every contract to supply goods by description is to be treated as including a term that the goods will match the description.

…

Section 19 – Consumer's rights to enforce terms about goods

…

(3) If the goods do not conform to the contract because of a breach of any of the terms described in sections 9, 10, 11 … the consumer's rights (and the provisions about them and when they are available) are-

    (a) the short-term right to reject (sections 20 and 22);

Contract

(b) the right to repair or replacement (section 23); and

(c) the right to a price reduction or the final right to reject (sections 20 and 24).

(4) If the goods do not conform to the contract under section 15 or because of a breach of requirements that are stated in the contract, the consumer's rights (and the provisions about them and when they are available) are-

(a) the right to repair or replacement (section 23); and

(b) the right to a price reduction or the final right to reject (sections 20 and 24).

...

Section 31 – Liability that cannot be excluded

(1) A term of a contract to supply goods is not binding on the consumer to the extent that it would exclude or restrict the trader's liability arising under any of these provisions–

(a) section 9 (goods to be of satisfactory quality);

(b) section 10 (goods to be fit for particular purpose);

(c) section 11 (goods to be as described);

...

(2) That also means that a term of a contract to supply goods is not binding on the consumer to the extent that it would–

(a) exclude or restrict a right or remedy in respect of a liability under a provision listed in subsection (1),

(b) make such a right or remedy or its enforcement subject to a restrictive or onerous condition,

(c) allow a trader to put a person at a disadvantage as a result of pursuing such a right or remedy, or

(d) exclude or restrict rules of evidence or procedure.

(3) The reference in subsection (1) to excluding or restricting a liability also includes preventing an obligation or duty arising or limiting its extent.

...

Chapter 4
Services

Section 48 – Contracts covered by this Chapter

(1) This Chapter applies to a contract for a trader to supply a service to a consumer.

...

Section 49 – Service to be performed with reasonable care and skill

(1) Every contract to supply a service is to be treated as including a term that the trader must perform the service with reasonable care and skill.

(2) See section 54 for a consumer's rights if the trader is in breach of a term that this section requires to be treated as included in a contract.

Appendix

Section 51 – Reasonable price to be paid for a service

(1) This section applies to a contract to supply a service, if–

    (a) the consumer has not paid a price or other consideration for the service,

    (b) the contract does not expressly fix a price or other consideration, and does not say how it is to be fixed, and

    (c) anything that is to be treated under section 50 as included in the contract does not fix a price or other consideration either.

(2) In that case the contract is to be treated as including a term that the consumer must pay a reasonable price for the service, and no more.

(3) What is a reasonable price is a question of fact.

...

Section 52 – Service to be performed within a reasonable time

(1) This section applies to a contract to supply a service, if–

    (a) the contract does not expressly fix the time for the service to be performed, and does not say how it is to be fixed, and

    (b) information that is to be treated under section 50 as included in the contract does not fix the time either.

(2) In that case the contract is to be treated as including a term that the trader must perform the service within a reasonable time.

(3) What is a reasonable time is a question of fact.

...

Section 57 – Liability that cannot be excluded or restricted

(1) A term of a contract to supply services is not binding on the consumer to the extent that it would exclude the trader's liability arising under section 49 (service to be performed with reasonable care and skill).

(2) Subject to section 50(2), a term of a contract to supply services is not binding on the consumer to the extent that it would exclude the trader's liability arising under section 50 (information about trader or service to be binding).

(3) A term of a contract to supply services is not binding on the consumer to the extent that it would restrict the trader's liability arising under any of sections 49 and 50 and, where they apply, sections 51 and 52 (reasonable price and reasonable time), if it would prevent the consumer in an appropriate case from recovering the price paid or the value of any other consideration. (If it would not prevent the consumer from doing so, Part 2 (unfair terms) may apply.)

(4) That also means that a term of a contract to supply services is not binding on the consumer to the extent that it would–

    (a) exclude or restrict a right or remedy in respect of a liability under any of sections 49 to 52,

    (b) make such a right or remedy or its enforcement subject to a restrictive or onerous condition,

    (c) allow a trader to put a person at a disadvantage as a result of pursuing such a right or remedy, or

    (d) exclude or restrict rules of evidence or procedure.

(5) The references in subsections (1) to (3) to excluding or restricting a liability also includes preventing an obligation or duty arising or limiting its extent.

...

Reading 3

SALE OF GOODS ACT 1979

Section 8 – Ascertainment of price

(1) The price in a contract of sale may be fixed by the contract, or may be left to be fixed in a manner agreed by the contract, or may be determined by the course of dealing between the parties.

(2) Where the price is not determined as mentioned in sub-section (1) above the buyer must pay a reasonable price.

(3) What is a reasonable price is a question of fact dependent on the circumstances of each particular case.

Section 13 – Sale of description

(1) Where there is a contract for the sale of goods by description, there is an implied term that the goods will correspond with the description.

(1A) As regards England and Wales and Northern Ireland, the term implied by subsection (1) above is a condition.

(2) If the sale is by sample as well as by description it is not sufficient that the bulk of the goods correspond with the sample if the goods do not also correspond with the description.

(3) A sale of goods is not prevented from being a sale by description by reason only that, being exposed for sale or hire, they are selected by the buyer.

...

(5) This section does not apply to a contract to which Chapter 2 of Part 1 of the Consumer Rights Act 2015 applies ...

Section 14 – Implied terms about quality and fitness

(1) Except as provided by this section there is no implied term about the quality or fitness for any particular purpose of goods supplied under a contract of sale.

(2) Where the seller sells goods in the course of a business, there is an implied term that the goods supplied under the contract are of satisfactory quality.

(2A) For the purposes of this Act, goods are of satisfactory quality if they meet the standard that a reasonable person would regard as satisfactory, taking account of any description of the goods, the price (if relevant) and all the other relevant circumstances.

(2B) For the purposes of this Act, the quality of goods includes their state and condition and the following (among others) are in appropriate cases aspects of the quality of goods–

(a) fitness for all the purposes for which goods of the kind in question are commonly supplied.

(b) appearance and finish,

(c) freedom from minor defects,

(d) safety, and

(e) durability.

(2C) The term implied by subsection (2) above does not extend to any matter making the quality of goods unsatisfactory-

(a) which is specifically drawn to the buyer's attention before the contract is made,

(b) where the buyer examines the goods before the contract is made, which that examination ought to reveal, or

(c) in the case of a contract for sale by sample, which would have been apparent on a reasonable examination of the sample.

(3) Where the seller sells goods in the course of a business and the buyer, expressly or by implication, makes known-

(a) to the seller, or

(b) ...

any particular purpose for which the goods are being bought, there is an implied term that the goods supplied under the contract are reasonably fit for that purpose, whether or not that is a purpose for which such goods are commonly supplied, except where the circumstances show that the buyer does not rely, or that it is unreasonable for him to rely, on the skill or judgment of the seller.

...

(6) As regards England and Wales and Northern Ireland, the terms implied by subsection (2) and (3) above are conditions.

...

(9) This section does not apply to a contract to which Chapter 2 of Part 1 of the Consumer Rights Act 2015 applies ...

Reading 4

SUPPLY OF GOODS AND SERVICES ACT 1982

Part I

Supply of Goods

Contracts for the transfer of property in goods

Section 3 – Implied terms where transfer is by description

(1) This section applies where, under a relevant contract for the transfer of goods, the transferor transfers or agrees to transfer the property in the goods by description, and other than a contract to which Chapter 2 of Part 1 of the Consumer Rights Act 2015 applies.

(2) In such a case there is an implied condition that the goods will correspond with the description.

Section 4 – Implied terms about quality or fitness

(1) Except as provided by this section ... and subject to the provisions of any other enactment, there is no implied condition or warranty about the quality or fitness for any particular purpose of goods supplied under a contract for the transfer of goods.

(2) Where, under such a contract, the transferor transfers the property in goods in the course of a business, there is an implied condition that the goods supplied under the contract are of satisfactory quality. ...

(4) Subsection (5) below applies where, under a contract for the transfer of goods, the transferor transfers the property in goods in the course of a business and the transferee, expressly or by implication, makes known–

(a) to the transferor; ...

any particular purpose for which the goods are being acquired.

(5) In that case there is (subject to subsection (6) below) an implied condition that the goods supplied under the contract are reasonably fit for that purpose, whether or not that is a purpose for which such goods are commonly supplied.

(6) Subsection (5) does not apply where the circumstances show that the transferee does not rely, or that it is unreasonable for him to rely, on the skill or judgment of the transferor.

Part II
Supply of Services

Section 13 – Implied term about care and skill

In a relevant contract for the supply of a service where the supplier is acting in the course of a business, there is an implied term that the supplier will carry out the service with reasonable care and skill.

Section 14 – Implied term about time for performance

(1) Where, under a relevant contract for the supply of a service by a supplier acting in the course of a business, the time for the service to be carried out is not fixed by the contract, left to be fixed in a manner agreed by the contract or determined by the course of dealing between the parties, there is an implied term that the supplier will carry out the service within a reasonable time.

(2) What is a reasonable time is a question of fact.

Section 15 – Implied term about consideration

(1) Where, under a relevant contract for the supply of a service, the consideration for the service is not determined by the contract, left to be determined in a manner agreed by the contract or determined by the course of dealing between the parties, there is an implied term that the party contracting with the supplier will pay a reasonable charge.

(2) What is a reasonable charge is a question of fact.

Reading 5

UNFAIR CONTRACT TERMS ACT 1977
Part I

Section 2 – Negligence liability

(1) A person cannot by reference to any contract term or to a notice given to persons generally or to particular persons exclude or restrict his liability for death or personal injury resulting from negligence.

Appendix

(2) In the case of other loss or damage, a person cannot so exclude or restrict his liability for negligence except in so far as the term or notice satisfies the requirement of reasonableness.

...

(4) This section does not apply to-

   (a) a term in a consumer contract, or

   (b) a notice to the extent that it is a consumer notice,

   (but see the provision made about such contracts and notices in sections 62 and 65 of the Consumer Rights Act 2015).

Section 3 – Liability arising in contract

(1) This section applies as between contracting parties where one of them deals on the other's written standard terms of business.

(2) As against that party, the other cannot by reference to any contract term-

   (a) when himself in breach of contract, exclude or restrict any liability of his in respect of the breach; or

   (b) claim to be entitled-

   (i) to render a contractual performance substantially different from that which was reasonably expected of him, or

   (ii) in respect of the whole or any part of his contractual obligation, to render no performance at all, except in so far as (in any of the cases mentioned above in this subsection) the contract term satisfies the requirement of reasonableness.

(3) This section does not apply to a term in a consumer contract (but see the provision made about such contracts in section 62 of the Consumer Rights Act 2015).

Section 6 – Sale and hire purchase

...

(1A) Liability for breach of the obligations arising from-

   (a) section 13, 14 or 15 of the 1979 Act (seller's implied undertakings as to conformity of the goods with description or sample, or as to their quality or fitness for a particular purpose);

   cannot be excluded or restricted by reference to a contract term except in so far as the term satisfies the requirement of reasonableness.

...

(5) This section does not apply to a consumer contract (but see the provision made about such contracts in section 31 of the Consumer Rights Act 2015).

Index

A

Acceptance 6-7, 19-20
    battle of the forms 11, 12
    certainty 13
    communication of 14-15
    completeness 13
    definition of 10-11
    by electronic communication 17
    by post
        postal rule 15-16
        retraction 16-17
    problem question on formation 22-24
    and silence 14-15
Advertisements
    invitations to treat 3-4
    offers 3-4
Affirmation
    and recission 155
    and termination of
        contract 108
Agency 51-52
    authorised agent 47
    authority
        actual 45
        apparent or ostensible 46
    creation 45-46
    definition of 45
    effects 47
    unauthorised agent 47
Agreements 6-7, 22-24
    commercial 21-22
    discharge by 127
    domestic 21
    objective test 1, 7
    social 21
Anticipatory breach 108-109
Auctions
    reserve price 5
    without reserve 5

B

Battle of the forms 11, 12
Bilateral contracts 4
Breach of contracts, and termination.
        See Termination of contract

C

Capacity 48
    corporations 49-50
    mental incapacity 48-49
    minors 48
Commercial agreements 21-22
Common law rule
    effect of frustration at 139-140
    exemption clauses on 69-74
    illegal contracts 185
    modified
        construction theory 130
        implied term theory 129-130
    original 129
Complete performance doctrine 119-120
    exceptions 120-127
Conditions
    advantages and disadvantages 66
    choice 67
    effects 66
    and warranties, differences
        between 65
Consideration 50-51
    adequacy 28-30
    alteration promises 35
    benefit and detriment 27-28
    complete failure of 112
    definitions of 27-28
    existing duties 43-44
        legal 31-32
        owed to a third party 32-33
        owed to the other party 33-36
    Foakes v Beer 36, 37, 43-44
    part payment of undisputed
        debts 36-42
    past consideration 30
        insufficiency, exception to 30-31
        sufficiency 30
    Pinnel's Case 36-37
    privity of contract 44-45
    promises 27-28
    promissory estoppel. *See* Promissory
        estoppel
    Stilk v Myrick 33-34, 43-44
    sufficiency 28-30
    Williams v Roffey Bros 34-35

Consumer Rights Act 2015 83
    exclusion and restriction of liability 83
    exemption clauses 84–85
    implied terms 62–64
    rights to enforce terms about goods 63
    rights to enforce terms about services 64
    sales contracts 62–63, 83
    services contracts 63, 83
    third parties 84–85
    unfair terms 84
Contracts (Rights of Third Parties) Act 1999 44
Contractual intention. *See* Intention
Corporations 49
    limited liability partnerships 50
    registered companies 49
    statutory 49
Counter offer 9
Custom, terms implied by 55

D

Damages 89–90
    as an adequate remedy 109
    compensation 90
    in contracts and torts 98–99
    contributory negligence 102
    cost of cure 92–93
    difference in value 92
    disappointment 95
    expectation loss 90–93
    loss of opportunity 94
    loss of profit 94
    measure and assessment of 90–94
        time for 102–103
    mental distress 95
    misinterpretation 157–160
        for fraudulent 157–158
        for non-fraudulent 158–160
    mitigation of loss 101–102
    penalty clauses 103–104
    physical injury 94
    to property 94
    reasonably foreseeable 98
    reliance loss 93–94
    remedies. *See* Remedies
    remoteness rule 96–101
    restitutionary 114–115
    specified (liquidated/agreed) damages
        clause 103–104
Deceit, misrepresentation 157, 158
Delays
    and frustration 133–135
    and recission 155
Description, sale of goods by 59–60

Discharge
    by agreement 127
    by frustration. *See* Frustration
    by performance. *See* Performance of contract
Duress 176–178
    burden of proof 165
    commercial pressure 166
    and consent 166
    constituents of 165–167
    economic 166–167
    effect of 167–168
    hard bargaining 166
    illegitimate threats 166
    ingredients of actionable 167
    meaning of 165
    physical violence 166
    remedy 167–168
    rescission 167–168
    voidable contract 167, 168

E

Economic duress. *See* Duress
Electronic communication
    acceptance by 17
Exemption clauses
    bargaining positions 78
    business liability 75
    common law rules on 69–74
    construction (or interpretation) of 73
    Consumer Rights Act 2015 83–85
    contra proferentem rule 73
    contractual nature 70
    definition of 68
    establishing liability 68–69
    incorporation
        by notice 70–72
        by previous consistent course of
            dealing 72
        by signature 69–70
    limitation clauses 74
    and negligence 73–74
    non-incorporable situations 69
    onerous clause 71
    party's knowledge about 70–71
    reasonable steps, timing of 72
    'regrettably small' print 69
    sold note 72
    Unfair Contract Terms Act (UCTA) 1977 74–82
    unusual clause 71
    and very serious breaches of contract 74
Expectation loss 90–93
Express terms 54, 147
Expression, definition of 1

F

False preliminary statements 161–163
    actionable pre-contractual statements 150
    assurance of vital importance 149
    availability of 151
    burden of proof 153
    conduct and silence, distinguishing between 151
    factuality 151–152
    inducing factor 152
    made by contracting party 147–148
    maker of 152
    misinterpretation 151
    negligent misstatements 160–161
    non-expert 148–149
    relative skill and knowledge of parties 148–149
    representations and terms, distinguishing between 148–150
    time lapses 150
    verbal and written contracts 149
    verification by other party 150
Foakes v Beer, rule in 36, 37, 43–44
Fraudulent misrepresentation 157–158
Frustration
    absolute obligations 144
    already-occurred events 136–137
    burden of proof 138
    common law rule
        effect at 139–140
        modified 129–130
        original 129
        original position at 139–140
    constituents of 127
    and delays 133–135
    event beyond the parties' control 137–138
    express provision 136–137
    force majeure clause 136, 138
    foreseeable events 136–137
    government intervention 133
    illegality 135
    and land leases 138–139
    Law Reform (Frustrated Contracts) Act 1943 140–143
    non-occurrence of a fundamental event 131–133, 139
    radically different 127–129
    restriction on doctrine of 136–138
    review 130
    self-induced 137, 138
    unavailability of a specific thing or person 130–131

G

Guarantee 115–116

H

Honourable Pledge Clause 22

I

Illegal contracts
    at common law 185
    meaning of 184–185
    restraint of trade 185–186
    under statue 185
Implied terms 54–55
    business efficacy test 56
    by the courts 55–57
        local custom 55
        presumed intention of the parties 56
        previous course of dealings between the parties 55–56
        trade usage 55
        type of contract 56–57
    officious bystander test 56
    reasonable fitness for purpose 58–59
    sale of goods by description 59–60
    satisfactory quality 58–59
    by statue 57
        Consumer Rights Act 2015 62–64
        Sale of Goods Act 1979 57–60
        Supply of Goods and Services Act 1982 61–62
Indemnities 116
Injunctions 110–111
    discretion of court 110
    negative promise 110
    realistic approach 111
Innominate terms 66–67
    choice 67
Intention
    commercial agreements 21–22
    creation of legal relations 20–24
    definition of 1–2
    domestic agreements 21
    problem question on formation 22–24
    social agreements 21
Invitation to treat
    advertisements 3–4
    auctions 5
    and offer, distinction between 2
    self-service displays 3
    unilateral or bilateral contracts 3–4

K

Knowledge, imputed and actual 98

L

Law Reform (Frustrated Contracts) Act 1943 140, 142–143
    expenses 141, 142
    money paid and/or payable before the event 140–142
    valuable benefit 141, 142
Limitation clauses 74, 79
Loss
    expectation 90–93
    mitigation of 101–102
    pre-estimate of loss 104, 105
    reliance 93–94
    types of 94–96
Lost opportunity damages 94

M

Mental distress 95
Mental incapacity 48–49
Mere puff statements 147
Misrepresentation 148
    burden of proof 160
    damages 157–160
    deceit 157, 158
    definitions of 150–153
    false statement 151
        availability of 151
        burden of proof 153
        conduct and silence, distinguishing between 151
        factuality 151–152
        inducing factor 152
        maker of 152
    Misrepresentation Act 1967 160
    reasonable grounds 160
    recission 153–157
    remedies for 153–160
Mistake
    common (or identical/shared) 181, 182
    cross-purpose 181, 182–183
    definitions of 181
    types of 181–182
    unilateral 182, 183–184

N

Negligent misstatements 160–161

O

Offer 6–7, 18–19
    acceptance of terms in. *See* Acceptance
    advertisements 3–4
    and auctions 5
    definition of 1–2
    inquiry in response 9
    and invitation to treat, distinction between 2
    lapse of time 10
    problem question on formation 22–24
    promise to keep open 7
    rejection by offeree 9–10
    self-service displays 3
    shop window displays 3
    tenders 6
    unilateral contracts 3–4

P

Part payment of undisputed debts 36–37
    promissory estoppel. *See* Promissory estoppel
Penalty clauses
    and specified damages clause 103–104
Performance of contract
    complete performance doctrine 119–120
        exceptions 120–127
    divisible obligations 124–127
    order of 119
    substantial performance 122–123
    voluntary acceptance of partial performance 122
    wrongful prevention of performance 121–122
Pinnel's Case, rule in 36–37
Post
    acceptance by 15–16
        limitations 16
        retraction of 16–17
Privity of contract
    Contracts (Rights of Third Parties) Act 1999 44
    doctrine 44–45
Promissory estoppel 37
    behaviour of parties 38
    cause of action 38
    clarity 38
    and continuing obligations 39
    as a defence 38
    effect of 38–39
    and one-off debts 39–40
    'promisee must act on the promise' 38

reliance on promise 38
review of 40–42
waiving a strict legal right 38

Q

Quality
satisfactory 58–59

R

Reasonableness test
Unfair Contract Terms Act (UCTA) 1977 77–78, 79–80
Rejection by offeree 9–10
counter offer 9
Remedies 117–118
action for an agreed sum 106
and duress 167–168
injunctions 110–111
for misinterpretation 153–160
restitution 111–115
specific performance 109–110
Remoteness rule 96, 100–101
definition of 96–97
interpretation of 97–100
test for 101
Representations 147
and terms, distinguishing between 148–150
See also Misrepresentation
Rescission 153
affirmation 155
bars of 154–156
bars to 167–168
bona fide purchaser has acquired rights in the property 154
damages in lieu of 157
duress 168
economic duress 168
effect of 154–155
impossibility to restore goods or property 155–156
indemnity 156–157
method 154
undue delay 155
Reserve price 5
Resource materials 187–197
Restitution 111–112
broken contract 113
compensations 112–113
complete failure of considerations 112
damages 114–115
never-formed contract 113
recovery of money paid 112

Revocation of offer 7, 22–24
communication 7–8
normal office hours 8
notice of 8
withdrawal through third party 8

S

Sale of Goods Act 1979
implied terms 57–60
reasonable fitness for purpose 58–59
sale of goods by description 59–60
satisfactory quality 58–59
Self-service displays 3
Shop window displays 3
Silence
and acceptance 14–15
and conduct, distinguishing between 151
Smith v Eric Bush, guidelines in 80–81
Specific performance 109
continuous supervision requirement 109
damages, as an adequate remedy 109
discretion of court 109
just and equitable 110
restrictions on the availability of 109
and services 109–110
Standard terms and conditions 11
Stilk v Myrick, rule in 33–34, 43–44
Supply of Goods and Services Act 1982
implied terms 61–62

T

Tenders 6
Termination of contract
anticipatory breach 108–109
circumstances 106–108
effect of affirmation 108
effect of termination 108
election of the innocent party 108
special rules for sale of goods contracts 108
Termination of offer 6–7
lapse of time 10
rejection by offeree 9–10
counter offer 9
revocation
communication 7–8
normal office hours 8
notice of 8
withdrawal through third party 8

Terms of contract
- battle of the forms 11, 12
- classification of terms 65-68
- false statements. *See* False preliminary statements
- identification 54
- innominate terms 66-67
- limitation clauses 74
- penalty clauses 103-104
- and representations, distinguishing between 148-150
- warranties 65-67

Third parties
- enforcement of contract 44
- and exemption clauses 84-85
- existing contractual duty owed to 32-33
- undue influence
  - basic principles 171-172
  - non-spouse 173-175
  - position of lenders 174
  - spouse 171-173

U

Undue influence 168-169, 176-178
- acceptable influence 168
- actual 169
- *Barclays Bank v O'Brien* 172
- *CIBC Mortgages plc v Pitt* 172
- non-spouse 173-175
- position of lenders 174
- presumed 169-170
- rebuttable presumption 170
- *Royal Bank of Scotland v Etridge (No 2)* 172-173
- spouses 171

third parties
- basic principles 171-172
- transaction must call for an explanation 170
- trust and confidence, relationship of 169

Unfair Contract Terms Act (UCTA) 1977 74
- areas of operation 75-76
- bargaining positions of the parties 78
- customer's knowledge about the clause 79
- express terms, breach of 76
- implied terms, breach of 77
- inducement to agree to the exemption clause 78-79
- liability exemptions 75, 76-77
- limitation clauses 79
- negligence 75
- reasonableness test 77-78, 79-80
- scope of 75
- *Smith v Eric Bush* 80-81
- special order 79

Unfair terms 84

Unilateral contracts
- offers 3-4
- and revocation of offers 8-9
- and tenders 6

W

Warranties
- advantages and disadvantages 66
- choice 67
- and conditions, differences between 65
- effects 66

Williams v Roffey Bros 34-35

Without reserve auction 5